17.5.85

Venice
The American View
1860 - 1920

Venice
The American View
1860-1920

Margaretta M. Lovell

The Fine Arts Museums of San Francisco

This catalogue has been published in conjunction with the exhibition
Venice: The American View, 1860-1920.

The Fine Arts Museums of San Francisco
California Palace of the Legion of Honor
20 October 1984 through 20 January 1985

The Cleveland Museum of Art
27 February 1985 through 21 April 1985

The exhibition has been organized by The Fine Arts Museums of San
Francisco. The presentation in San Francisco was funded, in part, by
generous grants from Barbro and Bernard Osher, the National Endowment for the Arts, a Federal agency, and the California Arts Council.

The publication of this catalogue was supported by a generous grant
from The Henry Luce Foundation, Inc., through The Luce Fund for
Scholarship in American Art, with additional funds contributed by the
Italian Institute of Culture, San Francisco, and by David Nisinson.

Frontispiece: James McNeill Whistler, *Nocturne*, 1879/80. The Fine Arts
Museums of San Francisco. Achenbach Foundation for Graphic Arts,
William H. Noble Bequest Fund. Cat. no. 99

Front cover: Charles Caryl Coleman, *The Bronze Horses of San Marco,
Venice*, 1876. The Minneapolis Institute of Arts. Gift of the Regis
Collection. Cat. no. 12

Back cover: Maurice Brazil Prendergast, *St. Mark's, Venice (The Clock
Tower)*, 1898/99. The William A. Farnsworth Library and Art Museum,
Rockland, Maine. Cat. no. 35

Photo credit: Photograph for cat.no.28 courtesy of Ira
Spanierman, Inc.

ISBN 0-88401-044-9
Library of Congress Catalogue Card No. 84-81857

Contents

Foreword

This exhibition, focusing on American nineteenth-century artists abroad, is one of a series of important projects undertaken in this field by The Fine Arts Museums of San Francisco since the opening of the American Galleries in 1977.

The seed for *Venice: The American View, 1860-1920* was planted almost a decade ago when the curator, Margaretta M. Lovell, studied a watercolor by John Singer Sargent of Santa Maria della Salute (cat. no. 65) and soon discovered that it belonged to a large family of works that were both masterful aesthetic achievements and culturally resonant documents. Moreover, beyond passing inclusions in monographic studies, these paintings, watercolors, pastels, and etchings of Venice had, for the most part, evaded scholarly study. The literature focused on the impact of the native landscape on American artists, eliding their European achievements. The questions prompted by that Sargent watercolor blossomed into a dissertation, a book (soon to be published), a symposium, and this exhibition. Although she feels these questions have scarcely been resolved, this exhibition succeeds admirably in identifying and diligently pursuing some of the issues prompted by the cultural phenomenon of self-consciously New World artists responding to the palpable historic presence of the Old World.

The achievement of this project could not have been possible without the generosity of sixty individuals and institutions from throughout the United States and Europe who have lent their treasured works to this exhibition. Our gratitude for their willingness to share these objects is profound, as it enables a wide audience to appreciate and learn from this unique gathering of masterworks.

Since it is by no means common practice in American museums for individuals to sponsor exhibitions, it is a particular pleasure to thank Barbro and Bernard Osher for their generosity, in this instance, in funding the basic costs of the exhibition, and the Bernard Osher Foundation for making possible the symposium, "American Artists and Writers in Italy in the Nineteenth Century." The exhibition also received generous grants from the National Endowment for the Arts, a Federal agency, and the California Arts Council. We are equally grateful to The Henry Luce Foundation for sponsoring the research and production of this catalogue and to the Italian Institute of Culture, San Francisco, for providing funds for additional color illustrations.

I must mention also the enduring support and encouragement of Ednah Root who established a Chair in American Art at The Fine Arts Museums of San Francisco in 1979. We are grateful to her for the wide range of activities made possible by that gift.

In the largest possible sense this exhibition is a response to the challenge of the gift by Mr. and Mrs. John D. Rockefeller 3rd of their extraordinary collection of American paintings to The Fine Arts Museums of San Francisco in 1979. It is one of a number of major undertakings recently initiated in our effort to cooperate in an active interinstitutional program for American art on the West Coast.

Ian McKibbin White
Director of Museums

Acknowledgments

Venice: The American View, 1860-1920 has been accomplished with the assistance of many people and institutions around the country to whom we extend our deepest gratitude. Space does not permit us to acknowledge each one, but a few need special mention. To our generous lenders, and to our sponsors – Barbro and Bernard Osher, The Henry Luce Foundation, the National Endowment for the Arts, a Federal agency, the California Arts Council, and the Italian Institute of Culture, San Francisco – our warmest gratitude is due.

Several key area resources have been invaluable to the research phase of the project: the Archives of American Art, Western Regional Office, Smithsonian Institution, housed in the de Young Museum; the Inventory of American Art, based in the National Museum of American Art in Washington, D.C.; The Bothin Helping Fund American Art Library Collection, also at the de Young, which provided essential texts; the University of California, Berkeley, which lent a number of graduate students trained in American art, as well as in-depth library resources, to the research effort.

Every member of the staff of The Fine Arts Museums has participated in the project, and we gratefully acknowledge the effort and professionalism each has contributed. Special recognition is due to Debra Pughe who, as Exhibitions Coordinator, has been the prime facilitator in achieving this exhibition from the outset. Similarly, Marc Simpson, Assistant Curator of American Paintings, provided indispensable support in every phase of the project and, most important, co-authored the catalogue entries on James McNeill Whistler. Research Assistants Paula Freedman, Kimerly Rorschach, and Lynn Federle Orr ably handled sections of the research task; and Curatorial Aides Linda Graham, Celeste Connor, and Courtney Damkroger contributed much-needed office and detail assistance. Paula Shields, Intern in the Department of American Paintings on a grant from the National Endowment for the Arts during the fall of 1983, gathered background material, while Jean Givens, as Symposium Coordinator, has handled that task with model proficiency. Special appreciation is due to Ann Karlstrom for her careful editing of the manuscript, to Fronia Wissman who assisted her so ably, and to Joseph Koerner, who read sections of the manuscript. It is interesting to note that all but three of the above team did their graduate work at the University of California, Berkeley, or at Yale University, notable centers for training in the field of American art.

The Registration department, orchestrated by Virginia Mann, deserves special recognition and thanks, as do William White and the careful crew of technicians who installed the exhibition. Andrew Woodd, who escorted the works in transit, and Eileen Petersen, who patiently typed the manuscript, deserve warm thanks for their detailed professional attention to their difficult but critical tasks. I would also like to note my gratitude to Max Chance and Desne Border, of the Museum's Design Department, and Jack Werner Stauffacher, The Greenwood Press, for their elegant solutions to the problems of architectural, graphic, and catalogue design.

Last, it is appropriate to extend my warmest thanks to Jonathan H. Lovell who graciously gave supportive assistance thoughout the project, most significantly in his timely and careful reading of the manuscript. In every sense this has been a team effort, and it is a pleasure to see the work of so many come to fruition.

Margaretta M. Lovell
Ednah Root Curator of American Painting

Lenders to the Exhibition

Addison Gallery of American Art, Phillips Academy,
  Andover, Massachusetts
Albright-Knox Art Gallery, Buffalo, New York
Mr. and Mrs. Arthur G. Altschul
The Art Institute of Chicago, Illinois
Mrs. Mary Bell
James Biddle
The Brooklyn Museum, New York
Cincinnati Art Museum, Ohio
Sterling and Francine Clark Art Institute, Williamstown,
  Massachusetts
The Cleveland Museum of Art, Ohio
Corcoran Gallery of Art, Washington, D.C.
The Detroit Institute of Arts, Michigan
Mr. and Mrs. Dale F. Dorn
William A. Farnsworth Library and Art Museum,
  Rockland, Maine
The Fine Arts Museums of San Francisco, Achenbach
  Foundation for Graphic Arts, California
Fitzwilliam Museum, Cambridge, England
Judy Goffman Fine Art, New York, New York, and Blue
  Bell, Pennsylvania
The Heckscher Museum, Huntington, New York
Hirshhorn Museum and Sculpture Garden, Smithsonian
  Institution, Washington, D.C.
Alice M. Kaplan
Mr. and Mrs. Harry A. Lockwood
Lyman Allyn Museum, New London, Connecticut
The Metropolitan Museum of Art, New York
The Minneapolis Institute of Arts, Minnesota
Mount Holyoke College Art Museum, South Hadley,
  Massachusetts
Museum of Art, Carnegie Institute, Pittsburgh,
  Pennsylvania
Museum of Art, Rhode Island School of Design,
  Providence, Rhode Island
Museum of Fine Arts, Boston, Massachusetts
The Museum of Modern Art, New York
National Gallery of Art, Washington, D.C.
National Gallery of Ireland, Dublin
National Museum of American Art, Smithsonian
  Institution, Washington, D.C.
National Museum of Wales, Cardiff
New York State Historical Association, Cooperstown
David Nisinson Fine Art, New York
North Carolina Museum of Art, Raleigh
Philadelphia Museum of Art, Pennsylvania
The Phillips Collection, Washington, D.C.
Royal Academy of Arts, London
The Saint Louis Art Museum, Missouri
The Tate Gallery, London
Peter G. Terian
Terra Museum of American Art, Evanston, Illinois
Thyssen-Bornemisza Collection, Lugano
The Toledo Museum of Art, Ohio
Victoria and Albert Museum, London
The Walters Art Gallery, Baltimore, Maryland
Washington University Gallery of Art, Saint Louis,
  Missouri
Wellesley College Museum, Massachusetts
Westmoreland Museum of Art, Greensburg,
  Pennsylvania
Wichita Art Museum, Kansas
Worcester Art Museum, Massachusetts
Yale University Art Gallery, New Haven, Connecticut
Mr. and Mrs. Julius L. Zelman
Anonymous lenders

Robert Frederick Blum
No Doubt this is ''Jimmy,'' [Whistler] Venice, 1880
Pencil on paper, 6⅞ × 4⅛ in. (17.5 × 10.2 cm)
Cincinnati Art Museum

Introduction

Poised between sea and sky, the city of Venice provided a seemingly endless source of subjects for a wide variety of American artists during the late nineteenth century. Tree-less, hill-less, almost season-less Venice gave its observers uninterrupted opportunities for interpreting architectural structure and architectural space. It also gave them a chance to explore and interrogate the Past, and clearly this elusive quality was a major element in their painterly quest. How Venice figured in the work of a handful of the many Americans who captured this eccentric cityscape is the subject of this exhibition. Why and how that work is memorable on the one hand, and culturally telling on the other, is the subject of this catalogue.

Venice

In 452, we are told, the residents of the Roman colony of Aquileia fled before the onslaught of Attila and found refuge on a cluster of offshore islands protected alike from the foe and the sea by a sheltering lagoon. The climate was mild, the natural resources abundant, the geographical position auspicious, and the necessary maritime aspect of the culture a virtue. The founders created a civilization, a Byzantine and Gothic city, which was to be the admiration of many, most notably in the nineteenth century, of John Ruskin:

The remains of their Venice lie hidden behind the cumbrous [architectural] masses which were the delight of the nation in its dotage: hidden in many a grass-grown court, silent pathway, and lightless canal, where the slow waves have sapped their foundations for five hundred years . . . [This ancient Venice was] not created in the day-dream of the prince, nor by the ostentation of the noble, but built by iron hands and patient hearts, contending against the adversity of nature and the fury of man, so that its wonderfulness cannot be grasped by the indolence of imagination, but only after a frank inquiry into the true nature of that wild and solitary scene, whose restless tides and trembling sands did indeed shelter the birth of the city.[1]

Those "iron hands and patient hearts" Ruskin reads in the stones of the city as one might read human character in a diary or in a portrait. For many of her latter-day visitors, these historic ghosts were as present as Venice's architectural heritage and her contemporary populace.

Having risen to preeminence in wealth and power among her European neighbors by the fifteenth century, the far-flung Venetian empire began to collapse as the center of power and commerce shifted from the Mediterranean to the Atlantic. But her Republican (more strictly speaking, oligarchical) form of government, her extraordinary achievements in the arts, and her forbidding reputation for secret and grim justice in matters related to the state remained intact until the last years of what Ruskin refers to as the city's "dotage." In 1797 Napoleon conquered the impotent city; the last doge was deposed, and the flag of the Republic was ceremoniously burned in the Piazza San Marco. Ceded by France to Austria late in 1797, Venice chaffed under foreign rule until 1866 when the city was united with the kingdom of Italy.

The whole tale of Venice afforded her nineteenth-century observers a clearer and nearer case of linear historic development than even Edward Gibbon's Rome, and the eccentric facts of her longevity, her splendor, and her Republican form of government insured their interest in her past history and in her present condition. As the noted collector James J. Jarves put it:

Over her, from first to last, in the mystery of her remote beginnings, the splendor of her prime, and the beauty of her slow decline, there is a glamour of romance which makes her continued existence one bewitching poem.[2]

And he goes on to comment on the intellectual appropriation of Venice by the world:

Not even the fate of Rome or Jerusalem touches the imagination more vividly than that of the Queen of the Seas. Every fresh mishap to her palaces, or whatever threatens to hasten her decay or change the poetical likeness of the past into the prosaic present, awakens a sympathetic thrill of regret or indignation throughout Christendom, as if Venice now belongs more to mankind than to its own impoverished citizens.[3]

But this sense that "Venice now belongs . . . to mankind" was slow to develop among Anglo-American observers and travelers. As late as 1818, Lord Byron was reveling in the isolation of the city, the absence of Englishmen and other travelers who found their way so regularly to Rome but left Venice quite unvisited.[4] Ironically, his poems and plays helped to awaken the English-speaking audience to the present and historic facts of the city. He spoke of its literary associations and visual magic in such passages as Canto IV of *Childe Harold's Pilgrimage:*

I loved her from my boyhood – she to me
Was as a fairy city of the heart,
Rising like water-columns from the sea;
Of joy the sojourn, and of wealth the mart;
And Otway, Radcliffe, Schiller, Shakespeare's art,
Had stamp'd her image in me. . . .[5]

But for Byron, the critical issues concerning Venice were political, centering on the claims of the state upon individuals and on the sanctity of the republican form of government. And the appropriate heir to Venice's ancient republicanism was, in his view, America, as he made clear in the ode to Venice of 1821.

While Byron was, early in the nineteenth century, almost alone among Englishmen in his enthusiasm for Venice, American interest in Italian culture in general, and Venice in particular, was at an even lower ebb. During the half-century between 1750 and 1800, only three Italian books were translated in America, and fewer than a dozen Americans are known to have visited Italy.[6] During the first half of the nineteenth century, Americans were only slightly more in evidence in Venice. Boston portraitist Amasa Hewins noted in his travel diary on 4 July 1831:

The only Americans in Venice were Mr. [Samuel F. B.] Morse and myself, and although we could not make a very large dinner party, we could not forget the day of our independence. I volunteered for a sentiment [toast], "The political and religious regeneration of Italy," and Mr. Morse, "Success to our principles throughout the world."[7]

That Hewins and Morse were the only two Americans in Venice that July evening is particularly notable in view of the enormous numbers of American artists and travelers to visit the city during the second half of the century. It is equally significant to note that their errand in the city was to study and copy the works of the great Venetian colorists, Titian, Tintoretto, Giorgione, and Paul Veronese. Hewins spent little time observing the city and apparently no time painting it. He clearly saw Venice through the lens of Byron's poetry, and the political element is prominent in his understanding of the city. For Hewins as for many others, Venice's present decay was directly associated with the decadence of her religious, social, and political institutions.[8]

Ten years later, there were more American artists in Venice; Thomas P. Rossiter notes in a letter of 27 August 1843 that his compatriots that summer included James Deveaux, Louis Lang, Luther Terry, Miner K. Kellogg, Daniel Huntington, and Emanuel Leutze. But he goes on to note that, although he finds Venice pleasurable and memorable, "it is not . . . a place to paint original pictures in, unless it be architectural compositions. . . . It, therefore, is a place essentially for Copies and Sketches [after Old Masters], and of these there is no end."[9]

The fact that Venice was not, for Rossiter and his generation, "a place to paint original pictures in," and then, within thirty years it became *the* place to paint original pictures, presents us with one of the central issues of this exhibition and of the large body of work from which it is drawn. What, indeed, prompted American artists and, for that matter, American writers and travelers to visit Venice in unprecedented numbers during the second half of the nineteenth century? As many as ninety American artists are known to have worked in Venice, and approximately 3000 works attest to the tremendous draw the city had for them and for their patrons during the period between 1860 and 1920 – and this despite the fact that Venice had no established art school, no sale galleries, and, until late in the period, no contemporary art exhibitions. A number of factors conspired to produce the phenomenon. The first is the fact that, in general, American artists were moving away from figurative compositions and toward landscape, and this enthusiasm for landscape, bred so close to home on the Hudson River, grew increasingly exotic as the nineteenth century progressed, drawing artists far from their homes and markets to the unsettled West, the rugged Andes, the frozen polar regions, and urban Europe for their subjects. All remote from daily American experience, these subjects became increasingly popular with an ever-widening public. Second, Venice represented an exoticism of a distinct kind – not only was it physically remote and very beautiful, it was also clearly, more than any other European or American urban center, non-industrial and technologically archaic. In a world altered elsewhere so dramatically and swiftly by industrialization, it offered an experience distinctly unlike bourgeois urban daily existence. But its radical otherness from America had not, in its essence, shifted. It had in itself changed little from the period of the eighteenth and early nineteenth century when most Americans regarded Venice with complete indifference. The shift had occurred not in any external circumstance, but in the dawning of an avid interest among Americans (and, indeed, among Europeans as well) in the past. And this enthusiasm for history seems to have grown increasingly keen among Americans as the century progressed.

For them, the virtue of Europe in general, and Venice in particular, in the second half of the nineteenth century was its almost miraculous preservation as a sort of time capsule. It was seen as a kind of semi-extinct species along the chain of evolutionary development toward Americanness; in terms of sequence, it ought not exist, but still, charmingly, and almost for their benefit, it did. As one observer put it, "Americans have a special call to travel. It is the peculiar privilege of their birth in the New World, that the Old World is left for them to visit."[10] This is not to say that their mood on viewing Europe was nostalgic, although that, of course, was a potent element; rather, they regarded it with a kind of wonder, as an instructive curiosity against which they could measure the modernity of American political and social institutions, read the 'lessons' of empire lost, and take instruction in the realm of art.

Travel literature was immensely popular even before the era of mass tourism.[11] One constant aspect of the American experience of Venice is the fact that 'all' Americans 'knew' the city even if they never visited it. Travel writers often interjected such remarks as "I should certainly attempt to give you some slight sketch of this peculiar and romantic city, were you not already quite familiar with it. Every American knows. . . ."[12] This preknowledge was primarily based on the work of three important British mediators: Lord Byron's poems, Joseph Mallord William Turner's canvases (he exhibited his *Venice* paintings on an almost annual basis in London during the 1830s and 1840s, events well chronicled in the American popular press), and John Ruskin's *The Stones of Venice* (published in London, 1851-1853, and excerpted in *The Crayon* as early as 1855). Countless lesser lights contributed to this sense of familiarity with the city: "We found the Piazza of St. Mark so familiar to us, through the medium of engravings and photographs, as to feel by no means a stranger to it," marks a recurrent refrain.[13]

But if Venice was, in a degree, familiar to Americans from a distance, it was also strange and eccentric on close inspection. In an attempt to relate it to their native experience of space, structure, and technology, many commentators struggled for appropriate similes; one found the gondola as appropriate to its "conditions and environment as the light canoe which Adirondack guides pick up at the shore of the lake," while Herman Melville remarked that the Grand Canal "winds like the Susquehanha [River]."[14] It is interesting to note that their comparisons were habitually drawn from nature, rather than from American urban experience, right down to Mark Twain's description of the cathedral of San Marco: "Propped on its long row of low thick-legged columns, its back knobbed with domes, it seemed like a vast warty bug taking a meditative walk."[15] As bizarre as they are telling, these similes point to an extraordinary American self-consciousness; in the face of a potentially overwhelming foreign cultural presence, they assert the primacy of nature as an intellectual and physical territory uniquely their own.

This flood of published travelers' accounts increased as the century progressed and artists shifted their attentions from Rossiter's paintings in the churches and in the Accademia (their specific painterly heritage) to the city at large (that time capsule of the western past). By 1860 they had come to the conclusion that "in spite of the marvels of Titian and Tintoretto, nothing in Venice is half so beautiful as Venice itself and the impressions it gives."[16] Artists set about recording those impressions in unprecedented numbers from the 1860s. They came from Spain, England, Germany, and France, as well as from America, and they became prominent, omnipresent fixtures in the cityscape, enthusiastic for their subject but necessarily haunted by a sense of belatedness. Edmund Gosse aptly described this sweet dilemma:

Venice has been so conspicuously the center of the plastic world, has occupied the art of the describer and cataloger and impressionist for so many centuries, that to attempt to add anything to the great store of pictorial record seems at first sight preposterous. Yet, as each observer comes to Venice with a certain paralyzing sense of everything having been long ago seen and recorded, so, too, there rises in him an ambition to seize the almost intangible emotions which she awakens in him, and which are – so far as he is individually concerned – new and intense and hitherto unconceived of. The consequence is that still every nook of the "sun-girt city" is hung with artists trying to recover that rapture of her beauty which is peculiar to themselves.[17]

The Venetians

Although by the 1860s every nook of Venice was "hung with artists," each brought his or her own visual training and intellect to the problem; their cultural preconceptions conditioned their perceptions and are visible in the products. The selection of subjects and the treatment of subjects are central considerations in this study, and the question of subjects overlooked is a pertinent element. From the evidence of the paintings, it is clear that late-nineteenth-century artists focused with far greater intensity on the "stones" of Venice, those palpable past events surviving into modern time, than on the inhabitants of the city; and this pattern is consistent with their understanding of Venice as a largely historical and aesthetic matter. Contemporary Venetians were regarded with some ambivalence, even hostility. Insofar as their city exhibited to its Anglo-American observers the "iron hands and patient hearts" of her founders in her architecture, the city's present decay and impotence seemed attributable to a weak, misguided, or self-indulgent progeny. Few expressed this sentiment as strongly as Byron in his Venetian ode:

In contrast with their fathers – as the slime,
The dull green ooze of the receding deep
Is with the dashing of the spring-tide foam,
That drives the sailor shipless to his home,
Are they to those that were; and thus they creep,
Crouching and crab-like, through their sapping streets.[18]

The matter was not helped by the fact that few Anglo-American travelers spoke sufficient Italian to venture to test the proposition, and such polite and intellectual Venetian society as existed remained, in large part, invisible to the visitors. Although few voiced Byron's antipathy to the current custodians of Venice, most writers, travelers, and artists refused to focus on them as equally sentient human beings. For many, they scarcely existed: "The masque or ballet, you will soon find," writes one observer of Venice, "is over. The scenery is still there, the lights have been left on; only the actors, the dancers, are gone."[19] For others, they were present but incongruous with their habitat: "The Venetians of to-day seem out of time and place, as if the inhabitants of one of our own towns had suddenly taken possession."[20] Most artists omitted figures from their compositions, or introduced them as minor elements in the distance; a few made figural studies of Venetian models, and in these we recognize the taste for the picturesque that characterizes many American and northern European interpretations of Italy and Spain in the nineteenth century. These figure studies were largely costume pieces, and we read in them the same impulse that led one writer to remark on a group of

old men, with tattered, yet still dignified cloaks, huge brigandish hats, their bright red stockings showing like an ornament through the gaps in their boots. They were terribly dirty; but in Venice, where everything has its own way of becoming beautiful, dirt, at the right distance, gives a fine tone to an old face.[21]

In such a description we recognize the cultural awareness-at-arms-length that suggests interest in, but little comprehension of, the observed group.

Very few writers and even fewer artists attempted to observe, capture, and interpret Venetians integrated with their ancient city, moving through it, working in it, participating fully in the complexities of human life. John Singer Sargent is unique in his pursuit of this question and in his ability to suggest the quality of light and space, of life and movement within the city as it was known and understood by the Venetians themselves. His Venetians display themselves, but they also experience boredom, and, what is more interesting, they confront us, they recognize us as culturally other. Sargent views them without pathos or accusation, just as he sees their architectural context frankly and ahistorically. For him – and in this he announces a new era – Venice moves from the provenance of the past into the immediate present.

The American View

Henry James tellingly remarks in *Transatlantic Sketches* of 1888,

Meeting on the Piazza, on the evening of my arrival, a young American painter, who told me that he had been spending the summer at Venice, I could have assaulted him, for very envy. He was painting, forsooth, the interior of St. Marks! To be a young American painter, unperplexed by the mocking, elusive soul of things, and satisfied with their wholesome, light-bathed surface and shape; keen of eye; fond of color, of sea and sky, and anything that may chance between them; of old lace, and old brocade, and old furniture (even when made to order); of time-mellowed harmonies on nameless canvases, and happy contours in cheap old engravings; to spend one's mornings in still, productive analysis of the clustered shadows of the Basilica, one's afternoons anywhere, in church or campo, on canal or lagoon, and one's evenings in starlight gossip at Florian's, feeling the sea-breeze throb languidly between the two great pillars of the Piazzetta and over the low, black domes of the church, – this, I consider, is to be as happy as one may safely be.[22]

Clearly the situation of an American artist in Venice

touched a chord with him; his pleasure attendant on the visual feast is palpable. He relishes empathetically the artist's "productive analysis of . . . clustered shadows," and it is in this element of analysis that we recognize the potential uniqueness of James's friend's contribution. While literally hundreds of artists confronted Venice during these decades, their interpretations of the same city, even the same sites, differ radically. Were these differences in any degree national in nature? Did they reflect artistic schools of training or were they simply personal? The questions are complicated, and not unrelated to the larger question of the presence of the past, a pressing issue for Europeans and Americans alike in the face of accelerating urbanization and industrialization. It is clear from the paintings and the literature, however, that Venice offered to Americans an important realm of discovery and self-discovery more dramatically different from their quotidian and national experience than it was for Europeans. While their personal experience was necessarily constituted of the undiluted present, Venice presented itself as the distilled essence of the past.

American paintings of Venice offer us a broad range of styles, subjects, and quality, just as do the Venetian works of such European artists as Martin Rico, Walter Sickert, and many others. Yet in the work of a few Americans we recognize something we miss in that of their European counterparts, and that is, curiously, the clear, frank, irreverent note of modernity. The three artists in whose work this quality is detectable – in different degrees – are Whistler, Prendergast, and Sargent, those whose works constitute the core of this exhibition, artists who were clearly perplexed by the "mocking elusive soul of things." Not irrelevantly two were expatriate, cosmopolitan men whose situation did not include the central element of national rootedness. One could conclude that it was just their chameleon-like personal identity, exaggerating as it did certain aspects of American civilization, that provided the circumstances in which their tendencies toward that perplexity in the face of the "soul of things" that we call modernism could flower. Among the many views of Venice by Americans, these eccentric examples, in which historically associated subjects are treated in a subtly or dramatically ahistorical manner, stand out. Their works include singularly successful and memorable images in a wide variety of media, for the interest in Venice coincided with a widespread revival of interest in etching, pastel, and watercolor – media that successfully rivaled, during this period, the long-acknowledged primary medium of oil painting.

While it was an interest in possessing the past that impelled Americans to Venice during the second half of the nineteenth century, the advent of the First World War marked the ascendency of modernism with its attendant repudiation of the past. Beyond the delicate play with the past that we experience in such works as Sargent's genre paintings or architectural watercolors, lay an era in which the past became a non-issue and, as one might expect, Venice retreated as a cultural subject to the indifference from which it had emerged with such force for a few brief, but intense, decades.

This exhibition focuses on the extraordinary cultural effort and aesthetic achievement inherent in this large body of work. Not a few represent remarkably successful efforts, and the present undertaking attempts to rescue from art historical limbo a category of works that fits only uneasily into the 'progress' of American art as it is usually understood and written. Even while this exhibition was being assembled, important paintings were deaccessioned from major cultural institutions because their non-native subject matter fit so ill with the familiar chronicle of American art. One could argue that it is the chronicle that is amiss and that if we permit these works to instruct us, we will see how the tale has been skewed by a long diogenean search for the American character of American art and the necessary nationalism attendant on that quest.

At the center of the issue are the artists and their work, but their enthusiasm for Venice represents only the tip of a broad-based pyramid that included their patrons, the many who traveled to Venice, and the infinite numbers who never left America but who 'knew' the city well from travel literature and from such illustrations in the popular press as Joseph Pennell's careful drawings and Maxfield Parrish's fictionalized illustrations.

It is difficult to reconstruct a precise picture of the patronage situation that supported the artists represented in this exhibition and their many compatriots who also painted Venice, but a few outlines can be discerned. First, because of its custodianship of the formidable Western painterly tradition and the presence of the foremost contemporary art instruction, Europe was, to the late-nineteenth-century collector or casual purchaser, the most straightforward field in which to browse for pictures. A few American collectors, such as Thomas B. Clarke, consciously strove to avoid both European artists and European subjects by American artists, but he was an exception in his era.[23] Most, like the Reverend F. Ward Denys, who bought Frank Duveneck's *Water Carriers, Venice* (cat. no. 15) from the artist in Venice, purchased Italian Old Masters, British portraits, and a few views of Italy by English and American artists.[24] Capitalizing on this tendency, many Americans, after the completion of their professional training, stayed, even for some years, abroad where models were cheaper, markets were readier, and the culture more welcome to those who elected to become professional artists. In several instances, we know of mature artists, such as George Inness and Emil Carlsen, who were, in effect, sent abroad by their American dealers with the assurance that the canvases they sent back would sell better than anything inscribed with a native city.[25] The phenomenon of artists flocking to Venice was, in part, a response to this very real market prejudice. As the editors of *The Art Amateur* put it rather cynically and specifically in 1891,

Mr. F. Hopkinson Smith hopes to return to Venice, with which paradise of painters he is even more infatuated than he was, in turn, with Mexico, Holland and Spain. "It is the only place in the world for an artist," he declared. Remembering the rapidity with which he sold all the pictures he made there last summer, one cannot doubt his sincerity.[26]

Hop Smith's sincerity was based not only on his own enthusiasm, but also on that of at least one large and active segment of the art-purchasing public. It is difficult to determine whether it was at the outset the artists who

Fig.1

educated their public or vice versa, but in either case the result was collaborative. One case in which it is clear that it was the artist who, not without struggle, educated his public in the ways one could look at and interpret Venice is Sargent. His architectural watercolors and genre oils imposed on his audience the strain of readjusting their ideas about objects and people once thought to be familiar and well understood. But he stands at one end of a wide spectrum of American artists, all of whom — whether Romantic or anti-Romantic, whether they sold their work abroad or in New York — sold primarily to American purchasers.

Most paintings of Venice by American artists found their way into modest households, those in which there were only a few pictures. As in the case of landscape paintings of the unsettled West, they were more frequently purchased by urban dwellers than by rural families, but in at least one case, we know of a Venetian view transported, almost before the paint was dry, deep into Indian territory.[27] A few Venetian subjects were purchased by truly distinguished collectors — Duncan Phillips (cat. no. 41), William T. Walters (cat. no. 82), La Grand Lockwood (cat. no. 29), and John Jacob Astor — but these were the exceptions. Not a few were exchanged among the artists themselves, and this is to be expected when they lived and worked in such close proximity.

Although we know Charles C. Coleman was correct when he observed in a letter of 1871 to Elihu Vedder that

"Venice swarms with artists," one of the most curious aspects of this large group of paintings is that the figure of the artist at work is not visible in the pictures.[28] While nineteenth-century landscapes often included a small study of an artist at his easel within the image, these paintings are entirely void of that self-conscious reenactment of the creative and interpretive process. The cause of this curious absence might be found in the difference of an urban rather than a pastoral or a wilderness setting, or in the relatively late date of these images, but it is probably more complex and more interesting. One notable exception is Thomas Moran's *Splendor of Venice* of 1889 (fig. 1, Philbrook Art Center, Tulsa, Oklahoma) in which he has placed an artist in the foreground, improbably perched with his full-scale easel in the prow of a gondola. As is customary with these figures of the artist-traveler-observer, his face is turned away from us and toward the object of our gaze. For other artists, this familiar figure — found in the landscapes of artists as disparate as Thomas Cole and Winslow Homer — is entirely absent, although one cannot help but feel that avoiding or deleting the omnipresent white umbrellas and concentrated figures of their fellows must have been a conscious, even difficult, effort.

In one instance we have a record — but only a sketch — of an artist at work, and true to tradition his back is turned to us as we glimpse his subject over his shoulder: Whistler in a drawing by Robert Blum (p. 10). Inscribed

15

"Venice/80/no doubt this is 'Jimmy' " – the name by which Whistler was known to his friends – the small drawing was preserved by fellow artist W. J. Baer. The picture records Whistler leaning out an upper window, probably of the Casa Jankowitz where he lodged with Frank Duveneck's "Boys," drawing or etching the Riva below (cat. nos. 106, 115). As a portrait of an artist at work in Venice, it is surprisingly rare.

They came from all parts of the United States, they stayed varying lengths of time, utilized many media, and found an audience in patrons from the most discriminating to the most popular. Their interpretations of the city, its structures, and its population exhibit no uniform posture. Yet collectively they alert us to the prominent presence of Venice in American thinking late in the nineteenth century, and to the sense of the past for which it so eloquently stood. Further, they suggest that we reinspect our sense of what it was to be an American artist at that period. For the city clearly did draw them, and, more important, in many cases it drew out their most memorable work. Even more curious, it is arguable that for some, such as Prendergast, Sargent, and Whistler, Venice provided the occasion for their most innovative work, work touched more clearly with the stamp of modernism than that produced in far less archaic environments. These facts and these paintings, watercolors, prints, and pastels give us a new perspective on these artists which we have only begun here to explore.

1. John Ruskin, "The Approach to Venice," excerpted from *The Stones of Venice*, in *The Crayon* 2, no. 1 (4 July 1855), p. 7.

2. James Jackson Jarves, *Italian Rambles: Studies of Life and Manners in New and Old Italy* (New York: Putnam's, 1883), p. 190.

3. Jarves, p. 190.

4. George G. Byron, *Byron's Letters and Journals, 1818-1819*, Leslie A. Marchland, ed., 12 vols. (Cambridge: Belknap Press, 1976), vol. 6, p. 65.

5. Byron, *Childe Harold's Pilgrimage*, IV, xviii.

6. Howard R. Marraro, "Italian Culture in Eighteenth-Century American Magazines," *Italica* 22, no. 1 (1945), pp. 24-25.

7. Francis H. Allen, ed., *Hewin's Journal: A Boston Portrait-Painter Visits Italy: The Journal of Amasa Hewins, 1830-1833* (Boston: The Boston Athenaeum, 1931), p. 74.

8. Allen, pp. 65-74.

9. Thomas B. Brumbaugh, "A Venice Letter from Thomas P. Rossiter to John F. Kensett–1843," *The American Art Journal* 5, no. 1 (1973), pp. 75-76.

10. *The North American Review*, 1856, quoted in Marcia Jean Pankake, "Americans Abroad: A Bibliographical Study of American Travel Literature 1625-1800," Ph.D. diss., University of Minnesota, 1975, p. 132.

11. Ahmed M. Metwalli, "Americans Abroad: The Popular Art of Travel Writing in the Nineteenth Century," in Steven E. Kagle, *America: Exploration and Travel* (Bowling Green, Ohio: Bowling Green State University Popular Press, 1979), pp. 68-82.

12. *Sketches of a Summer Tour* (New York: William J. Read, 1866), p. 181.

13. Felix O. C. Darley, *Sketches Abroad with Pen and Pencil* (New York: Hurd and Houghton, 1869), p. 175.

14. Ellen Olney Kirk, "In a Gondola," *Lippincott's Monthly Magazine* 50 (November 1892), p. 644; Herman Melville, *Journal of a Visit to Europe and the Levant, October 11, 1856-May 6, 1857*, Howard C. Horsford, ed. (Princeton: Princeton University Press, 1955), p. 234.

15. Quoted in Waller Barrett, *Italian Influence on American Literature* (New York: The Grolier Club, 1962), p. 21.

16. Kirk, p. 647.

17. Edmund Gosse, "Impressions of the Venetian Lagoon," *Independent* 53 (26 December 1901), p. 3077.

18. "Ode" I: 8-13, *The Works of Lord Byron* (London: John Murray, 1821), vol. 2, p. 274. Similar sentiments were expressed by Byron's American contemporaries; see Emilio Gioggio, "Italy and Some of Her Early American Commentators," *Italica* 10, no. 1 (March, 1933), pp. 4-10.

19. Arthur Symons, *Cities of Italy* (New York: Dutton, 1907), p. 77.

20. Darley, p. 181.

21. Symons, p. 86.

22. Henry James, *Transatlantic Sketches* (Boston: Houghton, Mifflin, 1888), pp. 86-87.

23. Linda Henfield Skalet, "The Market for American Painting in New York: 1870-1915," Ph.D. diss., The Johns Hopkins University, 1980, p. 133.

24. William H. Holmes, *Smithsonian Institution, The National Gallery of Art: Catalogue of Collections* (Washington, D. C.: Government Printing Office, 1922), vol. 1, p. 89.

25. George Inness, Jr., *Life, Art and Letters of George Inness* (New York: The Century Co., 1917), p. 75; Gertrude Sill, "Emil Carlsen: Lyrical Impressionist," *American Art and Antiques* (March-April 1980), p. 91.

26. "My Notebook," *Art Amateur* 25, no. 1 (June 1881), p. 2.

27. John F. Weir, *A Memorial Catalogue of the Paintings of Sanford Robinson Gifford, N. A.* (New York: The Metropolitan Museum of Art, 1881), p. 40.

28. Regina Soria, *Elihu Vedder: American Visionary Artist in Rome* (Cranbury, N. J.: Fairleigh Dickinson University Press, 1970), p. 84.

Note to the Reader

The Introduction and each artist's section of the catalogue are treated as discrete elements: after the first full
reference to a source in a note, all subsequent references
are shortened within that section.

In all text, words enclosed within single quotation marks
represent special usage of a term by the author. Quotations from other sources appear within double quotation
marks. All block quotations are set in italics.

Both Provenance and the Exhibition History and Bibliography for each work were compiled from the lender's
records, with additions provided in some instances by
the author. For traveling exhibitions, references are to
the publication and the initial venue only.

Abbreviations for Frequently Cited Sources

AAA	Archives of American, Smithsonian Institution
Clement and Hutton	Clara Erskine Clement and Laurence Hutton. *Artists of the Nineteenth Century and Their Works.* 2 vols. Boston: Houghton Mifflin, 1884
Dictionary of American Biography	Allen Johnson, Dumas Malone, et al., eds. *The Dictionary of American Biography.* American Council of Learned Studies. Reprint, 11 vols. New York: Scribner's, 1955-1964
Inventory of American Paintings	*Inventory of American Paintings Executed before 1914.* National Museum of American Art, Smithsonian Institution, Washington, D. C.
NAD	Maria Naylor, ed. *The National Academy of Design Exhibition Record, 1861-1900.* New York: Kennedy Galleries, 1973
Soria, *Dictionary*	Regina Soria. *Dictionary of Nine-teenth-Century American Artists in Italy, 1760-1914.* East Brunswick, N. Y.: Fairleigh Dickinson, 1982

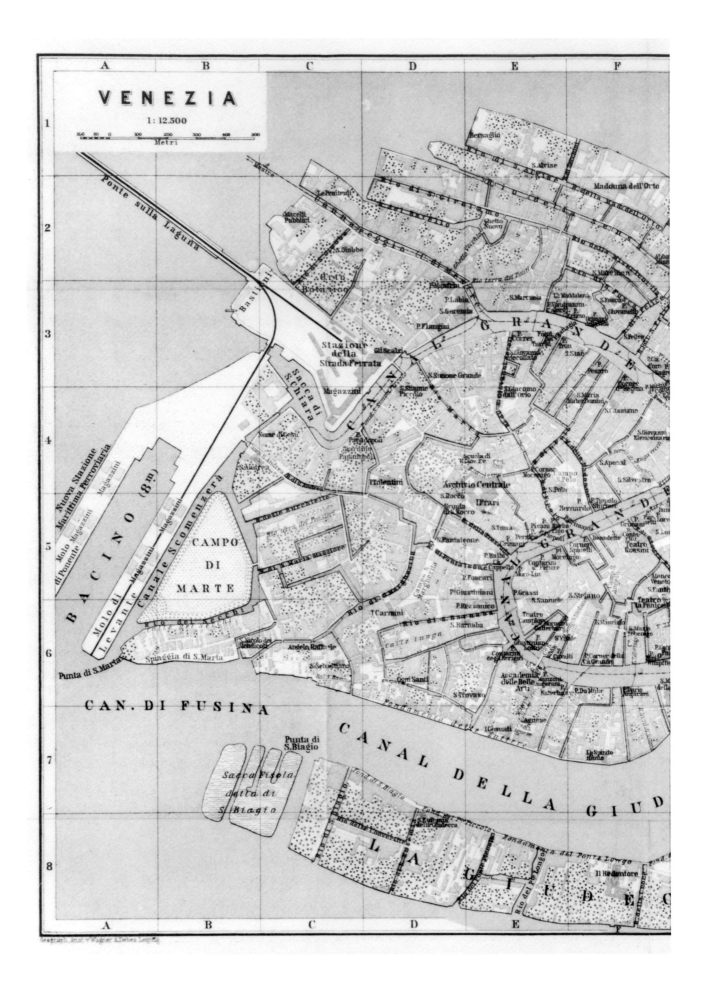

VENEZIA

1:12.500

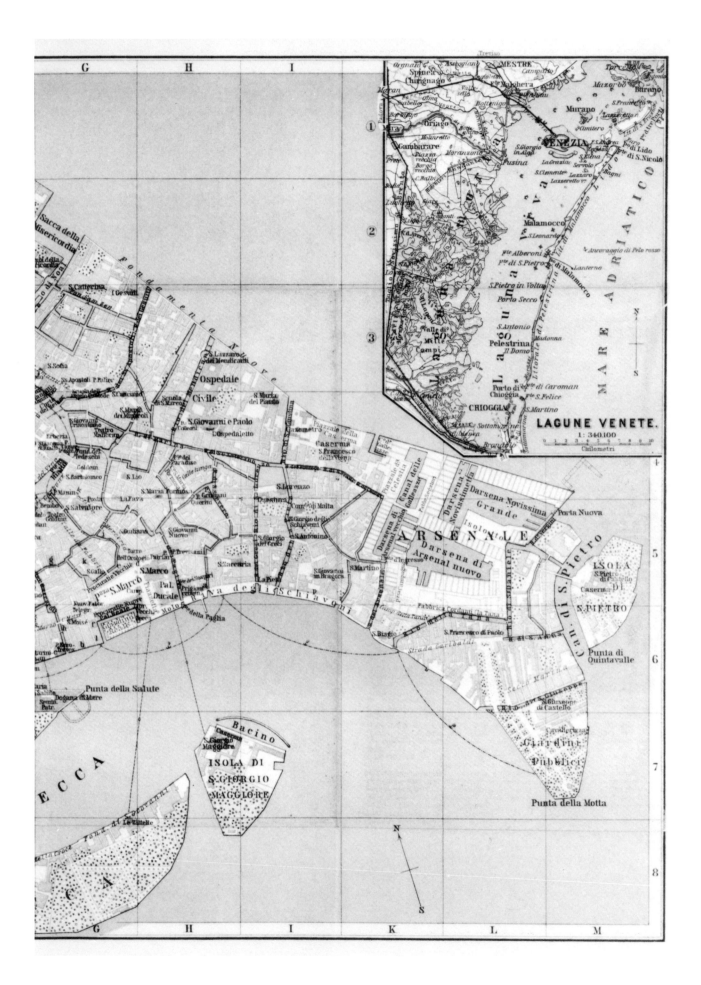

LAGUNE VENETE.

1 : 340,100

1

Anonymous

1   Venice, ca. 1840
Watercolor on paper, 14¾ × 19¾ in. (37.5 × 50.2 cm)
New York State Historical Association, Cooperstown

One of Venice's best-known monuments, the sixteenth-century marble Rialto bridge which arches over the Grand Canal is the subject of this watercolor by an unknown mid-nineteenth-century American artist. As much a symbol of Venetian civic pride as the Doge's Palace, and the center of the Republic's commercial life, the Rialto was widely known through Shakespeare's *Merchant of Venice*, Canaletto's many eighteenth-century paintings of the subject, and other less celebrated sources.

Whether the artist in fact visited Venice or worked from available pictorial sources (such as prints or daguerreotypes) is not clear from internal evidence, but the artist has thoroughly translated the scene into his own idiom.[1] Innocent of linear perspective, shading, and Renaissance canons of proportion, the image is, nevertheless, straightforward and descriptive of architectural form and human incident. Consistent with naive or 'folk' design conventions, the bridge, the boats, and most of the faces are presented in profile. Carefully describing of the most characteristic aspect of each form, the painter has depended on crisp outline and bold local color for effect. Keeping his palette to black, white, and the three primaries – blue, red, and yellow – the artist insists on the immediacy and significance of his subject. Against the carefully ruled lines of the architectural forms two red curtains flutter, introducing a random note of specificity into a timeless scene.

Unlike his more academically schooled fellow artists who were often at pains to disguise their position on land (implying instead a gondola perspective on their scene), this painter has introduced a fictive quay into the foreground assuring us of a firm foothold from which to behold the extraordinary bridge. But perhaps the most unusual thing about this painting is the assertion it makes that Venice (and the Western tradition in architecture and painting that the city so emphatically represents) was of interest to the rural artist. We tend to think of these community-oriented artists as very much bounded by and bound to the homely subjects of local garden, farm, and physiognomy. Clearly. however, their imaginative leaps were, on occasion, leaps in the direction of the very center of the Western tradition, a tradition that they, in formal terms, so emphatically discarded.

1. Daguerreotypes of the Rialto were made as early as Alexander John Ellis's *Bridge of the Rialto and the Riva dei Carbon, Venice* of 20 July 1841; see Wendy M. Watson, *Images of Italy: Photography in the Nineteenth Century*, exh. cat. (South Hadley, Mass.: Mount Holyoke College Art Museum, 1980), p. 29.

Provenance: Gunn Collection; Stephen C. Clark

Exhibition History and Bibliography: Agnes Jones and Louis C. Jones, *New Found Folk Art of the Young Republic*, New York State Historical Association, 1969, p. 16, pl. 19; Jean Lipman and Alice Winchester, *The Flowering of American Folk Art, 1776-1876*, New York: The Viking Press, in cooperation with The Whitney Museum of American Art, 1974, no. 67, p. 54; Century Association, 2 January-15 February 1961; Roberson Memorial Center, Binghampton, 1 November-15 December 1961; Union College Art Gallery, Schenectady, January-March 1962; Museum of American Folk Art, New York, *Folk Art from Cooperstown*, 21 March-6 June 1966.

2

Otto H. Bacher
1856 – 1909

When Otto Bacher first visited Venice during the summer and fall of 1880 with Frank Duveneck and other Duveneck pupils, his stay overlapped that of James McNeill Whistler. Bacher was an experienced etcher, and his printing press was useful to the older artist and to the company as a whole in their etching and monotype projects.[1] Evidence of these important experiments remained in his possession until his death.[2] The Duveneck group – joined by Whistler – was located in the Casa Jankowitz on the Riva degli Schiavoni.

Bacher's etchings of Venetian subjects were included in several exhibitions that year and the next, including the exhibition of the Society of American Artists in New York and the Society of Painters-Etchers in London. Their relative 'freedom' was a cause for both applause and complaint among critics.[3]

Bacher revisited Venice in 1882/83, again in 1885/86, and then returned permanently to New York.[4] However, the city remained a significant subject for him throughout the decade, as he exhibited Venetian oils at the Royal Academy in London in 1882 and at the National Academy of Design in New York in 1884 and 1888.[5] His autobiographical account of the eventful year 1880/81, *With Whistler in Venice*, and his papers and letters from this decade provide us with useful insights into the lives of Whistler, Bacher, Duveneck, and their circle.[6]

1. Margery Ryerson Papers, roll 962, frames 2-4, AAA: letter of 17 August 1920 from Henry M. Rosenberg to Margery Ryerson.

2. Otto Bacher Papers, roll 1654, frames 478-500, AAA: *Art Property of the Late Otto H. Bacher of Laurence Park, N. Y., Painter – Etchings, Original Drawings, Rare Whistler Items, Seymour Haden Etchings, Etchings by Rembrandt, Books and Letters, Associated Items* (New York: Anderson Art Galleries, 1910).

3. S. R. Koehler, "Mr. Bacher's Venetian Etchings," *The American Art Review*, vol. 2, second division (1881), pp. 231-232.

4. *Dictionary of American Biography*, vol. I, pp. 465-466; Soria, *Dictionary*, p. 59.

5. *NAD*, p. 19; Soria, *Dictionary*, p. 59.

6. Otto Bacher, *With Whistler in Venice* (New York: The Century Co., 1909); Bacher Papers, roll 1654, passim, AAA; Dennis R. Barrie, "Detroit," *Archives of American Art Journal* 19, no. 3 (1979), pp. 24-25.

2 A Wet Evening in Venice (Rainy Night, Venice), ca. 1880
Etching and drypoint (black ink on oriental paper), plate 5⅛ × 12 in. (13 × 30.5 cm), sheet 9¼ × 16¾ in. (23.5 × 42.6 cm)
Signed in pencil, lower left: *Otto H. Bacher*
The Fine Arts Museums of San Francisco, Achenbach Foundation for Graphic Arts. Gift of A. S. MacDonald

Seen from the Riva San Biagio, the Bacino San Marco – lined with the ghostly nocturnal forms of Venice's most distinguished buildings – is transformed by Bacher into a melancholy expanse of still water. In the dusky light, form and reflection merge indistinguishably, and small points of light gleam out of the rainy darkness, making a narrow, human-inhabited zone between sea and sky. Raising his horizon line very high and extending the format horizontally, Bacher emphasizes the wide expanse of water. Against its reflective surface and the light sky, all the concrete forms – boats, buildings, a solitary figure – are darkly silhouetted, with the marked exception of the Doge's Palace. Exempted from the dusk that enshrouds the surrounding scene, its marble surface seems to emanate a spectral light, reminding us of Turner's similar liberties with light and substance.

One of at least forty Venetian subjects etched by Bacher, *A Wet Evening in Venice* exhibits the *"over-abandon"* the New York critic S. R. Koehler finds in his work from this Whistler-Duveneck circle period.[1] Nevertheless, he goes on to defend, "that sense of a *first impression* which the artist has striven to call up in us."[2] Interestingly, Koehler expands upon his discussion of Bacher's etchings with a perceptive comment on the nature of Impressionism. It is a somewhat precocious analysis for New York in 1881 and suggests the flexible mind of a generation for whom Salmon's *Venice* (cat. no. 51) was beginning to look 'wrong' and Bacher's *A Wet Evening in Venice* was beginning to look interesting:

Impressionism is simply a new attempt at solving the problem of pictorial representation, which problem is very far yet from being completely solved. It is easy enough to say that the picture must produce upon the retina the same effect as the objects seen in nature. Superficially considered, it seems self-evident that, if the objects are represented on the picture plane, where it cuts the cone of rays, exactly as they would be represented by a camera lucida, the result on the retina must be the same as that produced by nature. This reasoning, however, is fallacious; for not only do the phenomena of binocular vision come in as a disturbing element, but it must also be recollected that the image on the retina is continually shifting, that no line is fixed on it, and that the blurring increases with the distance. It follows that a small, fixed object near by cannot produce the same effect upon the eye in its natural, unconstrained condition, as a large object at a great distance, and the impressionist is right, therefore, in avoiding definition.[3]

This marked avoidance of definition is also clear in Bacher's choice of a scene obscured by rainfall and darkness.

1. Koehler, p. 231.
2. Koehler, p. 232.
3. Koehler, p. 232.

Robert Frederick Blum
1857–1903

Robert Blum's first trip to Venice occurred in 1880 – *the critical year* for so many American artists in Venice. There he met James McNeill Whistler, Otto Bacher, Frank Duveneck, and others.[1] One of Blum's eloquently drafted pencil sketches catches Whistler drawing at the window of the Casa Jankovitz on the Riva, recording this important conjunction of Americans in Venice (see Introduction, fig. 2, Cincinnati Art Museum). We can glimpse a more complete portfolio of his first impressions of the city in the sketchbook of 1880-1881 preserved at the Cooper-Hewitt Museum.[2] During the decade of the 1880s, Blum returned to Venice many times: 1881, 1885, 1886, 1887, and 1889 saw extended visits, and in many cases he seems to have deliberately lingered through the more unpleasant winter months. His letters of 1885 suggest that the ''summer'' aspect of Venice presented by F. Hopkinson Smith was only a partial story; they give us (with a decided tone of good sportsmanship) glimpses of Venice in the off-season: ''Last week we had snow. Venetians walk about as if they didn't like it,'' and ''Twachtman is doing a large canvass of ships & boats in midsummer to keep warm. Lots of foggy effects now – don't have to draw in so damned much detail, just sort of blurr over the thing and there you are. . . . We are seeing some pretty lively times here what with the cholera and the earthquake we had last night.''[3]

His lodgings shifted, but it is clear from his letter of 12 June 1885 to William M. Chase that among the most satisfactory were the ''five rooms in the Palazzo Contarini di Scrigni, San Trovaso, on the Grand Canal near the Iron Bridge.''[4] Blum was at the center of a wide circle of American artists who visited Venice during the decade – his letters refer to the comings and goings of Walter Launt Palmer, Charles Ulrich, William Gedney Bunce, John Henry Twachtman, as well as Duveneck, Bacher, Whistler, and Chase.[5] The Spaniard Martín Rico was also ensconced in the Palazzo Contarini di Scrigni, according to Blum, in ''the room next to mine . . . doing some charming things.''[6]

Blum clearly found in Venice a congenial subject. Beyond a corpus of delicate etchings and pencil drawings, substantial works in oil, watercolor, and pastel survive. The 1913 Blum retrospective exhibition included nine paintings, four pastels, four watercolors, and six etchings of Venetian subjects.[7] His first important oil was *Venetian Lacemakers* (cat. no. 7), exhibited with remarkable success at the National Academy of Design (1888) and the Exposition Universelle in Paris (1889).[8] Although his output was not large, it was exquisite. As Royal Cortissoz put it, ''No painter of Venice has surpassed Blum in the fragility of his impressions, in their delicacy of fibre, in their ravishing precision.''[9]

1. *A Retrospective Exhibition: Robert Blum, 1857-1903*, exh. cat. (The Cincinnati Art Museum, 1966), p. 1.
2. Cooper Union Museum Papers, roll NCUd2, frames 1904-16-34 to 44, AAA.
3. L. R. McCabe, ''Illustrated Epistolary Art of Robert Blum,'' *Arts and Decoration* 4, no. 1 (November 1913), p. 21; Otto Bacher Papers, roll 1654, frames 153-155, AAA.
4. Chapellier Galleries Papers, roll N68-101, frame 13, AAA.
5. Chapellier Papers, frames 5-7, 11-13, 20-22.
6. Chapellier Papers, frame 37.
7. Bacher Papers, roll 1654, frames 611-622, AAA: *Catalogue of a Memorial Exhibition of the Works of Robert Frederick Blum*, Introduction by Martin Birnbaum (New York: Berlin Photographic Company, 1913), pp. 5-16.
8. Martin Birnbaum, *Introductions: Painters, Sculptors, and Graphic Artists* (New York: Frederick Fairchild Sherman, 1919), p. 93; *NAD*, p. 71.
9. Royal Cortissoz, *Personalities in Art* (New York: Scribner's, 1925), p. 411.

3 A Morning in St. Mark's (Venice)
Watercolor on paper, 9½ × 12⅞ in. (24.1 × 32.7 cm)
Inscribed, lower left: *A Morning in St Marks*
Cincinnati Art Museum. Gift of Henrietta Haller.

One of the many works placed in museum collections (particularly the Cincinnati Art Museum) by the artist's sister in 1905, this delicate watercolor is characteristic of Blum's work in this medium. Distinct forms and figures loom out of an overall indistinctness; catching a glint of sunshine, they shimmer momentarily in a rarified atmosphere.

Blum seems haunted in this work – probably executed in the early or mid-1880s – by a well-known passage from John Ruskin's epochal *Stones of Venice* which was excerpted in *The Crayon* as early as 1855:

Through the heavy door . . . let us enter the church [of San Marco] itself. It is lost in still deeper twilight, to which the eye must become accustomed for some moments before the form of the building can be traced; and then there opens before us a vast cave, hewn out into the form of a cross, and divided into shadowy aisles by many pillars. Round the domes of its roof

3

4 Canal in Venice, San Trovaso Quarter, 1885

Oil on canvas, 34⅛ × 23⅛ in. (86.7 × 58.7 cm)
National Museum of American Art, Smithsonian
Institution. Gift of William T. Evans
Color plate

Seated on the *fondamenta* that runs along the Rio di S. Trovaso, Blum looks down the Rio Ogni Santi, capturing the bright sun, irregular buildings, and eccentric waterways for which Venice is so noted. His vibrant brushwork describes opaque water, sparkling marble, and patient loiterers with equal dexterity. Keeping his palette rather subdued with dull reds, greens, and brown tones, Blum captures the timeless quality of this archetypical scene with its balanced composition and crooked vista. Eccentrically, he has left large areas of bare canvas which read as 'wall' here almost as readily as do areas of bare paper in his (and Whistler's) Venetian pastels.[1] Simultaneously constructing and calling attention to his fiction, Blum expresses a certain proto-modernism in this contradiction.

At the center of the composition Blum has placed one figure in action, a man who propels forward his small craft, a sandolo, with an oar only faintly suggested. Smaller in size and more maneuverable than the gondola, the sandolo was used by boys, artists and, if Elizabeth Pennell is to be trusted, by women:
Whatever may be the real or poetic beauty of the gondola, its sister boat, the sandolo, is without doubt one of if not the most graceful of all Venetian craft. It also is flat-bottomed, but it is very small and light, and instead of a ferro it has a steel knob at its prow. Moreover, it can carry a sail better than a gondola. Its very lightness makes it more desirable for the amateur gondolier, and after you have been in Venice a short time you begin to recognize the different artists who are their own gondoliers, rowing alone in their sandolos from canal to canal or from studio to trattoria, and the mere pleasure-seeker, who unfurls his tiny canvas, and spends the long lazy summer afternoons in sailing toward the main-land, or through the channels to the islands. You learn, too, to know the few women – artists and idlers – who have mastered the not easy art of rowing Venetian fashion.[2]

Although several of Blum's Venetian works were intended for public exhibition and were acquired by prominent collectors, this canvas was bought by fellow-artist Otto Bacher (as were *The Gondolas* and other works) and others were owned by William M. Chase; in this popularity with his colleagues, Blum was unusual.[3] Among the many sketches Blum included in his letters to Chase (often figure sketches and caricatures) is a rather detailed drawing very similar to this painting in subject, composition, and tone.[4]

the light enters only through narrow apertures like large stars; and here and there a ray or two from some far away casement wanders into the darkness, and casts a narrow phosphoric stream upon the waves of marble that heave and fall in a thousand colors along the floor. What else there is of light is from the torches, or silver lamps burning ceaselessly in the recesses of the chapels; the roof sheeted with gold, and the polished walk covered with alabaster, give back at every curve and angle some feeble gleaming to the flames....

Nor is the interior without effect on the minds of the people. At every hour of the day there are ... solitary worshippers scattered through the darker places of the church, evidently in prayer both deep and reverent, and for the most part profoundly sorrowful.[1]

Ruskin's *Stones* was known to Blum and to virtually all foreign visitors in the late nineteenth century, for writer and book made a deep impression on European and Anglo-American culture. Ruskin dictated to many the terms – of celebration or excoriation – on which Venice's key monuments were to be taken. Although in *A Morning in St. Mark's* Blum clearly adopts Ruskin's persona and reverence for the great Byzantine-Gothic church, in at least one private instance – a drawing embellishing a letter entitled "Sights in Venice" – he satirized a monocled British tourist who conscientiously peruses, among other books, Ruskin's *Stones* (Cincinnati Art Museum).

As in his better-known *Venetian Lacemakers*, Blum in this painting takes advantage of stark, lateral, natural lighting on a cool, dark interior space. A decade later John Singer Sargent depicted virtually the identical scene in oils with rather different effect (*The Pavement*, 1898, private collection).

1. John Ruskin, "St. Mark's," *The Crayon* 2, no. 5 (1 August 1855), pp. 69-70; *The Stones of Venice* was published 1851-1853.

Provenance: Gift of Henrietta Haller

Exhibition History and Bibliography: Cincinnati Art Museum, *A Retrospective Exhibition: Robert F. Blum, 1857-1903*, 1 April-7 May 1966, no. 41.

1. See, for instance, Blum's *A Street in Venice*, pastel, 8⅛ × 12 in., Sterling and Francine Clark Art Institute, Williamstown, Massachusetts.
2. Elizabeth Robins Pennell, "Venetian Boats," *Harper's New Monthly Magazine* 80, no. 478 (March 1890), p. 552; Mary Peixotto, "A Summer in a Sandolo," *Harper's Monthly Magazine* 51, no. 633 (February 1903), pp. 431-437.
3. Letter of 21 April 1909, from William T. Evans to Prof. Richard Rathbun, National Museum of American Art files; Otto Bacher Papers, roll 1654, frames 618-621, AAA: *Memorial Catalogue*, pp. 14, 16.
4. Katherine Metcalf Roof, *The Life and Art of William Merritt Chase* (New York: Charles Scribner's Sons, 1917), p. 342.

4

5

Provenance: Otto Bacher; from whom obtained by William T. Evans; gift of William T. Evans, New York, 1909

Exhibition History and Bibliography: Richard Rathbun, *Smithsonian Institution, United States National Museum, Bulletin 70: The National Gallery of Art, Department of Fine Arts of the National Museum*, Washington, D.C.: Government Printing Office, 1909, p. 117; National Gallery of Art, Washington, D.C., Catalogue for opening of the National Gallery of Art, 1910, p. 6; *International Studio* 48 (February 1913); National Gallery of Art, Washington, D.C., Catalogue, 1916, p. 123; William H. Holmes, *Smithsonian Institution, The National Gallery of Art: Catalogue of Collections*, 2 vols., Washington, D.C.: Government Printing Office, 1922, vol. 1, p. 32; American Federation of Arts Traveling Exhibition, 1923-1924; Corcoran Gallery of Art, Washington, D.C., National Academy Exhibition, 1925; Grand Central Art Galleries, New York, National Academy Exhibition, 1925; National Gallery of Art, Washington, D.C., Catalogue, 1926, p. 42; National Museum of American Art, Washington, D.C., *Descriptive Catalogue of Painting and Sculpture in the National Museum of American Art*, Boston: G. K. Hall, 1983, p. 19.

5 Lady Boarding a Gondola from a Palazzo, 1885

Watercolor, brush and black ink, over pencil on paper, 11⅞ × 9⅝ in. (30.2 × 24.4 cm).
Signed, dated, and inscribed with pen and purple ink at right: *Blum / 85 / Venice*; annotated on reverse with pencil: *Blum* (followed by instructions for framing)
Sterling and Francine Clark Art Institute, Williamstown, Massachusetts

Painted during the summer of 1885 when Blum was renting rooms in the Palazzo Contarini di Scrigni on the Grand Canal, this little watercolor incorporates that lightness of touch which we associate with his work in watercolor and pastel. Bordering on the narrative, the painting captures, nevertheless, a single momentary glimpse, a situation. A lady stands at the foot of the watersteps of a palace, one that is unusual for its set-back façade and front garden (this may be the fifteenth-century Palazzo Falier rented by William Dean Howells early in his consulship during the administration of Abraham Lincoln and which stood directly across the Grand Canal from Blum's own residence).[1] She is assisted into a waiting gondola by a dark figure – probably a gondolier – while a second gondolier steadies the narrow black craft. It is a simple act, this stepping into a gondola, yet one imbued with a magic uniquely Venetian. One writer described the experience in decidedly poetic terms:
You bear your weight on Giorgio's bent elbow and step into his boat.

It is like nothing else of its kind your feet have ever touched – so yielding and yet so firm; so shallow and yet so stanch; so light, so buoyant, and so welcoming to peace and rest and comfort.

How daintily it sits the water! How like a knowing swan it bends its head, the iron blade of the bow, and glides out upon the bosom of the Grand Canal! You stop for a moment, noting the long narrow body, blue-black and silver in the morning light, as graceful in its curves as a bird.[2]

This aquatic "bird" and its little human drama are observed by a second woman, with a red fan in her hand, who leans on the balustrade on the left; she watches the scene – as we do – with concentrated interest.

Blum has succeeded in giving this modest scene a palpable sense of hot sun and deep shadows. The water is dark and still, reflective and not transparent. Unlike many of his contemporaries, Blum was particularly adroit and eloquent in his use of black. In the areas in which black is most intense – the dark water, the shadowed doorway, half-hidden window, and gondola *felze* – he has heightened the otherworldly shimmering quality of the scene by including flecks of gold in his pigment.

A 'genre' scene which focused on a figure of fashion was, surprisingly, an unusual subject for Blum and his contemporaries. Here he has succeeded in injecting vibrancy, life, and a touch of mystery into this fleeting glimpse of a young visitor or elegant Venetian.

1. William Dean Howells, "An Old Venetian Friend," *Harper's Magazine* 138, no. 827 (April 1919), p. 638.
2. F. Hopkinson Smith, *Gondola Days* (Boston: Houghton Mifflin, 1902), p. 13.

Provenance: Perhaps acquired by Robert Sterling Clark from his father, a friend and patron of the artist

Exhibition History and Bibliography: Egbert Haverkamp-Begeman, et al., *Drawings from the Clark Art Institute*, 2 vols., New Haven and London: Yale University Press, 1964, no. 311; University Gallery, University of Massachusetts at Amherst, *Late Nineteenth Century American Drawings and Watercolors*, 14 May-5 June 1977, no. 1; Soria, *Dictionary*, p. 107; Rafael Fernandez, *A Scene of Light and Glory: Approaches to Venice*, Sterling and Francine Clark Art Institute, 20 March-25 April 1982, no. 62.

6 Venetian Scene, ca. 1885

Watercolor on tan wove paper, 6⅝ × 2⅝ in.
(16.8 × 6.7 cm)
Inscribed with pencil on verso: *Venezia Italia*
The Fine Arts Museums of San Francisco. Achenbach Foundation for Graphic Arts purchase

A tiny vignette capturing a small glimpse of Venice, this modest watercolor depicts sections of buildings, masts, apertures, and a dry-docked boat. Deliberately fractured and incomplete, the composition suggests an important aspect of Venice often commented upon but rarely painted: its baffling, labyrinthine character. As one contemporary put it,
A single wrong turning may lead one to the other end of Venice. This movement, the tangles of the way, the continual arresting of one's attention by some window, doorway, or balcony, puts a strain upon one's eyes, and begins after a time to tire and stupefy the brain. There is no more bewildering city, and, as night comes on, the bewilderment grows almost disquieting. One seems to be turning in a circle, to which there is no outlet, and from which all one's desire is to escape.[1]
Blum's little sunset here captures some of this quality of visual and spatial disorientation.

This picture was once owned by Willis Seaver Adams, a minor artist from western Massachusetts who painted dozens of watercolors of Venice between 1885 and 1907 and who may have been an acquaintance of Blum's.[2]

1. Arthur Symons, "The Waters of Venice," *Scribner's Magazine* 39, no. 4 (April 1906), p. 386.
2. *Inventory of American Paintings*; American Studies Group, *Willis Seaver Adams Retrospective* (Deerfield, Mass.: The Hilson Gallery, Deerfield Academy, 1966).

Provenance: Willis Seaver Adams (1842-1921); purchased by the Achenbach Foundation for Graphic Arts from David and Constance Yates, New York, 1982

6

7 Venetian Lacemakers, 1887

Oil on canvas, 30⅛ × 41¼ in. (76.5 × 104.7 cm)
Signed and dated, lower right: *Robt Blum/87.*
Cincinnati Art Museum. Gift of Mrs. Elizabeth S. Potter
Color plate

Toward the end of January 1886 Blum wrote to his friend Otto Bacher describing his life in lonely winter-bound Venice:
Well I'm, as you can well imagine, pretty lonely now he [Twachtman] is away and don't know what to do with my evenings as I hardly care to sit with that German gang at the Florian's and act mummy. So after dinner at the Capellonero which I spin out as long as a cheap dinner can be I saunter forth chewing a toothpick and ogle the Raggazzi for a while up and down the Mercerie then for a cup of Capuchina at the Orientale and then home. . . . Well there is a little bit of life going on here on account of the Carnival but I'm out of that sort of thing – as it doesn't interest me much. I'm at work on a "lace makers" picture but am hardly progressing with it.[1]

Blum's enthusiasm for the "Raggazzi" – in his ragged Italian, "girls" – of Venice clearly informed his daytime labors as it lightened his evening strolls, for this major "'lace makers' picture" which he mentions to Bacher

7

is touched at every point by the artist's awareness of the delicacy, youth, and charm of his subjects.

Not so much an ancient craft survival as a recent revival, lacemaking among Venetian women in the late nineteenth century was something of a novelty. A primary innovator and world-supplier of laces in the six-teenth, seventeenth, and eighteenth centuries, Venice's needlework industry had declined to the point of extinc-tion by the mid-nineteenth century. Two lace schools were founded during the 1870s, probably indirectly in-spired by John Ruskin's and William Morris's influential enthusiasm for handicrafts. Moreover, the government and private sponsors hoped to relieve permanently the distress of a single-resource economy severely threat-ened by winter freezes and poor fishing.[2] These lace schools were founded in Venice for many of the same philanthropic, aesthetic, and socially conscious reasons that the Rookwood Pottery works were established in Blum's native Cincinnati at this time.[3] From a mere eight students in 1872, the number of lacemakers in Venice boomed to 3,400 by 1897, and it is this new-found eco-nomic and human resource that Blum celebrates in *Venetian Lacemakers*.

Attentive to their meticulous handwork, to each other, and to the artist-observer, the two clusters of young women are arranged in an interesting and complex com-position dominated by a steeply receding diagonal line. Blum has given himself a difficult pictorial problem by backlighting the subject, which gives him the oppor-tunity to use the sharp value contrasts and sparkling points of illumination for which he is well known. A few years earlier Edgar Degas had given himself a similar problem in *The Rehearsal* (1879, Frick Collection, New York), but where the Frenchman permits the window light to etch his dancers' features in its harshest, most unflattering manner, Blum carefully orchestrates the spotlit contours of face, hair, and shoulder to enhance rather than negate his sitters' beauty. The whole com-position emphasizes the exquisiteness of the young women and suggests the beauty of their unseen handi-work. In a minor key, Blum has juxtaposed to the lacemakers – the buoyancy of their spirits, the gaiety of their dress, and the elegance of their product – the humbleness of their straight-backed, reed-bottomed chairs, the aged irregularity of the Venetian blinds, and the fact of their necessary labor.

According to the record left in his letters, *Venetian Lace-makers*, always intended to be a major statement of his art, experienced at least one false start and considerably taxed its author.[4] The problem of the light source, and the action of that light on his subject, was clearly one of the difficulties. We can see him at work on this problem in the 180-degree shift of the direction of the light source from his preparatory oil sketch for two figures to their incorporation in the rear group of the finished painting.[5] At least two other "lacemakers" oil sketches exist and may relate to earlier versions of the Cincinnati picture.[6]

Whatever difficulties Blum had with pictorial problems, the absence of models, the interruptions in his work to finish other pictures, and the move back to New York, the finished painting was a success. It was exhibited with favorable comment and congratulatory medals in New York in 1887, in both London and Paris in 1889, in Chicago in 1890, and was acquired by the notable collector Alfred C. Clark.[7] A British reviewer of the Royal Academy exhibition summed up the contemporary reception of the work:

This, though not specially well-observed as a study of life and manners, furnishes one of the most consummately realized studies of the qualities of light and of chiaroscuro to be found in the whole exhibition.[8]

In 1887/88 Blum painted a pendant, *The Italian Bead Stringers* (The Otesaga Hotel, Cooperstown, N.Y.), which clearly embodies the prescribed closer "study of life and manners." Here the women's gestures and posture more clearly relate to their specific manual task. The paintings are similar in size and subject, and one of the models for the earlier work reappears in the later painting. In both we feel not only the charm which Blum responded to so enthusiastically in his *ragazze* but also, as one critic put it, Blum's "exquisite execution . . . carried to its highest point."[9]

1. Otto Bacher Papers, roll 1654, frames 200-202, AAA.

2. Mrs. Bury Palliser, *History of Lace* (London: Sampson Low, Marston & Co., Ltd., 1910), pp. 45-63.

3. Robert Judson Clark, ed., *The Arts and Crafts Movement in America, 1876-1916*, exh. cat. (Princeton: The Art Museum, Princeton University, 1972), pp. 119-120, 144.

4. Letters of 7 October 1886, 5 November 1886, 10 November 1886, 27 November 1886, 6 March 1887, 18 April 1887 (private collection), noted in *The Golden Age: Cincinnati Painters of the Nineteenth Century Represented in the Cincinnati Art Museum*, exh. cat. (Cincinnati: Cincinnati Art Museum, 1979), pp. 39-40.

5. The oil sketch (oil on board, 9¼ × 6¾ in.) is illustrated in *The Magazine Antiques* 123, no. (April 1983), p. 663.

6. *Venetian Lacemakers* (oil on canvas, 16¼ × 12¼ in., collection of Mr. and Mrs. Raymond J. Horowitz) and *Venetian Lacemakers* (oil on wood panel, 5 × 18 in., Canajoharie Library and Art Gallery, Canajoharie, N.Y.); a large-scale pastel related to the Cincinnati picture was executed in 1887 and is in a private Cincinnati collection (*Golden Age*, p. 40).

7. *Golden Age*, p. 39.

8. Claude Phillips, "Fine Art: The Royal Academy II," *The Academy* 33 (January-June 1888); supplement to *The Academy* (28 July 1888), p. 365.

9. Frank Jewett Mather, Jr., et al., *The American Spirit in Art* (New Haven: Yale University Press, 1927), p. 140. The record of a related watercolor study, *Venetian Bead Stringers* (10½ × 10 in.), "Eight women seated in a group, the pencilled outlines filled with a suggestion of color," is found in the catalogue of Otto Bacher's "Art Property," 1910 (Bacher Papers, roll 1654, frame 487, no. 60, AAA).

Provenance: Alfred C. Clark; Mrs. Alfred C. Clark (Elizabeth S. Potter), ?-1905

Exhibition History and Bibliography: American Art Galleries, New York, *Third Prize Fund Exhibition*, 1887, no. 24; "The American Art Association," *The Nation* (26 May 1887), p. 457; "Prize Fund Exhibition," *Art Age* (June 1887), p. 69; Royal Academy of Arts, London, Royal Academy Exhibition, 1888, no. 49; Claude Phillips, "Fine Art, The Royal Academy, II," *Academy* 33 (26 May 1888), p. 365; "The Royal Academy Exhibition," *Art Journal* (London, 1888), p. 181; Paris, *Exposition Universelle*, 1889, no. 20; "The Fine Arts at the Paris Exposition," *The Nation* 17 (October 1889), p. 311; *Chicago Interstate Exhibition*, 1890, no. 19; Charles H. Caffin, "Robert Frederick Blum," *International Studio* 21, no. 82 (December 1903), p. clxxxi; Mrs. Charles Mason Fairbanks, "Robert Blum, An Appreciation," *Metropolitan Magazine* (July 1904), p. 509; St. Louis, *Universal Exposition*, 1904, no. 65; *Illustrations of Selected Works of the Department of Art, Universal Exposition*, St. Louis: Louisiana Purchase Exposition Co., 1904, pp. 64, 65; *Exhibition of Paintings and Studies by the Late Robert Frederick Blum*, 1905, no. 1; Berlin Photographic Co., New York, *Memorial Loan Exhibition of the Works of Robert Frederick Blum*, 1913, p. 5; Martin Birnbaum, *Introductions: Painters, Sculptors, and Graphic Artists*, New York: Frederic Fairchild Sherman, 1919, p. 93; Ernest Bruce Haswell, "Cincinnati as an Art Center," *Art and Archaeology*, September-October 1919, p. 255; Carnegie Institute, Pittsburgh, *An Exhibition of Works by Robert Blum*, 18 January-18 February 1923, no. 40; Lorinda Munson Bryant, *What Pictures to See in America*, New York: John Lane, 1925, p. 299; Frank Jewett Mather, Jr., et al., *The American Spirit in Art*, New Haven: Yale University Press, 1927, p. 140; Cincinnati Art Museum, *Fiftieth Anniversary Exhibition of Work by Teachers and Former Students of the Art Academy of Cincinnati*, 27 November 1937-2 January 1938, no. 14; Cincinnati Art Museum, *Cincinnati Artists of the Past*, 16 January-19 April 1942, no. 15; "Cincinnati De-Dusts Artists of Her Past," *Art Digest* 16 (1 March 1942), p. 15; Marquette University, Milwaukee, *American Paintings of the Last 75 Years*, 22 April-3 May 1956, no. 7; Cincinnati Art Museum, *A Retrospective Exhibition: Robert F. Blum, 1857-1903*, 1 April-7 May 1966, no. 5; Richard J. Boyle, "From Hiram Powers to Laser Light," *Apollo* 93 (April 1971), pp. 309, 313, 314; William H. Gerdts, "Revealed Masters, 19th Century American Art," *American Art Review* 1 (November-December 1974), p. 90; Michael Quick, *American Expatriate Painters of the Late Nineteenth Century*, Dayton Art Institute, 4 December 1976-16 January 1977, p. 41 (not in exhibition); Cincinnati Art Museum, *The Golden Age: Cincinnati Painters of the Nineteenth Century Represented in the Cincinnati Museum*, 6 October 1979-13 January 1980, no. 18; New York University, Grey Art Gallery and Study Center, *Walter Gay: A Retrospective*, 16 September-1 November 1980, fig. 15; Jane Durrell, "A Museum Is Its Collection," *Cincinnati Historical Society Bulletin* (Spring 1981), p. 22.

Edward Darley Boit
1840 – 1916

It is curious that we know Edward Darley Boit best not as a watercolorist or as a friend of the most distinguished writers and artists of his day, but rather as the father of the four girls immortalized by John Singer Sargent in his masterpiece *The Daughters of Edward Darley Boit* (1882, Museum of Fine Arts, Boston). That painting was executed in Paris, but the Boits also frequently resided in Italy.

Visiting Venice for the first time in March 1867, Boit stayed at the fashionable Hôtel de l'Europe, a former palazzo at the mouth of the Grand Canal patronized by French and American visitors. He was not to take up painting for another four years, but his letters indicate a lively appreciation of the old masters and a keen eye for pictorial effect as well as a general delight in the eccentricity of the place.[1]

As he was a friend of William S. Haseltine, Elihu Vedder, Joseph Lindon Smith, Henry James, and, most important, John Singer Sargent, it was perhaps inevitable that Boit would become a painter.[2] He took up watercolors in 1871 after finding himself deeply moved by an exhibition of the paintings of Jean-Baptiste-Camille Corot (in the gallery of Towle and Ward in Boston), yet his surviving work, focusing on architectural subjects seen under a hot summer sun, has very little Corot in it.[3] Among the watercolors preserved at the Museum of Fine Arts in Boston are nine Venetian subjects executed in 1910 and 1911. They are unusual in the occasional inclusion of such attributes of modernity as the *vaporetto* (water-bus) piers which other artists avoided.[4]

1. Edward Darley Boit Papers, roll 83, frame 443, AAA.
2. Boit Papers, roll 2395, frames 273-296, AAA; Guest Book 1901-1914, from Cernitoio, Boit's Italian villa. According to Robert Apthorp Boit, *Chronicles of the Boit Family and their Descendants and of other Allied Families* (Boston: S. J. Parkhill & Co., 1915), p. 121 (Boit Papers, roll 83, frame 8, AAA), Boit graduated from Harvard in 1863 and then took a degree from Harvard Law School in 1864; how much law he actually practiced is not recorded.
3. Boit Papers, roll 85, frames 137-138, AAA.
4. *Catalogue of Paintings and Drawings in Water Color* (Boston: Museum of Fine Arts, 1949), pp. 36-38, 216-218.

8   Rio di San Barnaba, Venice, 1911
Watercolor on paper, 19 × 14 in. (48.3 × 35.6 cm)
Signed, dated, and inscribed, lower left: *Boit Venice – 1911*
Museum of Fine Arts, Boston. Purchased, Picture Fund

A group of Boit watercolors of Venice and other subjects was purchased by the Museum of Fine Arts in Boston in 1912, the same year that institution acquired a large group of John Singer Sargent watercolors. The close association of the two artists was remarked on at the time: "It is well known," J. G. reports, in the *Museum of Fine Arts Bulletin* announcing the acquisition of the two groups of watercolors, "that Mr. Boit was one of the first to appreciate and encourage Mr. Sargent, whose work he brought to the attention of his friends."[1] Nevertheless, in terms of handling of the medium, they are very different,

8

and the influence we might expect Sargent to have had on Boit is not evident. Where Sargent's brush is fluid and inferential, Boit's is linear and descriptive.

Rio di San Barnaba is very characteristic of Boit's choice of subject (almost always architectural), and treatment (a series of sharply juxtaposed individual strokes over washes descriptive of local color). The view that he has chosen here is particularly apt for his technique. Waterborne, he sits between the grand Palazzo Rezzonico (1667, Baldassare Longhena) on the right and the more modest but more ancient Palazzi Contarini-Michiel on the left. The buildings all along the north side of the canal are brightly etched by the summer sun. Punctuating the skyline and orienting us, as they have generations of Venetians, are bell towers, or campanili – on the left that of San Barnaba, on the right that of S. Maria del Carmine. It is both a typical Venetian scene (a secondary canal with ranged buildings), and a distinguished one (the Rezzonico successively housed celebrated popes, poets, and artists). And in terms of Boit's work, it is at once characteristic of his approach and of his era.

1. J. G., "The Watercolors of Edward D. Boit and John S. Sargent," *Museum of Fine Arts Bulletin* 10, no. 57 (June 1912), pp. 18-21.

Provenance: Purchased from Brooks Reed Gallery, Boston

Exhibition History and Bibliography: J. G., "The Water-Colors of Edward D. Boit and John S. Sargent," *Museum of Fine Arts Bulletin* 10 (June 1912), pp. 18-21; Museum of Fine Arts, Boston, *Catalogue of Paintings and Drawings in Water Color*, 1949, p. 38; Art Association of Newport, Boit Exhibition, 1-30 June 1967.

Emil Carlsen
1853 – 1932

Very little is known about Carlsen's sojourn(s) in Venice. An émigré from Denmark at the age of nineteen, he returned to Europe in 1884 and remained until 1886 for study in Paris; he again returned in 1908 and 1912.[1] It is probable that the 1908 trip was the only one that brought him to Venice.

Although better known for his Chardinesque still lifes and vibrant seascapes, he executed a few architectural subjects, reflecting perhaps his early training in architecture.[2] These include French and American buildings as well as four known Venetian views.[3]

1. *The Art of Emil Carlsen 1853-1932* (San Francisco: A Rubicon-Wortsman Rowe Publication, 1975), passim.
2. Gertrude Sill, "Emil Carlsen: Lyrical Impressionist," *American Art and Antiques* (March-April 1980), p. 88.
3. Examples include *Courtyard in Grez, France* (1885, *The Magazine Antiques* 110, no. 900 [November 1976]), and *Windham Church, Connecticut* (ca. 1911, *Arts* 55, no. 167 [November 1980]); *Inventory of American Paintings*.

9 Venice
Oil on canvasboard mounted on laminated support, 8½ × 10 in. (21.6 × 25.4 cm)
North Carolina Museum of Art, Raleigh. Gift of Mr. and Mrs. Fabius B. Pendleton in Memory of Katherine Clark Pendleton Arrington

The smallest of Carlsen's known Venetian canvases, *Venice* captures in miniature a prospect of the church of Le Zitelle on the tip of the Giudecca. An island known among artists for its fisherfolk and for vernacular views of warehouses and fishing boats, the Giudecca is here summarized in a broad *fondamenta*, a cluster of vertical buildings, and a distant oblique view of Palladio's San Giorgio Maggiore. Carlsen's monochromatic treatment eloquently describes the leaden sky, the opaque water, and the gray-tinted rose stucco which characterize Venice's palette in bleak weather. It is high tide and a wave from the Giudecca Canal, which has splashed up the landing steps in the foreground, retreats across the *fondamenta*. The whole little study has a unity of mood, of a single caught impression; it is a round and complete précis of geometric architectural forms within the context of fog and mist.

Carlsen's treatment of large expanses of canvas as two-dimensional blocks of almost uniform hue – as we see here in the water – reminds us of the artful use of this form of abstraction in the painting of Arthur Mathews, a California artist with whom he was associated from 1886 to 1891.[1] Carlsen's suppression of atmospheric perspective and deliberate summarization (rather than description) of form helped his work look 'modern' but nevertheless acceptable to contemporaries who were perplexed by some of the developments in painting during the first two decades of the twentieth century. As Duncan Phillips, founder of the Phillips Memorial Gallery in Washington, D.C., and an early enthusiast for Emil Carlsen's work, put it, "Carlsen is a constant student of nature and a laborious and devout technician . . . his pictures are outwardly faithful representations of things as they are without any insane befuddlement of abstractization."[2]

1. Sill, p. 92.
2. Duncan Phillips, "Emil Carlsen," *International Studio* (June 1917), reprinted in *The Art of Emil Carlsen 1853-1932*, pp. 66-70.

9

Provenance: Feragil Galleries, New York (?); Mrs. Katherine Clark Pendleton Arrington; Fabius B. Pendleton

Exhibition History and Bibliography: *North Carolina Museum of Art Bulletin* 12, nos. 1 and 2 (December 1973), p. 40; Asheville Museum of Art, *American Paintings from the Permanent Collection of the North Carolina Museum of Art: Inaugural Exhibition*, 16 May-27 June 1976, no. 6; St. John's Museum of Art, Wilmington, N.C., 5 December 1980-25 January 1981.

John Linton Chapman
1839 – 1905

Little is known of Chapman. He was the elder son of the artist John Gadsby Chapman and was named after John Linton, the patron who had sent his father (a painter of landscapes and historical subjects) to Rome in 1828 on a study tour.[1] Chapman senior moved his family to Europe in 1848, settling in Rome in 1850 where, patronized by Anglo-American visitors to the city, he enjoyed modest success.[2] Both his sons became artists; John, also a landscapist, settled in New York in 1878 and exhibited Italian views at the National Academy of Design in the 1880s.

1. Charles Eldredge, *The Arcadian Landscape: Nineteenth-Century Painters in Italy*, exh. cat. (Lawrence, Kansas: Spencer Museum of Art, University of Kansas, 1972), n.p.
2. *John Gadsby Chapman: Painter and Illustrator*, exh. cat. (Washington, D.C.: National Gallery of Art, 1963), pp. 15-16.

10　**Venice in the Distance**, ca. 1870
Oil on panel, 8 × 19¼ in. (20.3 × 48.9 cm)
Signed, lower right: *J. Linton / Chapman*
Collection of the Heckscher Museum, Huntington, New York. Gift of August Heckscher

Borrowing much from the Italianate pastoral landscape tradition of earlier centuries, Chapman offers us here a miniaturized version of the Venetian cityscape with pensive laborers adding interest in the foreground. Eccentrically, he has, at the far right, juxtaposed these archaic technological and human elements with a large two-funneled, steam-assisted sailing vessel.

A convenient small size for a traveler's purchase, the painting, nevertheless, includes the full catalogue of significant buildings: the domes of Santa Maria della Salute and the Punta della Dogana (or Custom-House Point) on the left; the Campanile, Doge's Palace, the church of San Marco, and the Prisons on the right. This view of the city as it is seen from the Giudecca has been slightly distorted; the pavilion supporting the silhouetted welcoming statue of Fortuna and sheltering a festive gathering of Venetians has been greatly enlarged and brought forward to balance the gaily decked-out two-masted *bragozze* (or fishing boat) in the center of the composition. Remarking on these brightly decorated sails, Elizabeth Pennell noted in 1890 that one soon came *to know all the different sails – the orange sheets, with galloping steeds, or spear-pierced hearts, or simple crosses; the red canvases, with orange corners, or white lines and circles . . . and the more ambitious sails, with pictures of the Madonna or of patron saints. Almost every sail has its own peculiar design. They say the art of sail-painting is in its decline, and men who have lived long in Venice will tell you that year after year they have watched its splendor growing less. But for all who have not known it in its better days, this is hard to believe. Indeed, so lovely are the sails that it seems as if they must belong, not to an everyday life of toil and struggling, but to a great festival like that which graced the lagoon of old on Ascension morn, when the Doge went in the Bucentoro to wed the sea.*
She goes on to add, significantly,
But the fact that their boats are a joy forever to poet and painter and tourist cannot, after all, make up to the fisherman for the days of bitter cold and piercing wet which are but too often his portion. . . . The whole existence of these poor men is

10

*one long battle against hunger and discomfort with, for-
tunately, pleasant interludes of unclouded sunshine and good-
luck.*[1]

Curiously, while travelers in their journals, poets, and
other verbal interpreters of the facts of Venice remarked
on this bleaker aspect of Venetian life, the painters almost uniformly insisted on depicting the brave sails
unfurled in "pleasant interludes of unclouded sunshine."

1. Elizabeth Robins Pennell, "Venetian Boats," *Harper's New Monthly
Magazine* 80, no. 478 (March 1890), pp. 554-555.

Provenance: August Heckscher, New York, by 1920

Exhibition History and Bibliography: Heckscher Museum, Huntington,
N. Y., *Huntington Fine Arts Building Catalogue*, ca. 1920, no. 46; idem,
American Paintings from the Heckscher Museum, ca. 1959, p. 13; idem,
Changing Vision of Space, 1962-1963; Guild Hall, East Hampton, N. Y.,
Paintings from the Collection of the Heckscher Museum, 1975; Katherine
Lochridge, ed., *Catalogue of the Collection: Paintings and Sculpture*,
Huntington, N. Y.: Heckscher Museum, 1979, pp. 13-14; Parrish Art Mu-
seum, Southampton, N. Y., *Americans Abroad*, 1981; Soria, *Dictionary*,
p. 113.

William Merritt Chase
1849 – 1916

William M. Chase visited Venice for the first time in 1877.
On a break from art studies in Munich, Chase arrived in
the city for a nine-month sojourn, accompanied by Frank
Duveneck and John Twachtman. Despite severe illness,
Chase accomplished a great deal during his stay. According to Kenyon Cox, Chase went to Venice "for the
purpose of copying in the museums," and we know that
he did copy a Giorgione in the Giovanneli Palace.[1] However, he also finished quite a few small oil studies of
architectural subjects and one large still life, *A Fishmarket
in Venice* (1878 – ca. 1890, The Detroit Institute of Art).
This latter work was well received and entered the collection of Mr. S. A. Coale, Jr., of St. Louis, one of four
patrons who supported Chase's study abroad, apparently
with the understanding that each would receive a painting.[2] Beyond studying the Old Masters and painting
glimpses of the city around him, Chase spent his time in
Venice acquiring objets d'art, monkeys, and other attributes of the aesthetic life.[3] His painting *The Antiquary
Shop* (ca. 1877, The Brooklyn Museum) reflects in its subject Chase's enthusiasm for this pursuit, one celebrated in
his later, better-known paintings of the Tenth Street
Studio. Other Venetian works of this period record interiors, including *In the Baptistery of St. Mark's*, (ca. 1877,
location unknown) and studies toward a painting of
laceworkers.[4]

As a mature artist Chase returned to Venice several
times, most notably as the teacher and leader of "The
Chase Class in Italy."[5] He briefly visited the city in 1907
and 1910 and returned in 1913 for a seven-week stay with
a group of students – his last, as it happens, of numerous
such European summers.[6] During this trip he stayed at
the Grand Hotel et Monaco, a sumptuous hostelry oc-
cupying the Monolesso, and at the Flangini-Fini palaces
on the Grand Canal directly across from Santa Maria
della Salute.[7] For his own work, according to his letters
home, he contented himself with painting from his hotel
balcony, and – returning to the subject of his still-life
success of thirty-six years before – searching "for a
studio to paint fish in."[8]

We know by title about twenty Venetian paintings by
Chase, but less than half of these have been located.[9]
With the exception of the interior scenes and still lifes,
they tend to be quite diminutive, loosely brushed, and
focused on a very narrow cluster of architectural elements.

1. Kenyon Cox, "William M. Chase, Painter," *Harper's New Monthly
Magazine* 78, no. 466 (March 1889), p. 552; Thurman Wilkins, *Thomas
Moran: Artist of the Mountains* (Norman, Okla.: University of Oklahoma
Press, 1966), p. 186.
2. "The Public and Private Collections of the United States, III: The
Collection of Mr. S. A. Coale, Jr., St. Louis," *American Art Review* 1,
second division (1880), pp. 423-428; *The First West Coast Retrospective
Exhibition of Paintings by William Merritt Chase*, exh. cat. (Santa Barbara:
University Art Museum, University of California, 1964), n. p.
3. Katharine Metcalf Roof, *The Life and Art of William Merritt Chase*
(New York: Charles Scribner's Sons, 1917), pp. 45-51; Ronald G. Pisano,
A Leading Spirit in American Art: William Merritt Chase, exh. cat. (Seattle:
Henry Art Gallery, University of Washington, 1983), pp. 30-32.

4. Pisano, p. 30; M. G. Van Rensselaer, "William Merritt Chase," *The American Art Review* 2, first division (1881), pp. 136, 138, 139-140; *Chase Centennial Exhibition*, exh. cat. (Indianapolis: John Herron Art Museum, 1949), n. p.: "*Venetian Lace Maker*, o.c., Owner Unknown."

5. *The First West Coast Retrospective*, n. p.

6. Roof, pp. 233-234, 240-245; Pisano, pp. 138, 142; *The First West Coast Retrospective*, n. p.

7. William Merritt Chase Papers, roll N69-137, frame 5669, AAA.

8. Chase Papers, roll N69-137, frames 5669-5678, AAA: 11 July 1913, 16 July 1913, 26 July 1913.

9. *Chase Centennial*, n. p.; *Inventory of American Paintings; Loan Exhibition of Paintings by William M. Chase*, exh. cat. (New York: The Metropolitan Museum of Art, 1917), p. 20.

11

11 Street in Venice
Oil on board, 12½ × 6 in. (31.8 × 15.2 cm)
Signed, lower right: *Wm. Chase*
Lyman Allyn Museum

It is probable that this little study of a brazier's or coppersmith's shop in a narrow Venetian *calle* (street) dates from Chase's visit to the city in 1877 at the end of his student sojourn abroad. A wall shrine and a brightly costumed workman form the principal elements of visual interest in this cluster of partially and obliquely viewed vernacular structures. While the little courtyard is cast in deep shade, bright sunshine strikes a patchy piece of wall, picturesque chimney, and green wooden shutters above. The arbitrariness of this spotlight and the seeming casualness of Chase's composition point toward a deliberate artistic posture: he presents himself as a mere observer-recorder of a scene, not the organizer of an aesthetic achievement. In this he is distinctly modern. As his contemporary Kenyon Cox put it,

He is, as it were, a wonderful human camera – a seeing machine – walking up and down in the world, and in the humblest things as in the finest discovering and fixing for us beauties we had else not thought of. . . . His art is objective and external, but all that he sees he can render, and he sees everything.[1]

Radically different from such predecessors and contemporaries as Frederic Church and Thomas Moran, Chase was aware of his self-conscious unwillingness to interpret or interject meaning in his work. As he put it in an address at the American Federation of the Arts many years later at the end of his career, "The aim of every great artist, so far as technique goes, is, to as great an extent as possible, to do away with the intermission between his head and his hand."[2]

This willful unification of perception and execution has its roots deep in nineteenth-century thought (one thinks immediately of Ralph Waldo Emerson's "I become a transparent eyeball" in his essay *Nature*, 1836), but its secularized aesthetic implications were not apparent until the late nineteenth and early twentieth centuries. Pioneer in this move toward absolute optical experience and away from the concept of the painting as a story – whether anecdotal or historical – were the French Impressionists, whose records of immediate empirical reality startled and then attracted an ever-widening audience.

Sensing these new currents with the shrewdness of an ambitious as well as an immensely talented novice, Chase here – within the context of a very modest project – is utilizing a new and immensely powerful artistic voice.

1. Cox, p. 549.

2. William M. Chase, "Painting," *The American Magazine of Art* 8, no. 2 (December 1916), p. 50.

Provenance: Virginia Palmer Bequest

Exhibition History and Bibliography: The Parrish Art Museum, Southampton, New York, 14 June-19 September 1957.

Charles Caryl Coleman
1840 – 1928

A native of Buffalo, New York, Coleman traveled to Paris in 1859 and settled in Florence in 1860, but he returned to America to join the Union Army in September of 1862. He was discharged in November of the following year after suffering a severe wound and lost little time returning to Italy (the date is variously given as 1864 or 1866).[1] He established a studio in Venice near the clock tower but by December 1866 moved to Rome, then later to Capri, returning to Venice frequently, however, for summer painting excursions.[2]

Coleman's letter from Venice in October of 1871 to the artist Elihu Vedder and his wife, encouraging them to visit, makes it clear that the city's attraction for him at that time was primarily historical: *"I really think it positively necessary for Ved, and you too, to have a look at the Bellini, Paolo [Veronese], Tiziano, Bonifacio, and Carpaccio before returning to Rome. . . . Venice swarms with artists."*[3] The paintings that Coleman exhibited at the National Academy of Design in 1877, 1880, 1888, and 1894 clearly include historical Venetian fictions as well as Whistlerian records of contemporary Venice. His delight in costume pieces did not wane with age: an account of his rebuildings and redecorations of his villa on Capri (successively Baroque, Oriental, Medieval, and Greco-Roman) gives us a sense of his will to fabricate and re-enact an exotic personal context. Nor did he abandon his early Venetian enthusiasm: a portrait photograph taken late in life posed the artist in the manner of Titian and was published in *The American Magazine of Art* with the caption "Charles Caryl Coleman Wearing the Costume of a Venetian Senator in his Studio, The Villa Narcissus, Capri, Italy."[4]

Coleman's Venetian work includes genre scenes, historical tableaux, and pure architectural documentaries. His paintings were admired and received by a ready market at the Royal Academy in London and the annual Salon in Paris, but most were purchased by Americans enthusiastic for Coleman's interpretations of Europe's elusive past and its crystalline or poetic present.[5]

1. Soria, *Dictionary*, pp. 91-93; Edwin Cerio, *The Masque of Capri* (London: Thomas Nelson & Sons, Ltd., 1957), p. 111.

2. Soria, *Dictionary*, p. 91; Cerio, p. 111; Michael Quick, *American Expatriate Painters of the Late Nineteenth Century*, exh. cat. (Dayton Art Institute, 1976), p.91

3. Regina Soria, *Elihu Vedder: American Visionary Artist in Rome* (Cranbury, N.J.: Fairleigh Dickinson University Press, 1970), p. 84.

4. *The American Magazine of Art* 15, no. 9 (September 1924), p. 467; photographer: Morgan Heiskell.

5. Cerio, p. 112.

12 The Bronze Horses of San Marco, Venice, 1876

Oil on canvas, 40¼ × 32½ in. (102.2 × 82.5 cm)
Signed, dated, and inscribed, lower left center: *CCC Venezia 1876* (interlocking C's); also signed on the stretcher: *CC Coleman, 22 Via Margutta, Roma*
The Minneapolis Institute of Arts. Gift of the Regis Collection
Color illustration on cover (detail)

One of the most dramatic paintings of the monumental structures bordering the Piazza San Marco, Charles C. Coleman's *Bronze Horses* makes the most of a foreshortened oblique view of those noble steeds. Seated on the narrow balcony on the façade of San Marco, high above the Piazza, the artist has included the upper section of the Torre dell'Orologio, or clock tower, in his view. Still in the shadow of the great church, the gilt bronze horses glimmer in the shade while the tower beyond, spotlit by the early morning sun, glows with intense gold, lapis lazuli blue, and white marble.

Both the monumental horses (probably late Roman, and certainly booty of the sack of Constantinople in 1204) and the Renaissance clock tower (designed by Mauro Codussi and built between 1494 and 1500) were central symbols of the artistic and military power of the Venetian Republic. Placed on axis with the Piazza and the Piazzetta respectively, they are focal gems in Venice's most extraordinary civic space. By selecting his eccentric point of view and placing the two subjects in close conjunction, Coleman has succeeded in defamiliarizing these very recognizable, completely familiar forms and giving them new life. Heightening the effect by the use of dramatic chiaroscuro and silhouette, Coleman bestows upon his subjects a new intensity, a new value.

This early example of the use of a restricted or attenuated cone of vision, shortly to be eloquently exploited by John Singer Sargent, is eccentric for an American during the decade of the 1870s, and quite radical for Coleman, whose composition rarely departed so completely from more established conventions. The inventiveness evident here is possibly the result of either the intervention of Coleman's patroness, Lady Ashburton, who commissioned the work, or his study of contemporary photographs.[1] Exhibited at the Paris Salon and the Art Club in London during 1877, the painting was a success for Coleman.[2] A second version of the work, inscribed "Venetia 1883/Roma 1885," exhibits minute changes but is painted with less intensity and with much flatter brushwork.[3]

A painting in which sculptures – the horses, the great bronze bellringers, the lion of St. Mark, the Madonna, and the Magi – stand in for human actors, Coleman's work depends, for its effect, on our knowledge of the religious and civic iconographic meanings of these figures. They each evince majesty, even in the present when their function as signifiers of conquest and adoration is largely absent. Coleman avoids both irony (in majesty lost, now bathetic) and nostalgia (in majesty longed for). The tone is, rather, celebratory and emphasizes a telescoped conflation of time and cultures: classical Roman (the fabrication of the horses), Byzantine (the building of San Marco), Renaissance (the construction of the clock tower), and the present (marked most notably by the nineteenth-century numeration on the clock dial). Coleman suggests that time is at once specific (9:30 a.m.), cyclical (in the numerical and zodiacal dials), and still (in the fixity of art – his art, the brazier's art, the architect's art). The real conquest, Coleman suggests, is the conquest of time in art, and the appropriate adoration is that directed at canonical art objects.

1. Clement and Hutton, vol. 1, p. 146; Iris Drigo, *A Measure of Love* (New York: Pantheon, n. d.), pp. 169-185.

2. Gertrude Grace Sill, "Americans Abroad," *Portfolio* 5 (March-April 1983), p. 77.

3. It is not improbable that Coleman worked from photographs. A very similar view made by Carlo Ponti during the decade of the 1870s suggests that this subject and composition were of interest to photographers (see *Important Photographs of Landscape and Architecture*, Sotheby Parke Bernet, New York., Wed., 19 December 1979, 2 p.m., no. 74). Even more thought-provoking is the fact that the minute alterations in shadows, shutters, and clock between Coleman's 1876 painting and the 1883/85 version (illus. Christie, Manson & Woods, International Inc., Sale, New York, Fri., 11 December 1981, p. 81, no. 98) suggest that Coleman worked from two different photographs taken about one-half hour apart. F. Hopkinson Smith painted a very similar view (undated) in watercolor, entitled *From the Balcony of St. Mark's, Venice* (Kennedy Galleries, 1983).

Provenance: Commissioned by Lady Ashburton; W. Herron, Bugbrooke, Northampton, England; sold Sotheby's, London, 1978; James Maroney, Inc., New York; Regis Collection, Minneapolis, by whom given to The Minneapolis Institute of Arts

Exhibition History and Bibliography: Clement and Hutton, vol. 1, p. 146; *Antiques Magazine* 115 (March 1979), p. 415; *Minneapolis Institute of Arts Bulletin* 64, 1978-1980, p. 126; The Brooklyn Museum, *The American Renaissance, 1876-1917*, exh. cat. (The Brooklyn Museum, 1979; distributed by Pantheon Books, New York); Gertrude Grace Sill, "Americans Abroad," *Portfolio* 5 (March-April 1983), p. 76.

12

13

Samuel Colman
1832 – 1920

Samuel Colman was a painter and etcher of note, but his name also appears in the annals of architecture (he commissioned McKim, Mead, and White to build one of Newport's superb shingle-style houses of the 1880s), and interior design (he was an associate of Louis Comfort Tiffany).[1] He was also a shrewd judge and patron of the work of other artists; at the first exhibition of the Society of American Artists in 1878 he saw John Singer Sargent's *The Oyster Gatherers of Cancale* and purchased it. A contemporary records the incident:
When asked by a friend why he had purchased it, Mr. Colman replied, promptly: "Because I wanted to have it near me to key myself up with. I am afraid that I may fall below just such a standard, and I wish to have it hanging in my studio to reproach me whenever I do."[2]

An artist who gathered his subjects from far and wide, Colman is best known for his 'discovery' of Spain and his years in Morocco, but he also visited Venice during his longest stay abroad, 1871 to 1875.[3] Sketches made at the time resulted in oils exhibited at the National Academy of Design in 1876, watercolors exhibited in 1877 and 1881, and etchings exhibited in 1881.[4] His images done in these decades, and early in the twentieth century, tend to be broad in scope, marked by a bright array of sails punctuating a dignified display of monumental buildings. His reading of Venice could not be more diametrically opposed to that of John Singer Sargent, and yet it is clear that he perceived and valued the younger artist's choice of subject, treatment, and composition.

1. Wayne Craven, "Samuel Colman (1832-1920): Rediscovered Painter of Far-Away Places," *The American Art Journal* 8, no. 1 (May 1976), pp. 16-37.
2. G. W. Sheldon, *American Painters* (New York, 1878; reissued New York: Benjamin Blom, Inc., 1972), p. 72.
3. Clement and Hutton, vol. 1, p. 148.
4. Clement and Hutton, vol. 1, p. 148; Craven, pp. 27, 31; *NAD*, pp. 177, 178.

13 **San Giorgio Maggiore**, 1902
Oil on canvas, 31½ × 72 in. (80 × 182.9 cm)
Signed and dated, lower right: *Saml Colman, 1902*
Private collection

Viewed from the little *traghetto* pier across the Grand Canal from Santa Maria della Salute, the island of San Giorgio has been caught by Colman with the full mellow glow of the setting sun on the church's marble façade. Bathed in this warm evening light, the church, its campanile, and the clustered buildings of the Benedictine monastery possess themselves of a stillness and calm almost supernatural. Palladio's great ecclesiastical masterpiece, San Giorgio, was begun in 1565. Still noble and poised on its islet in the lagoon, the church clearly appealed to Colman's sense of architectural and pictorial formality. A quarter century before he painted this picture he had been mildly reproved by a critic who characterized Colman's method as "attractive" in technique, color, and all other respects, but noted, "A little seeming negligence or unstudied effect in composition would produce a more agreeable result."[1] Such "negligence" was clearly not an aspect of Colman's aesthetic temperament; there is nothing negligent or unstudied about Palladio's balanced Renaissance façade or about Colman's arrangement of his image of the church. The horizon line is low, the rectangle stable, and the buildings are carefully whole, uninterrupted by the picture's frame.

Colman's late theoretical writings reinforce our sense of an artist for whom the rules of symmetry, proportion, and reason are supreme: "Geometry is not only the gateway to science but it is also a noble portal opening wide into the realms of art."[2] And Renaissance geometry – complex, pleasurable, and reasonable – is the underlying model in this image, a model humanized and made evocative, but not mysterious, by the play of golden sunset light.

1. Professor Robert W. Weir, "Official Report of the American Centennial Exhibition of 1876," cited in Clement and Hutton, vol. 1, p. 148.
2. Samuel Colman, *Nature's Harmonic Unity, a Treatise on its Relation to Proportional Form* (New York: Putnam's, 1912), p. 1, cited in Craven, pp. 35-36.

Frank Duveneck
1848 – 1919

The sale of a painting to a Munich dealer in 1873 enabled Frank Duveneck to expand his artistic training with a trip to Italy. He had apparently intended to travel from city to city, but, pausing in Venice, he spent his allotted weeks there, studying in the Accademia, relaxing on the Lido, and observing the city.[1] Four years later he returned with William M. Chase and John Twachtman, fellow Americans and fellow students in Munich. Their nine-month sojourn was eventful (including a brief but significant visit from one Miss Boott), but there was evidently too much competition to enable them to support themselves – as they had hoped – by the sale of paintings.[2] Their poverty relieved at the eleventh hour by a portrait commission executed by Duveneck, they returned to Munich in 1878. Apprenticeship effectively concluded that summer for Chase, who accepted a teaching post at the Art Students' League in New York, and for Duveneck, who organized his own school in Munich.[3] In that same year Duveneck sent one of his Venetian canvases, *Interior of St. Mark's Venice*, to the first exhibition of the Society of American Artists.[4]

Convinced by Miss Boott – who had studied painting with William Morris Hunt in Boston and with Thomas Couture in Paris – to move his school to Italy, Duveneck, with his pupils, passed the next two years wintering in Florence and summering in Venice.[5] During the second summer, that of 1880, while staying at the Casa Kirsch on the Riva, he began etching under the influence of one of his students, Otto Bacher, in Bacher's studio in the Casa Jankowitz nearby.[6] James McNeill Whistler – in Venice with a commission to produce a set of etchings – attached himself to the group. Although in at least one instance Whistler seized on a subject Duveneck had developed, the "Riva" window views, it is clear that, in general, the younger man's approach to the medium during this initial encounter was distinctly Whistlerian[7] – so much so, that when an interested patroness sent three of Duveneck's prints to London in 1881, they were mistaken for Whistler's and caused that artist no little consternation.[8]

Duveneck returned to Venice in 1882, 1883, 1884, and 1885. During these visits he continued to etch and to paint: boats in the Bacino, figure pieces, and genre works. In 1886 – after a long engagement – he married Elizabeth Boott, but she died suddenly in 1888 and the pattern of his life changed. Shifting from a European base back to his native Cincinnati, he visited Venice rarely. During the spring and summer of 1894, however, between excursions to Florence to oversee the carving of a monument for his wife, he painted in Venice and nearby Chioggia.[9]

As for many painters, Venice presented Duveneck with distinct visual problems, certain opportunities for comradeship, and unusual learning experiences which were critical to his development as an artist. The most important phase of his Venetian experience, 1880 – 1885, saw the execution of virtually all his etchings and many of his major 'genre' projects.

1. Josephine W. Duveneck, *Frank Duveneck, Painter-Teacher* (San Francisco: John Howell Books, 1970), pp. 51-52.
2. Duveneck, pp. 66-70, 75-76.
3. Duveneck, pp. 68, 70; L. H. Meakin, "Duveneck, A Teacher of Artists," *Arts and Decoration* 1, no. 9 (July 1911), p. 382.
4. Clement and Hutton, vol. 1, p. 230.
5. W. Bilodeau, *Frank Duveneck* (New York: Chapellier Galleries, 1972), n. p.
6. Duveneck, pp. 89-90; Mahonri Sharp Young, "Duveneck and Henry James: A Study in Contrasts," *Apollo* 92 (September 1970), p. 213; Otto Bacher, *With Whistler in Venice* (New York: Century, 1909), passim.
7. *From Realism to Symbolism: Whistler and His World*, exh. cat. (New York: Columbia University, 1971), p. 74.
8. Emily Poole, "The Etchings of Frank Duveneck," *The Print Collector's Quarterly* 25 (October 1938), p. 321; James McNeill Whistler, *The Gentle Art of Making Enemies* (London: William Heineman, 1890), pp. 52-65.
9. Duveneck, p. 131.

14 Canal Grande, Venezia, 1883
Etching (brown ink on oriental paper),
plate 11⅞ × 19⅜ in. (30.2 × 49.2 cm),
sheet 14⅜ × 21⅞ in. (36.5 × 55.6 cm)
Inscribed, in plate, lower left: *Canal Grande/Venezia/FD 1883*; in pencil along bottom edge: *etched by Frank Duveneck of Cincinnati U.S.A. 1iere etat*
The Fine Arts Museums of San Francisco, Achenbach Foundation for Graphic Arts. Gift of Osgood Hooker

14

15

All of Duveneck's thirty etchings date from 1880 to 1885, and they are almost all of Venetian subjects.[1] He made use of his pupil Otto Bacher's experience and press to learn the art, and they both worked under the same roof with Whistler that first year. Unlike the etchings from 1880 which have much of the spatial ambiguity and suggestiveness that we associate with Whistler, the later works, such as *Canal Grande, Venezia*, are characterized by a density of texture, shading, and detail that is almost painterly in quality. Curiously, Duveneck chose markedly different subjects for his etchings and his paintings, the latter focusing on marine views and genre works, while the former are almost uniformly of architectural subjects.

Characteristic of Duveneck's etched work, the plate of *Canal Grande* is large, the horizon is high (eliminating all but a narrow strip of sky), and the details are worked with descriptive care. "Massive" and "more full of detail" are the terms one contemporary used to differentiate these later works from Whistler's "free and graceful linear beauty."[2] This same critic praised both artists for the modernity of their vision:

It should be noted – as a happy sign once more – that from Whistler and Duveneck down to their last young pupil, it is not the Venice of tradition or of fantasy which has inspired the needle, but the Venice of today, – that modern life where the nineteenth century utilizes the relics of the cinque cento; *where great ships loom up amid the hurrying gondolas, and where smoke and steam play their not ignoble part in the gorgeous panorama of Venetian skies.*[3]

Little smoke or steam interrupt this languid view of the extraordinary row of palaces opposite the Salute – Palazzo Venier-Contarini (fifteenth century), Palazzetto Contarini-Fasan (fifteenth century, known as "Desdemona's House"), Palazzo Monolesso and Palazzo Flangini-Fini (seventeenth century, the Grand Hotel), and the Palazzo Pisani-Gritti (fifteenth century) – but there is a sense of contemporaneity in the composition. For visitors to Venice, the etching evoked simultaneously the memory of Shakespeare's *Othello* and their own excursions in a canopied sandolo or *felze*-topped gondola on this most memorable waterway. In 1887 *Canal Grande, Venezia*, renamed *Desdemona's House*, was published in an edition of 100 by Frederick Keppel and Co.; all were promptly sold.[4]

1. L. H. Meakin, "Duveneck, A Teacher of Artists," *Arts and Decoration* 1, no. 9 (July 1911), p. 383; Emily Poole, "Catalogue of the Etchings of Frank Duveneck," *The Print Collector's Quarterly* 25, no. 4 (December 1938), pp. 447-463.

2. M. G. Rensselaer, "American Etchers," *The Century Magazine* 25, no. 4 (February 1883), p. 492.

3. Rensselaer, p. 493.

4. Poole, p. 325.

Provenance: Given to the Achenbach Foundation for Graphic Arts by Osgood Hooker, 1959

Exhibition History and Bibliography: Emily Poole, "Catalogue of the Etchings of Frank Duveneck," *Print Collector's Quarterly* 25 (December 1938), no. 19.

15 Water Carriers, Venice, 1884

Oil on canvas, 48⅜ × 73⅛ in. (122.9 × 185.7 cm)
Signed, lower left: *F. Duveneck. Venice. 1884.*
National Museum of American Art, Smithsonian Institution. Bequest of Reverend F. Ward Denys

During the winter of 1877/78 Elizabeth Boott, the future wife of Frank Duveneck, met the artist in his studio in Venice and reported to friends of her visit:
I could not see that he made any step in the direction of beauty which we hoped he would do – on the contrary the very genius of ugliness seems to possess him. In fact, this is characteristic of the school, but it is a great and living school and I have been much interested and excited by it.[1]
In the artist's large Venetian genre paintings – *Water Carriers, Venice* of 1884 and *Venetian Washerwomen* (exhibited at the National Academy of Design in 1888) – this ''genius of ugliness'' is quite evident, most obviously in the dirty feet and rough appearance of the male figures here juxtaposed with Palladio's serene San Giorgio. However, there is evidence, especially in the primary, female group, that Miss Boott's hopes for a ''step in the direction of beauty'' had been fulfilled in the intervening decade. Smoother brushwork, a brighter palette, and a generally optimistic tone can be attributed variously to the artist's removal from Munich to Italy, the influence of Impressionism, or the presence of Miss Boott herself.

Another traveler reports on the universality and picturesqueness of these women carrying water from the centralized wells to their homes:
We never tired of the busy scene in the early morning when the wells were opened, the flocks of women hurrying to get water and carrying it away on their heads in beautiful old jars and copper repoussé vessels, gesticulating, gossiping, and clamoring, in gayly colored groups.[2]
Duveneck's ambitious exhibition paintings of Venice, focusing as they do on the portage of water, the washing of clothing, even the washing of children, give us an image of labor, especially female labor, under preindustrial but socially humane, visually handsome, and atmospherically propitious conditions. Knowing that reality was often imperfect and painful, we welcome the dirty feet and the startling juxtapositions (Salute dome and common bucket, Baroque marble balustrade and common fishnet) as the artist's acknowledgment of the ''ugliness'' and diminution inherent in the picturesque subject.

The original owner of *Water Carriers, Venice*, Reverend F. Ward Denys, noted in 1921 that he had purchased the painting directly from the artist in Venice during 1884 when cholera had kept most visitors away from the city and artists were in unusual need. He further mentioned that Duveneck had worked on it for two years at great expense in terms of models and materials but had found it difficult to reach a point of satisfaction with the work.[3] One still feels, somewhat, this lack of resolution; indeed one feels it in most of Duveneck's multi-figure groups. Unlike the marvelously random placement of figures in such prints as *Riva degli Schiavoni, Number Two*, this composition seems somewhat overdetermined. Yet it is a problem to which he returned over and over during the mid-1880s: Venetians loitering or laboring by a balustrade, along the steps arching over a wide canal bridge, or on a set of water steps leading into a canal.[4] Within this narrow vocabulary of forms he attempted to reconcile his training as a figure-painter, his avoidance of overt anecdote or history, and his awareness of the social and physical facts of contemporary Venice.

1. Duveneck, p. 76.
2. Maitland Armstrong, *Day Before Yesterday: Reminiscences of a Varied Life* (New York: Scribner's, 1920), pp. 242-243.
3. Museum records, National Museum of American Art, Smithsonian Institution, Washington, D.C.
4. In fact, he returned to this subject the next year as Blum in Venice reports in a letter of 1885 to Chase: ''Duveneck has under way a large and very good canvas of a water stairway with woman [sic] getting water,'' Catherine Metcalf Roof, *The Life and Art of William Merritt Chase* (New York: Hacker Art Books, 1975), p. 145. Other associated works include *The Water Carrier, Venice*, pencil on paper (illus. *Frank Duveneck*, Chapellier Gallery, New York, 1972, no. 40); *Figures on Venetian Steps*, oil on canvas (illus. John Ashbery, ''The Indian Summer of Frank Duveneck,'' *Art News* 71, no. 1 (April 1972), p. 28; *Venetian Bathers*, oil on canvas (illus. *Art Journal* 41, no. 2, [Summer 1981], p. 110); *Venetian Washerwomen*, oil on canvas (illus. *Connoisseur* 182, no. 734 [April 1973], p. 103); *Grand Canal in Venice*, ca. 1884, oil on canvas (illus. in Duveneck, n.p.).

Provenance: Purchased from the artist in Venice by the Reverend F. Ward Denys; given by Denys to the museum, 1921

Exhibition History and Bibliography: Washington, D.C., National Gallery of Art Catalogue, 1916, p. 180; William H. Holmes, *Smithsonian Institution, The National Gallery of Art: Catalogue of Collections*, 2 vols., Washington, D.C.: Government Printing Office, 1922, vol. 1, p. 89; Washington, D.C., National Gallery of Art Catalogue, 1926, p. 106; Whitney Museum of American Art, New York, Duveneck Exhibition, May 1938; Chapellier Gallery, New York, *Frank Duveneck*, 1972, no. 7; National Museum of American Art, Washington, D.C., *Descriptive Catalogue of Painting and Sculpture in the National Museum of American Art*, Boston: G. K. Hall, 1983, p. 68.

Sanford Robinson Gifford
1823 – 1880

Sanford Gifford's first visit to Venice occurred in the summer of 1857. Arriving on 10 July, he stayed at the Hotel Luna near the Piazza San Marco and spent two weeks sketching and observing the city which he would later describe as the ''most peculiar and most beautiful of all.''[1] His first impressions are recorded in a letter to his father: ''I am sure there is no city in the world that has so much architectural beauty and splendor as there is in the palaces and churches of Venice.''[2] He clearly also spent time in the Accademia and the churches studying the great Venetian painters, for a decade later he recalled being ''charmed with the works of the Venetian masters – I thought them almost perfect.''[3]

In June of 1869 Gifford returned to Venice, this time on his way back to the United States from the Middle East. He stayed at the Hotel Vittoria in the Frezzeria, to the west of the Piazza San Marco. Intending to leave in a few days, he lingered weeks:
I did not know till now, when I am about leaving Venice forever, how strong a hold this dear old, magnificent, dilapidated, poverty-striken city has taken on my affections. Even in her rags and tatters and old age the ''Bride of the Sea'' is the loveliest, the most glorious and the most superb of cities. It wrings one's heart to see her poverty and her vain efforts to recover her commercial power. . . . Her material prosperity is gone, but the art which shed lustre upon it and made it

glorious is not to be extinguished. . . .

   I have made a few sketches about Venice, from some of which I may make pictures.[4]
Judging from his productivity in the decade of the 1870s, Gifford's "few sketches" were extremely valuable to him. He exhibited Venetian views at the National Academy of Design in 1870, 1871, 1874, and 1878. When he died, the catalogue raisonné of his known works (published by The Metropolitan Museum of Art in 1881) included thirty-two Venetian subjects. Five of these were canvases of exhibition scale, while others were tiny oil sketches. His paintings of Venice were dispersed among a wide range of patrons. These included John Jacob Astor in New York (*Venetian Sails*, 1873) and a Mrs. Thomas Sturgis of Cheyenne, Wyoming Territory, who purchased Gifford's last canvas, *Venice*, painted in June 1880. Few of these works can be located today.

   1. S. R. Gifford Journal, vol. 2, 10 August 1857, p. 175, quoted in Ila Weiss, *Sanford Robinson Gifford* (New York: Garland, 1977), p. 71.
   2. Sanford Robinson Gifford Papers, roll D21, AAA: European Letters, vol. 2, p. 171, July 1857.
   3. Gifford Papers, roll D21, AAA: European Letters, vol. 2, p. 129, letter of 17 July 1869; cited in Weiss, p. 291.
   4. Gifford Papers, roll D21, AAA: European Letters, vol. 3, pp. 128-130.

16   Venetian Sails: A Study, 1873

Oil on canvas mounted on panel, 13⅜ × 24 in.
(34 × 61 cm)
Signed and dated, lower right: *S. R. Gifford 1873*
Washington University Gallery of Art, St. Louis. Gift of Charles Parsons, 1905

An unsigned article in the 1877 *Art Journal* entitled "How One Landscape Painter Paints" tells us,
Mr. Gifford's method is this: When he sees anything which vividly impresses him, and which he therefore wishes to reproduce, he makes a little sketch of it in pencil on a card about as large as an ordinary visiting card. It takes him, say, half a minute to make this sketch; but there is the idea of the future picture. . . . While travelling, he can in this way lay up a good stock of material for future use. The next step is to make a larger sketch, this time in oil, where what has already been done in black-and-white is repeated in colour. To this sketch, which is about twelve inches by eight, he devotes an hour or two. It serves the purpose of defining to him just what he wants to do, and of fixing it in enduring material. . . .

   He is now ready to paint the picture itself. . . .

   First of all, on this first day, he removes the glaring white of his canvas by staining it with a solution of turpentine and burnt sienna. . . . Then he takes a white chalk crayon and makes a drawing of the picture he expects to paint.[1]

   If this is indeed "Gifford's method" during the mid-1870s, *Venetian Sails: A Study*, with its white ground and pencil underdrawing, is clearly not "the picture itself" but an oil sketch. It is larger and more finished than our author indicates, perhaps because the finished work, *Venetian Sails*, painted the same year and acquired by John Jacob Astor, was an ambitious full-scale exhibition work.[2]

16

Here the pencil underdrawing is clearly visible but not obtrusive; the fiction of cityscape, boats, and atmosphere is richly, convincingly, described. We feel not only Gifford's response to the scene before him but also his response to Turner's *Grand Canal of Venice* of two decades before: "This is indeed splendid in light and gorgeous in color. . . . There is great indefiniteness in the forms. I think this must be one of the best of the late Turners, and . . . it fully warrants the eulogiums on his splendid coloring."[3] Gifford's own "splendid coloring" is elegantly restricted here to multiple variations on a single color problem: the blue-orange set. Color opposites, these two hues vibrate against one another and emphatically heighten the visual effect. Gifford has given us infinite variations from the palest cream and gray-blue in the reflections to the deeply saturated orange and blue pigments side by side in the sails. Contemporaries have reported that Gifford was color blind, but probably we can surmise that, if this in fact was the case, his was a red-green 'blindness.'[4]

Seen from the side of San Giorgio Maggiore, the broad sweep of Venice's skyline is given here with more fidelity to topographical fact than most artists' views of the city from afar. Gifford makes the most of the sweeping horizontal line and its suggestion of peacefulness, a note of tranquility picked up in the slack sails of the fishing boats. In a letter of 17 July 1869, the artist wrote his father, "The richly colored sails of the Venetian and Chioggian fishing boats have interested me a good deal from the striking contrasts of color they afford with the sky and water. There is also a curious variety of quaint design in them."[5] Clearly it is as much the orange-amber sails against the blue as the verticals against the horizontal or the picturesqueness of the sail devices that arrested his attention. And the intensity of his original vision has been preserved in this masterful study.

1. "How one Landscape Painter Paints," *The Art Journal*, n. s. 3, (1877).
2. *NAD*, p. 342; John F. Weir, *A Memorial Catalogue of the Paintings of Sanford Robinson Gifford, N. A.* (New York: The Metropolitan Museum of Art, 1881), p. 40. The J. J. Astor painting was given to the New York Public Library and subsequently deaccessioned (apparently misattributed to R. S. Gifford): Parke-Bernet, New York, 14, 15, 16 April 1943.
3. S. R. Gifford, "Journal," letter of 14 June 1855, p. 23, cited in *Sanford Robinson Gifford*, exh. cat. (Austin: University of Texas Art Museum, 1970), p. 15.
4. Maitland Armstrong, *Day Before Yesterday: Reminiscences of a Varied Life* (New York: Scribner's, 1920), p. 245.
5. Gifford Papers, roll D21, AAA: European Letters, vol. 3, p. 130, 17 July 1869.

Cass Gilbert
1858 – 1934

Cass Gilbert, although best known as an architect, was also a talented watercolorist. His picturesque European subjects appealed to his contemporaries, as they do to us, for their evocative as well as precise rendition of architectural form. They were particularly important early in his career: their sale helped him through periods of scant commissions and their publication in architectural journals familiarized his colleagues with his name and work.[1]

Gilbert was in Europe from January until July or August of 1880 and visited Venice during the early spring; a memorable watercolor of the interior of San Marco (dated 12 February 1880) records his first impressions of the city's primary architectural monument.[2] In 1898 he went abroad again and definitely spent time in the city painting and sketching the principal monuments.[3] He was in Europe again in 1908 (apparently he was eager enough to secure the commission for the Woolworth building in Manhattan to book passage on Mr. Woolworth's liner and successfully pursue the client on shipboard), and may have returned to Venice.[4] Four years later he returned and again recorded buildings with his careful draftsmanship. Late in his career he spent most summers abroad although principally in Britain.

1. Francis S. Swales, "Master Draftsmen, XVIII," *Pencil Points* 7, no. 10 (October 1926), pp. 581-600.
2. Patricia Anne Murphy, "The Early Career of Cass Gilbert: 1878 to 1895," M. A. thesis, School of Architecture, University of Virginia, May 1979, pp. 10, 13-14, fig. 4; Robert A. Jones, *Cass Gilbert: Midwestern Architect in New York* (New York: Arno Press, 1982), p. 39.
3. Two works of this date are in the collection of the National Museum of American Art, Smithsonian Institution, Washington, D.C.
4. *Dictionary of American Biography*, vol. 11, pp. 341-343.

17 Bell Tower, St. Mark's Square, Venice, 1912
Watercolor and pencil on paper, 20 × 10⅝ in.
(50.8 × 27 cm)
Signed, lower left: *C. G.*; dated, upper right: *1912*
National Museum of American Art, Smithsonian Institution. Bequest of Emily Finch Gilbert through Julia Post Bastedo, Executor

The Campanile (or bell tower), which Gilbert so carefully delineated during his visit to Venice in 1912, was a new building. First erected in 900, the Campanile was rebuilt in 1329, and the top section was again rebuilt in the early sixteenth century. For almost six centuries its imposing mass served as a landmark, its smooth vertical brick façade acting as a foil to the highly encrusted, rounded forms of nearby San Marco. On 14 July 1902 the Campanile suddenly collapsed in a large brick heap. Plans for its rebuilding began almost immediately. Between 1905 and 1911 it was reconstructed, following the precise lines of the originial with one notable exception: the inclusion of an elevator. Hydraulic passenger elevators had been invented in the late nineteenth century, and their refinement early in the twentieth was the critical element in the development of the skyscraper. It was the American artist Francis Hopkinson Smith who proposed the construction of elevators in the Campanile, even offering to

17

rhetoric (the lobbies were adorned with gold mosaics recalling San Marco, and the building's exterior was encrusted with gothic details) and in his verbal rhetoric: "We ourselves are cathedral builders!"[2]

Gilbert's watercolor of 1912 could be seen as a record of the new Campanile, completed only the year before, and as a tribute to two other buildings: his own 'cathedral' of commerce, the Woolworth Building, to be opened the next year in Manhattan, and the ancient tower, so eloquently memorialized in both new structures. The artist has chosen dusk to portray the great piazza; the sky has deepened into purple, vividly contrasting with the brick-orange mass of the tower. The great cathedral is partially visible on the left while the Doge's Palace, just visible on the tower's right, glistens in the final rays of the sun. Lamps have been lit and a band plays at the foot of the Campanile, entertaining the throng of strollers that fills the great square so aptly described by Henry James as "the great drawing room of Europe."

1. Joseph Pennell, *The Adventures of an Illustrator* (Boston: Little, Brown, 1925) p. 286.
2. Cass Gilbert, *Reminiscences and Addresses* (New York: privately printed, 1935), p. 85.

Provenance: Gift of Emily Finch Gilbert, 1962

William Stanley Haseltine
1835 – 1900

A Philadelphia artist trained in Düsseldorf in the 1850s, Haseltine probably visited Venice for the first time in 1859. Although after 1867 he established the Palazzo Altieri in Rome as his base, "most summers and autumns," his daughter, Helen Haseltine Plowden, reports, "he would spend a few weeks in Venice."[1] His circle there included the Daniel Sargent Curtises at the Palazzo Barbaro and Robert Browning at the Palazzo Rezzonico.

Although his Venetian paintings do not constitute a large portion of Haseltine's surviving canvases, they bear a family similarity to his better-known works; Nahant, Mt. Desert, and Capri provide, like Venice, wide expanses of water with which foreground architectural or geological forms could be contrasted. He painted both the Bacino San Marco and, less often, the secondary, vernacular canals. His daughter recalled those memorable days,

when in search of subjects for study, his gondola would meander through the narrow canals, between ancient red and brown palaces picked out with pointed windows and white marble balconies, past doorways with elaborate coats of arms and marble steps against which the private, often dilapidated, gondola bumps and splashes; canals cross and recross, gondolas silently emerge from a sunless waterway and disappear under a dark tunnel; lights and shadows play with lightning rapidity on the vaults of the bridges and vivid streaks of blue cut through the deep green water.[2]

Three sketchbooks that record these searches, containing several studies of the Salute, gondoliers, the Grand Canal, and other Venetian subjects in pencil, watercolor, and wash, dating from the 1860s and 1875, are preserved in the Museum of Fine Arts, Boston, Karolik Collection.

Some of Haseltine's finished Venetian scenes were exhibited at the National Academy in New York (1885,

invest in the scheme himself, knowing how popular the ascent would be for a tourist public accustomed, from their experiences at the great nineteenth-century expositions, to the idea of a tower prospect.[1]

This introduction of New York modernization in the reconstructed Campanile had its counterpart in the role that the original building played in changing the nature of Manhattan. It is probable that, in receiving the commission to design the Woolworth Building in 1908, Gilbert thought back to his 1898 visit to Venice, recalling the visual impact of the Campanile's dramatic vertical thrust in an urban environment, and used it as a model for his design. Credited with being America's first tower skyscraper, the Woolworth Building, 792 feet in height, held the record for the world's tallest building from its completion in 1913 until 1931. Its central section follows the lines of Venice's Campanile almost verbatim. That Gilbert was not solely focused on modernity and on the future in his Woolworth project is evident in his visual

18

1886); others were painted as specific commissions (as the painting of 1887 for Sir Henry Laird), but many, apparently, were neither for exhibition nor for sale, remaining in his studio until his death.[3] As the Italian art critic Diego Angeli reported in *Il Giorno* shortly after Haseltine's death, "Only a few [in Rome] recognised his intrinsic value as an artist, because he worked solely for the sake of his art, rarely exhibited his work, invited no criticism, and asked for no praise."[4] Angeli went on to remark,

He belonged to that set of American artists who, although they pass the greater part of their life "abroad," still preserve to the end the characteristics of their race: rapid conception of ideas, accurate reproduction of what they see and thorough knowledge of what they undertake. . . . As a consequence of . . . [his international education in America, Düsseldorf, and Paris] we find three elements in the character of Haseltine's paintings – Anglo-Saxon precision in drawing, French quest after atmosphere and light, and German romanticism. . . . Perhaps Anglo-Saxon precision is most evident in the drawings, French atmosphere in the water-colours, and German romanticism in the oil paintings.[5]

Clearly, his surviving Venetian works exhibit all three characteristics Angeli mentions: linear precision, a preoccupation with the qualities of light and atmosphere, and a tone at once positive and romantic.

1. Helen Haseltine Plowden, *William Stanley Haseltine: Sea and Landscape Painter* (London: Frederick Muller, 1947), pp. 150, 171; *The Crayon* (December 1859), p. 379.
2. Plowden, p. 150.
3. Plowden, pp. 151, 198.
4. Plowden, p. 198.
5. Plowden, pp. 198-199.

18   **Santa Maria della Salute – Sunset**, ca. 1880
Oil on canvas, 23 × 36½ in. (58.4 × 92.7 cm)
The Metropolitan Museum of Art. Gift of Helen Haseltine Plowden, 1954, in the memory of the artist

As early as 1859 *The Crayon* reported that "Haseltine's studio [in the Tenth Street Studio Building in New York] is filled with souvenirs of European scenery. The walls are hung with sketches of the . . . bay of Naples, and Salerno, added to which are Campagna and mountain views near Rome, and scenes in Venice; the whole forming a pictorial journey through the rare picturesque regions of Italy."[1] This early enthusiasm for "picturesque Italy" (recorded in an early sketchbook in the Museum of Fine Arts, Boston, Karolik Collection) became a dominant force in Haseltine's career, still visible in such mature works as *Santa Maria della Salute – Sunset* of two decades later.

Seen from the prospect of the point of the Giudecca, and silhouetted against the setting sun, the domes and towers of the Salute form the principal focus of the composition; to the right, the gilt ball carrying the weathervane figure of Fortuna at the mouth of the Grand Canal reflects the intense but unseen orb of the sun. Bracketing and blocking the low horizontal line of the customhouse (or Dogana) are three clusters of fishing boats, their colorful sails sharply punctuating the horizon. In its almost Baroque high key, its juxtaposition of the fishing boats with the monumental architecture, and its wide sweep of sea and sky, this painting is not unlike Venetian

19

views by Thomas Moran (cat. nos. 25-28). The color and brushwork are, however, rougher, less gem-like, and Haseltine seems reluctant to give us the deep void at the center which is so characteristic of Moran's compositions. Even more interesting, these fisherfolk, unlike Moran's, turn their backs to us, avoiding our gaze and any connection to our world.

In terms of painting techniques, Haseltine's canvas is full of variety and enthusiasm. The domes are thinly painted in subtle tones of violet-blue, while the sky behind displays an exuberant white-yellow impasto describing sun and cloud. Substance – the church – is suppressed, while that which is insubstantial – the atmosphere – is depicted as robust tactile substance; physical Venice is, here, subordinate to its expressive projected idea. Radiating out from the immediate area of the Salute, with its sunset penumbra and halo, are gestural rays – broad, visible brushstrokes – overlaying the cloud forms and reinforcing the emotionally-charged effect.

In the wide expanse of foreground water, however, Haseltine describes the reflected and refracted sunset with individual brushstrokes of pure color, most intensely in the complementary hues of blue and orange. Jarring and staccato, these patches of vibrating, contrasting hues suggest the optical and physical action of rippling water and intimate that the artist's gesture (in this section of the painting) is spontaneous. In distinct contrast to the top half of the painting where the action of the sun on the sky is described in Romantic Anglo-German terms, the bottom half offers something quite different. Here the action of the sun on the water is described in Impressionist, French terms. For Haseltine, clearly, the idea of Venice was a composite; it insisted on both the sense of yearning inherent in the older tradition and on an awareness of the vibrancy inherent in the newer French visual vocabulary. Venice was no longer, by 1880, for

Haseltine, only a "rare picturesque" Italian subject; it was also an immediate optical actuality to be artfully described.

1. *The Crayon* (December 1859), p. 379; also (November 1859), p. 349.

Exhibition History and Bibliography: Doll and Richards, Boston, *Paintings and Watercolors by William S. Haseltine*, 1954, checklist no. 26; The Phoenix Art Museum, *The Metropolitan Museum of Art Loan Collection*, "The River and the Sea," February 1967-February 1968, no. 9, illus.

19   Venice I
Oil on canvas, 23½ × 48½ in. (59.7 × 123.2 cm)
The Detroit Institute of Arts. Gift of Mrs. Roger H. Plowden, the artist's daughter

Working from almost exactly the same spot in front of the Public Gardens as Robert Salmon (cat. no. 51), Haseltine gives us, three decades later, a rather different interpretation of the Venetian cityscape. De-emphasizing the Salute, the Campanile, the Doge's Palace, and other recognizable landmarks, Haseltine focuses on the deeply hued fishing boats in the foreground. Here the linear precision of his elegant draftmanship is evident, while in the background the tints and architectural definition are affected by atmospheric perspective. Where Salmon treats the whole scene with a uniform crystalline clarity, bracketing the sharply etched architectural forms with glassy reflective water below and buoyantly crisp (if unmeteorological) cloud formations above, Haseltine gives us hazy, distant structures, their lines diffused and their forms bleached by water vapor in the atmosphere.

Haseltine's composition also differs from Salmon's; the panorama extends to the southwest only as far as the Salute, while Salmon includes the back of San Giorgio Maggiore and the Redentore on the Giudecca as well. Although the pentimento suggests that Haseltine considered including a single boat on the left, the finished composition, weighted heavily to one side, is quite successful and strikingly different from the more 'classical more symmetrical composition chosen by Salmon. It is also characteristic of their differing generations that Salmon's *Venice* is depicted at midday when the sun is brightest on his subject, while Haseltine chose a transitional time of day – dawn. This interest in marginal temporal dimensions also places Haseltine in the mainstream of the 1870s.

In one last important respect these canvases differ substantially. While Salmon places proportionately heavier weight on the familiar façades which invoke Venice's heroic history, he also includes foreign frigates and schooners (including one English vessel), suggesting the continuing commercial dignity of the city. Although his fishermen draw their nets in the foreground, the verandahed villa on the right has a distinctly suburban air. His interpretation of the city is, in other words, broader, including evidence of past greatness, present cosmopolitan prosperity, and interesting picturesqueness. Haseltine, on the other hand, gives a more polarized view of the city. His Venetians are uniformly picturesque; they tend their boats, or carry water vessels archaically on their heads, and their milieu is starkly contrasted to the misty city hovering on the horizon. By omitting the parapet which Salmon carefully includes in the foreground, Haseltine deliberately fails to ground us, to establish us as observer in the role of a third, alternate, socio-historic reality.

Donald Shaw MacLaughlan
1876 – 1938

Canadian by birth, Donald Shaw MacLaughlan grew up in Boston where he studied painting before his departure for Paris in 1898. The following year he visited Italy and began etching – two key developments for his future career.[1] In 1904 he moved to Italy, dividing his time between Venice and Asolo, high in the nearby hills, until 1914 when World War I forced him to leave.[2] From his dated etchings we know that he worked in Venice every year between 1908 and 1913. At the conclusion of the war he returned to Venice, "recalled," as one contemporary put it, by

that attraction which he cannot resist of the antique city of the Doges with its fairy palaces, its elaborate architecture rising from the water, its cupolas and its campaniles, the canals ploughed by gondolas laden with fruit and vegetables, its bridges which span them with a sturdy arch.[3]

Although a few watercolors and oils survive, his principal achievement was in the area of etching. And in this medium his major subject was Venice.[4] Exhibiting in Paris, London, New York, and Chicago, he was well known in his day and often was associated by his contemporaries with Charles Méryon, Seymour Haden, and James McNeill Whistler, three central figures in the nineteenth-century etching revival.[5] His Venetian etchings, produced in limited editions often on sixteenth-century or handmade Japanese papers, cover a wide variety of subjects including well-known landmarks and more modest domestic exteriors.[6] Artfully using his line to both describe form and evoke atmospheric tone, MacLaughlan was praised by his contemporaries for creating distinctive and superb effects in his prints, "effects mainly of dazzling sunlight on warm gray stone and rippling water, distilling that lyric intoxication which is the very soul and atmosphere of Venice."[7]

1. Donald Shaw MacLaughlan Papers, roll N97, frames 944-958, AAA: *Catalogue of a Retrospective Exhibition of the Etched Work of Donald Shaw MacLaughlan*, introduction by Léonce Bénédite (Chicago: Albert Roullier Art Galleries, 10-30 November 1925); "MacLaughlan Prints," *The Art Digest* 8, no. 4 (15 November 1933), p. 20; "138 MacLaughlan Prints a Toledo Treasure," *The Art Digest* 8, no. 7 (1 January 1934), p. 24.

2. Cleveland Palmer, "The Recent Etchings of Donald Shaw MacLaughlan," *The Print Collector's Quarterly* (February 1916), p. 124.

3. Bénédite, in MacLaughlan Papers, roll N97, frame 948, AAA.

4. "Gift of a MacLaughlan Watercolor," *Museum News: The Toledo Museum of Art*, no. 89 (March 1940), n. p.; "A Notable Gift of Fine Prints," *Museum News: The Toledo Museum of Art*, no. 67 (December 1933), n. p.; Bénédite, in MacLaughlan Papers, roll N97, frames 945-958, AAA.

5. Henri Beraldi, "Les Graveurs du XXième Siècle," *La Revue de l'Art Ancien et Moderne* 13, no. 70 (10 January 1903), p. 31; E. A. Taylor, "The Original Etchings of Donald Shaw MacLaughlan," *The Studio* 59 (1913), pp. 122-129; Palmer, "Recent Etchings," pp. 111-113.

6. James Laver, "The Etchings of Donald Shaw MacLaughlan," *The Print Collector's Quarterly* 13 (December 1926), p. 342; MacLaughlan Papers, roll N97, frame 920, AAA; Letter from D. S. MacLaughlan to New York dealer Arthur H. Hahlo & Co., 1911.

7. Palmer, "Recent Etchings," p. 114.

20   The Canal of the Little Saint, Venice, 1909
Etching (warm black ink on antique laid paper), plate 8⅛ × 11½ in. (20.6 × 29.2 cm), trimmed to plate mark
Signed in pencil, in margin, lower right:
D. S. MacLaughlan
The Fine Arts Museums of San Francisco, Achenbach Foundation for Graphic Arts

Evidently responding to an inquiry from Messrs. Arthur H. Hahlo & Co. who had recently installed an exhibition of his etchings in their New York galleries, MacLaughlan wrote with great precision about his working methods:
I always draw directly upon the copper plate from nature, for I believe that this is the only way in which one can etch with spontaneity; but before beginning the plate, every line has been arranged in my mind, even to the kind of print necessary. I sometimes make many drawings and studies for a particular movement of a figure, and then draw it upon the plate from memory.

I also wish to say that I never steel-face my plates, but print direct from the copper. The number of proofs in my editions is generally forty, a few were printed at sixty. Many of the early plates had but a few proofs pulled. Each proof is printed by myself, and when an edition is completed, I immediately destroy the plate. . . . The ink used is ground and prepared by myself, and the paper is from old manuscripts of the Renaissance (for the most part) which I have collected by endless searching through Italy and Europe.[1]
There is a self-consciousness evident in this report which suggests not only MacLaughlan's need for accuracy but also his awareness of the collectibility of his prints. Indeed, his works were as keenly sought after as they were

20

carefully crafted. Following in the wide wake of Whistler in etching Venice, MacLaughlan necessarily felt the challenge of his formidable predecessor and thus was exceptionally attentive to technique, tone, and subject. We have some curious evidence of MacLaughlan's sense of Whistler's role in his art and life from Elizabeth and Joseph Pennell. They report in *The Whistler Journal* that on 13 March 1910 MacLaughlan and his wife attended a séance which was visited by a spirit: "It said it had a message from Whistler for MacLaughlan. Whistler wished MacLaughlan to go on with his etching, to devote himself to it." On another occasion, "in Florence, the MacLaughlans attended a séance, to which Whistler's own spirit came and told MacLaughlan that he must go on with his etching."[2]

The Canal of the Little Saint, Venice is Whistlerian in many important respects including the depiction of a partial façade parallel to the picture plane and the tonal wiping of the plate in the foreground water areas. Yet there are important differences, which MacLaughlan's contemporaries were quick to point out:

His debt to Whistler is much less real than the Venice set would lead one at first to suppose. In reality the two artists looked at Venice with very different eyes and translated their vision into very different results. . . . One has only to compare his Canal of the Little Saint *with a very similar composition of Whistler's – * Two Doorways *– to understand this difference very clearly. Whistler's work is all broken lines, moiré darks, tenuous suggestion of distant shapes, a gondola which is a mere silhouette. The younger etcher is much more precise. His chosen moment is high noon with somewhat hard vertical shadows. His darks are blacker, his illuminated surfaces more summary, his gondola (for the parallelism of the two plates is extraordinary) more tightly drawn. He gets his effect, but it is an effect quite different from those sought by Whistler. Venice seen through the medium of two such opposite temperaments – yet both American, and both cosmopolitan – tempts one to linger over the comparison and the contrasts between their work.*[3]

Two things this perceptive critic does not mention but which decidedly set this work apart from Whistler's are the fully described "little saint" enshrined high on the wall, and the articulated interior vignettes. While Whistler often clusters and silhouettes figures at doorways and apertures, he rarely takes the viewer into the interior. Here we see the partial contents of three rooms, one of which seems hung with putti-like figures, suggesting that this might be a carver's or gilder's shop. Five men and women people this shabby Renaissance palace and suggest more activity and communication than one usually finds in a Whistler Venetian view.

However indebted he was to Whistler's composition, technique, and even his encouraging Spirit, MacLaughlan clearly saw the city and its inhabitants in a different light. As one contemporary put it,
The Canal of the Little Saint – *what an engaging name for an etching: what a delightful one for a canal! – is a favorable instance of the Venetian subjects; for in it Mr. MacLaughlan holds his own distinctly – he was pleased, I am sure, with his theme, and so, in a field so well tramped, apparently, from Carpaccio's days, through Canaletto's to Whistler's, his footsteps were still visibly his own.*[4]

1. MacLaughlan papers, roll N97, frame 920, AAA: 10 November 1911.
2. Elizabeth R. and Joseph Pennell, *The Whistler Journal* (Philadelphia: Lippincott, 1921), p. 159.
3. James Laver, "The Etchings of Donald Shaw MacLaughlan," *The Print Collector's Quarterly* 13 (December 1926), p. 332.
4. Frederick Wedmore, "MacLaughlan's Etchings," *Art Journal* 62, no. 49 (1910), p. 234.

Exhibition History and Bibliography: Marie Bruette, *Descriptive Catalogue of the Etched Work of Donald Shaw MacLaughlan*, Chicago: Albert Roullier Art Galleries, 1925, no. 126; Donald Shaw MacLaughlan Papers, roll N97, frame 954, AAA: *Catalogue of a Retrospective Exhibition of the Etched Work of Donald Shaw MacLaughlan*, Introduction by Léonce Bénédite, Chicago, Albert Roullier Art Galleries, 10-30 November 1925, no. 96.

Color plates

Robert Frederick Blum
Canal in Venice, San Trovaso Quarter, 1885.
Cat.no.4

Robert Frederick Blum
Venetian Lacemakers, 1887.
Cat.no.7

Thomas Moran
The Fisherman's Wedding Party, Venice, 1892.
Cat.no.26

Maurice Brazil Prendergast
Square of S. Marco, Venice (Splash of Sunshine and Rain), 1899.
Cat.no.34

Maurice Brazil Prendergast
Sunlight on the Piazzetta, Venice, 1898/99.
Cat.no.37

Maurice Brazil Prendergast
Umbrellas in the Rain, 1899.
Cat.no.39

Maurice Brazil Prendergast
Riva degli Schiavoni, Castello, 1898.
Cat.no.42

John Singer Sargent
Venetian Interior, ca. 1882.
Cat.no.54

John Singer Sargent
Venetian Women in the Palazzo Rezzonico, ca. 1880.
Cat.no.58

John Singer Sargent
Stringing Onions, ca. 1882.
Cat.no.59

John Singer Sargent
The Salute, Venice.
Cat.no.65

John Singer Sargent
Venetian Doorway.
Cat.no.76

John Singer Sargent
Campo S. Agnese, Venice.
Cat.no.79

James McNeill Whistler
The Doorway, Venice, 1879/80.
Cat.no.97

John Marin
1870 – 1953

John Marin was thirty-five before he discovered etching, Europe, and his first artistic success. A six-month stay in Venice during the spring of 1907 resulted in a few pastels and twenty delicate etchings which found a ready market through his New York dealer, Louis Katz.[1] Clearly the long shadow of Whistler, whose pastels and etchings of Venice from 1879 and 1880 had set new standards in the media, is visible in Marin's use of tinted papers for his pastels and in his vignetted, etched subjects. Although associated with the "Whistlerians" (as opposed to the Sargent enthusiasts) in his student days at the Pennsylvania Academy, he apparently declined to visit an exhibition of the master's work at the Accademia for fear of too direct an influence on his own choice of subject and artistic manner.[2]

Marin's etchings of Venice are small in scale, and although some see the germ of the radical late watercolors in these works, such sympathetic contemporaries as Charles Saunier valued them for their Old World picturesqueness.[3] Marin himself, viewing them retrospectively, saw a telling "freedom" in these works: "Some etchings I had been making before [Alfred] Stieglitz showed my work already had freedom about them. I had already begun to let go some. After he began to show my work [1909] I let go a lot more."[4] But in another mood, speaking of his European sojourn and his artistic production during these years, Marin somewhat cavalierly recalled in his "Notes Autobiographical" in 1922 that he had "played some billiards, [and] incidentally knocked out some batches of etchings which people rave about everywhere."[5] Most are quite elegantly, if casually, composed and executed with a masterful touch on delicately toned oriental paper.

1. Sheldon Reich, *John Marin: A Stylistic Analysis and Catalogue Raisonné* (Tucson: The University of Arizona Press, 1970), vol. 1, p. 17; MacKinley Helm, *John Marin* (Boston: Pellegrini & Cudahy, in association with the Institute of Contemporary Art, 1948), pp. 16, 17.
2. Carl Zigrosser, *The Complete Etchings of John Marin* (Philadelphia: The Philadelphia Museum of Art, 1969), p. 8; Helm, p. 16.
3. E. M. Benson, *John Marin: The Man and His Work* (Washington: The American Federation of the Arts, 1935), p. 31; Charles Saunier, "John Marin: Peintre-Graveur," *L'Art Décoratif* 18 (January-June 1908), pp. 17-24.
4. Quoted in Dorothy Norman, *The Selected Writings of John Marin* (New York: Pellegrini & Cudahy, 1949), p. xi.
5. Benson, p. 27.

21 Santa Maria della Salute, Venezia, 1907
Etching (black ink on oriental paper), plate 5⅛ × 7 in. (13 × 17.8 cm), sheet 6¾ × 9 in. (17.2 × 22.9 cm)
Signed in pencil in margin, lower right: *John Marin*; signed, dated, and inscribed in plate, lower right: *Marin/ 07*, and lower left: *Santa/Maria/della Salute/Venezia*
The Fine Arts Museums of San Francisco, Achenbach Foundation for Graphic Arts. California State Library long loan

Although most of Marin's Venetian etchings capture less recognizable and less celebrated sites, a few, such as this one, address the archetype. From a vantage point beside the stately Palazzo Corner della Ca' Grande (its water-steps just visible on the right), Marin looks out the last reach of the Grand Canal onto the Bacino San Marco. Punctuated by the vaulting domes of Santa Maria della Salute, this is one of Venice's most celebrated views. Marin has portrayed it delicately, lightly, concentrating his darkest, most emphatic lines in the dome in the middle distance. Objects near, and those remote, are elusive, vague, and partial. This strategy of understatement suits the diminutive scale of his plates and the suggestive (rather than topographical) line of his technique. Nonetheless, the dignified grace of the Salute is preserved. As one contemporary American architect enthused, "If any single building in Venice is conspicuous not only as a beautiful, but as a characteristic and unique landmark, it is this white-domed church. . . . It is not often that such signal success awaits the architect who conceives a general scheme so unusual and so fantastic."[1] Marin's

21

homage to the achievement of Longhena is clear: the ordered, generous symmetry of the two domes contrasts in form and density with the random, paler jumble of lesser, rectilinear structures below and the placid expanse of reflective canal.

As in his other Venetian etchings, Marin has pressed the architectural subject up high on the plate, abandoning, like Prendergast, the broad expressive sky characteristic of earlier views of the city. This composition is doubly eccentric in the inclusion of the suggestive figure of a gondolier who moves swiftly out of the image at the lower right.

1. Robert Swain Peabody, "An Architect's Vacation III: The Venetian Day," *Atlantic* 76 (1895), p. 477.

Exhibition History and Bibliography: Carl Zigrosser, *The Complete Etchings of John Marin*, Philadelphia Museum of Art, 1969, no. 53.

22 Palazzo Dario, Venezia, 1907
Etching (black ink on oriental paper), plate 7⅝ × 5¼ in. (19.3 × 13.4 cm), sheet 15¼ × 11 in. (38.7 × 27.9 cm)
Signed, dated, and inscribed in plate, lower left: *Marin/07*, and lower right: *Palazzo/Dario/Venezia*
The Cleveland Museum of Art. Dudley P. Allen Fund

Before undertaking training in painting, Marin studied architecture, and in such etchings as *Palazzo Dario* he exhibits his sympathy with the decorative, ancient structures of Venice. The little fifteenth-century palace is, for him, a thin, elegant, patterned curtain best portrayed with a nervous, 'spontaneous' line. Although the marble roundels are full of variety and vitality, his real interest is in the windows. Some shuttered, some wide open, some covered with leaded circles of crown glass, these apertures are described with a richness that solicits our minute attention. Balanced carefully between positive and negative shapes, between described and suggested forms, the windows seem at once familiar and mysterious.

On either side of the palace, deep, narrow alleyways retreat into dusky shadows, contrasting to and isolating the façade. Its vertical edges, silhouetted against the shadows, dramatize the irregular, canted lines of the whole building. As one contemporary points out:
One cannot fail to notice how many of these palaces are out of line. Side-walls lean noticeably out of plumb, cornices seen against the sky are decidedly crooked, and one is told of the steady, slow, but none the less sure, undermining of these foundations which extend so far below the water line, and will wonder if it can really be true that some day these monuments of past glories will totter into the waves and vanish from sight forever.[1]

In Marin's etching we sense the artist's response to both the glorious intricacy of a vibrant positive-negative pattern and this melancholy note of memento mori. Unlike the vigorous canted diagonal lines of energy that frame and strengthen his later watercolors, these irregular diagonals suggest a sweet but irreversible surrender. According to Charles Saunier, who announced these etchings to the Parisian public in 1908, it is precisely this out-of-plumb, non-rectilinear quality that appealed to Marin and will appeal to his patrons: "D'abord ingé-

22

nieur, puis architecte, M. John Marin . . . a fui les villes trop neuves et rectilignes du Nouveau-Monde pour les vieilles cités d'Europe" (First engineer, then architect, Mr. John Marin . . . fled the too new and too rectilinear cities of the New World for the old cities of Europe).[2]

1. Elise Lathrop, *Sunny Days in Italy* (New York: James Pott & Co., 1907), p. 281.
2. Saunier, p. 17, author's translation.

Exhibition History and Bibliography: Carl Zigrosser, *The Complete Etchings of John Marin*, Philadelphia Museum of Art, 1969, no. 67.

23 Le Pont, 1907
Etching (black ink on laid paper), plate 5 × 7 in. (12.7 × 17.8 cm), sheet 6¾ × 9 in. (17.2 × 22.8 cm)
Signed in pencil, lower right: *John Marin*; signed, dated, and inscribed in plate, lower center: *Marin/07*, and lower right: *Le Pont/Venezia*
The Fine Arts Museums of San Francisco, Achenbach Foundation for Graphic Arts. California State Library long loan

In his enthusiastic review of 1908, Charles Saunier speaks of the charm of Venice which he reads in Marin's etchings. He praises Marin's response to "l'imprévu d'une population qui n'a pas changé d'allure et presque de costume depuis les Canaletto et Guardi: mieux, depuis

Carpaccio'' (The surprise of a population that has not changed its demeanor and scarcely its costume since Canaletto and Guardi: better, not since Carpaccio).[1] And there is not a little Carpaccio in the figure of the gondolier who guides his craft and his passenger on a trajectory perpendicular to that of the gracefully arched bridge which forms the major focus of attention. A procession of pedestrians crosses the span to two invisible streets. It is not their destiny, however, but their mid-air transit that arrests Marin's attention. The print gives us a fragment, a fractional glimpse of Venetian space and life, isolated and marked off in a decorative, almost oriental pattern.

More than in most of the etchings from 1907 Marin here plays with the possibility of juxtaposed positive and negative forms. Figures at the middle of the span are delineated with black ink while those on either side read as white shapes against a dark ground. The bridge itself is only faintly described in line: a graceful negative which we read as stone.

Like that of most American artists in Venice, Marin's Italian was rudimentary and he slipped into the more familiar French when he titled the work *Le Pont*. And yet, as Saunier's article makes clear, he judges right to address himself to an Anglo-French audience in these works.

1. Saunier, p. 18, author's translation.

Exhibition History and Bibliography: Carl Zigrosser, *The Complete Etchings of John Marin*, Philadelphia Museum of Art, 1969, no. 59.

24   Della Fava, 1907

Etching (black ink on oriental paper), plate 9⅜ × 6⅞ in. (23.8 × 17.5 cm), sheet 13¾ × 11 in. (34.9 × 27.9 cm)
Signed and inscribed in pencil, lower right: *John Marin*, and lower left: *A/imp/Della Fava/Venice*; in plate, lower left: *Marin/07*, and lower right: *Della/Fava/Venezia*
The Fine Arts Museums of San Francisco, Achenbach Foundation for Graphic Arts

As in Marin's other etchings, the subject of *Della Fava* is primarily architectural with a lively genre element. Venetians propel their gondolas into the deep picture space or watch from windows and balconies overhead while a solitary, top-hatted, urban gentleman – a tourist perhaps – stands silhouetted on a distant landing. The Rio della Fava is a narrow canal marked at this site by the curving façades of buildings on the one side and the entrance of another secondary canal on the other. Drawing directly on the plate as was his wont (and hence reversing the image), Marin sat on a small landing to execute his print. He depicts a range of vernacular buildings while to the left, invisible, stands the imposing Palazzo Giustiniani Faccanon which is glimpsed in Sargent's *Venetian Doorway* (cat. no. 76). As in so many Venetian views, we are conscious, as Marin was no doubt conscious, that the sites he selected were pre-examined and pre-interpreted by others.

Although Sargent may have been, figuratively, sitting across the canal from Marin's perch, it is Whistler he has in mind here. His line is rougher, wirier, but the vignette effect, the suggestive rather than descriptive draftsmanship, and the overall 'sliced' composition owe much to Marin's influential predecessor. Nevertheless, he cannot resist the very un-Whistlerian recording of such particularized details as the incongruous stovepipe that issues from a balcony high on the right-hand wall. In such

23

touches and in the introduction of such figures as the dark, top-hatted tourist, Marin shows us a perception that has as little in common with the Whistler of 1880 as it has with the mature Marin. In these inclusions he displays, in its raw form, a quality every ambitious artist must find: an intense, even a witty, visual curiosity.

Exhibition History and Bibliography: Carl Zigrosser, *The Complete Etchings of John Marin*, Philadelphia Museum of Art, 1969, no. 64.

24

Thomas Moran
1837 – 1926

In a letter of 1888 Thomas Moran wrote to a friend, "Venice is an inexhaustible mine of pictorial treasures for the artist and of dreamy remembrance to those who have been fortunate enough to visit it."[1] And clearly the city was to be, for him, an "inexhaustible mine of pictorial treasures" over the next three and one-half decades, for this prolific artist painted more views of Venice than of any other subject.

Moran made his first trip to Venice at the age of forty-nine; he financed the expedition by the sale of sixty-four pictures at the galleries of Ortigies and Co. in New York City, a sale that netted $10,321.[2] He stayed at the Grand Hotel at the mouth of the Grand Canal throughout most of May and June of 1886, making preliminary sketches and watercolors but no finished pictures.[3] During the next four years he completed several Venetian canvases

and a large-scale etching. However, most of his paintings of the city postdate his second trip, taken in 1890. Imprinted on his "dreamy remembrance" from these two trips was a singularly romantic view of the city which would become a chief element in his repertoire. Not content to import only memories, however, Moran also brought back from his 1890 trip an elegantly carved gondola – said to have been owned by Robert Browning – for use on Hook Pond, near Moran's East Hampton, Long Island, home.[4] This eccentric conjunction of the native element with the exotic is an important aspect of Moran's oeuvre, for Venice, once entered into his repertoire, remained a constant and often appeared side-by-side with views of the American West in his exhibition lists.

As Moran carefully dated most of his paintings, it is possible to chart the frequency of his returns to Venetian subjects: we know of five painted in 1898, four in 1903, and three in each of the years 1893, 1897, 1904, and 1906. In most years between 1887 and 1907 he painted at least one, and between 1887 and 1900 his submissions to the National Academy of Design's annual exhibition were most frequently of Venetian subjects.[5] Most of Moran's Venetian canvases are moderate in size (many are 20 × 30 in.) and horizontal in format, but a few are quite large and several small vertical paintings vary the formula. There was a lull in Moran's preoccupation with the subject between 1907 and 1921, but in 1922 he submitted his last painting to the National Academy of Design, one entitled *Venice*, reinvoking the association between the city and his interpretation of it in the minds of his public. Moran's Venetian views were painted, exhibited, and bought in New York; the prices of those exhibited at the National Academy of Design varied from $300 to $5000 and were comparable to the prices asked for works of Western or Long Island subject matter.[6]

The titles of Moran's Venetian paintings, like those of many other artists, invoke the grandeur of the city (*Gate to Venice*, 1889; *Entrance to the Grand Canal, Venice*, 1893) and a cosmic temporality (*Sunset, Venice*, 1902, Newark Museum). More unusual is the presence of such titles as *The Bridge of Sighs* and *Ducal Palace and Prison – Venice* (exhibited at the National Academy of Design, 1890 and 1892, respectively). Specifically invoking the more macabre, more grandly sensational aspects of Venice's past, Moran alludes here to an aspect of the city's reputation often recognized and utilized by writers (such as James Fenimore Cooper in *The Bravo*, 1831) but, curiously, rarely by artists.

A second aspect of Moran's paintings that one might term Romantic – beyond looming allusions to the dark shadows of historic fact and fable – is his willingness to depart from visual fact, his insistence on the element of wistful or nostalgic dream. In fact, one might point to his *Dream of the Orient*, 1876, as the starting point of his Venetian enthusiasm and *Dream City*[7] of 1919 as its terminus. Between the two works he repeatedly returned to the subject of Venice but never, in fact, made a portrait of its topographical or architectural facts. His intention was to allude, infer, and dramatize, not to record or analyze.

Infused as they are with "dreamy remembrance," Moran's Venetian views are indebted to the earlier works of Joseph Mallord William Turner in their format, their suggestion of jewel-like color, their richly impastoed surface, and the frequent incorporation of the light source within the scene. Also like his great British predecessor, Moran concentrated on the recognizable public spaces of the city, especially the Bacino di San Marco and the mouth of the Grand Canal.

1. Letter to Christian Klackner, quoted in pamphlet *"The Gate of Venice" Etched by Thomas Moran, N. A.*, 1886, located in the Print Room, New York Public Library, and cited in Thurman Wilkins, *Thomas Moran: Artist of the Mountains* (Norman, Okla.: University of Oklahoma Press, 1966), p. 188.

2. Wilkins, p. 186. Although some authors have suggested that Moran may have visited Venice during his earlier trips abroad, it is evident from his letter of 3 May 1886 to his wife Mary that his first glimpse of the city was in that year (see Amy O. Bassford, ed., *Home-Thoughts, from Afar: Letters of Thomas Moran to Mary Nimmo Moran* [East Hampton, N.Y.: East Hampton Free Library, 1967], p. 77).

3. Wilkins, p. 187. Sketchbooks and letters relevant to the 1886 and 1890 trips to Venice are in the Moran Collection, East Hampton Free Library, East Hampton, New York; see Bassford, p. 76.

4. Bassford, pp. 144-145.

5. *Inventory of American Paintings; NAD*, pp. 654-656.

6. Moses Tanenbaum Papers, roll 97, frames 10 and 51, AAA; *NAD*, pp. 653-656.

7. Illustrated in *International Studio* 79, no. 327 (August 1924), p. 365.

25

25   View of Venice, 1891
Oil on canvas, 35⅛ × 25¼ in. (89.2 × 64.1 cm)
Signed and dated, lower left: monogram *TMoran. 1891*
National Museum of American Art, Smithsonian Institution. Transfer from the U.S. Department of the Interior

Unusual in its vertical format, this view of the Bacino di San Marco looking westward toward the mouth of the Grand Canal from the area of the Riva S. Biagio is otherwise very characteristic of Thomas Moran's interpretations of the city. The foreground with its dark and richly hued genre element contrasts sharply with the pale horizontal line of epic structures in the distance: the double-domed Salute marks one side of the Grand Canal while the Campanile, Doge's Palace, and Bridge of Sighs (all distorted in scale and inflected in direction to accommodate the viewer) mark the other. The whole scene – with its picturesque fisherfolk, their extraordinary globe-like fish baskets and gaudy vessels juxtaposed so sharply with the poised and aloof architectural remnants of Venice's grand and melancholy past – is presided over by a meteorologically auspicious sky reflected in opalescent waters.

Topographically a fiction (there is no sandbar or tidal spit in this section of the lagoon), this picture is simultaneously a plea to the imagination and a triggering mnemonic device, an image that could transport the American viewer not only into his memories of the foreign world of Europe but beyond that into the mood of sweet melancholy characteristic of Romance.

One of approximately one hundred views of the city painted by Moran between his first trip to the city in 1886 and his death in 1926, this example is an early treatment of the subject and possibly is the painting entitled *Morning – Venice* exhibited at the National Academy of Design in New York in 1891.[1]

1. *NAD*, p. 655.

Provenance: Transfer from the National Park Service, Springfield, Virginia, 1968

Exhibition History and Bibliography: Phyllis Braff, *Thomas Moran: A Search for the Scenic*, East Hampton, N.Y., Guidhall Museum, 29 November 1980-25 January 1981, p. 40; National Museum of American Art, Washington, D.C., *Descriptive Catalogue of Painting and Sculpture in the National Museum of American Art*, Boston: G. K. Hall, 1983, p. 142.

26

26 The Fisherman's Wedding Party, Venice, 1892
Oil on canvas, 24 × 33 in. (61 × 83.8 cm)
Signed and dated, lower right: monogram *TMoran./1892*
The Detroit Institute of Arts. Bequest of Alfred J. Fisher
Color plate

As in *View of Venice* (cat. no. 25) of the previous year,
Moran has chosen to portray the principal structures and
main waterway of Venice from a distant prospect, enrich-
ing the foreground with a chromatically intense cluster
of boats and figures. The foreground contributes a picturesque note, as before, but the tone of exoticism is
heightened in the rich use of fabrics, intense contrasts of
impastoed whites with crimson and gold tones, and the
introduction of elaborate costumes. The appeal here is
not just to the viewer's memory of Turner's brilliant rendering of water and atmosphere but also to an
orientalism reminiscent of Rembrandt. Invoking his two
formidable artistic predecessors as well as the architectural feats of a distant but still accessible Venetian past,
Moran bestows upon the scene a kind of supernatural
beauty. His intention is not to record perceivable facts
but to conjure a kind of dream vision. But curiously he
does not permit the vision to be passive: the fisherfolk
pause in their festivities to observe the observer and, in
doing so, solicit his collaboration in the fantasy.

Built up in layers of pigment and glaze on a pale brick-
toned ground, this work shows the full vocabulary of
Moran's painterly techniques. From the thinly painted,
invisibly stroked, distant water to the rough, active, and
spontaneous brushstrokes of the lower right and the
artfully layered pigments of the Rembrandtesque areas,
we can observe his painterly versatility. Although it
might be argued that once Moran achieved his pictorial
voice – in terms of subject and technique – he produced
formula works with little variation or struggle, it is clear
from internal and secondary evidence that one might
more properly see them as serial images reinvestigating a
single question. In such passages as the top segment of
the ruddy right-hand sail it is evident that the artist
rethought and altered his composition. Speaking of another painting, Moran wrote to a New York collector in
1896, "I have made some small changes in your Venetian
picture – I tried some radical ones, that did not seem to
improve the picture and therefore took them off."[1] Such
evidence of active rethinking, remaking of his paintings,
as well as their consistently high quality, suggests that
the subject continued to be as interesting to Moran as to
his patrons.

27

1. Moses Tanenbaum Papers, roll 97, frame 51, AAA.

Provenance: Howard Young Galleries, New York; bought in 1927 or 1928 by Alfred J. Fisher

Exhibition History and bibliography: Graham Hood, Nancy Rivard, and Kathleen Pyne, "American Paintings Acquired During the Last Decade," *Bulletin of The Detroit Institute of Arts* 55 (1977), pp. 101-102, illus.

27   View of Venice, 1895

Oil on canvas, 16½ × 26½ in. (41.9 × 67.3 cm)
Signed, lower right: *Moran, 1895*
Collection of the Wellesley College Museum

As in most Moran cityscapes, the artist offers two competing primary subjects: a procession of grandly heroic, orderly buildings and clusters of picturesque vernacular fishing vessels. These boats and their colorful accoutrements (best seen from Riva and the area of the Public Gardens) were much commented upon by travelers and enthusiastically painted by Moran and his fellow artists. As Elizabeth Robins Pennell records in a magazine article of 1890 entitled "Venetian Boats":

Down by the Public Gardens you are always sure to find a number of them [fishing boats] *lying idly by the shore, a wonderful confusion of many-colored, many-shaded nets hanging from mast to mast, while almost as many artists are painting or trying to paint them from under the trees of the gardens, or from gondolas fastened to the great red buoy, or from the steam-boat pier. And in the evening, when the sun sinks behind the Salute, the lagoon, which it has set afire, seems to break out in flames in the brilliant sails of the homeward-bound boats.* [1]

Capturing the scene at sunset, Moran includes the orb of the sun, its energy radiating into the sky overhead and into the water below. Few but the Romantics consistently set for themselves the problem of placing the source of light (especially the sun) within the painting itself. The effect here is to backlight both major and minor elements, silhouetting the Salute and the fishing boats alike. Exempted from the simplifying and darkening effect of this pictorial situation are the luminous sky, the "flames" of a few sails, and the dramatic, glowing façade of the Doge's Palace. Termed by John Ruskin "the central building of the world," this stately Gothic fourteenth-century structure seems to stand for all the power and dignity of Venice's historic past, a past abruptly contrasted to and muted by a diminished but colorful present represented by fisherfolk and their picturesque but impotent vessels. [2]

1. *Harper's New Monthly Magazine* 80, no. 478 (March 1890), p. 554.
2. John Ruskin, *The Stones of Venice*, 3 vols. (New York: John W. Lovell, n. d.), vol. 1, p. 38.

Provenance: Bequest of Mrs. Harry H. Walter (Ella Mason, Class of 1900)

Exhibition History and Bibliography: Phyllis Braff, *Thomas Moran: A Search for the Scenic*, East Hampton, N.Y., Guildhall Museum, 29 November 1980-25 January 1981, no. 72, illus. pp. 38-39.

28

28　View of Venice, 1903
Oil on canvas, 12¼ × 20⅛ in. (31.1 × 51.1 cm)
Signed, lower right: monogram *TMoran./1903*
Collection of Mr. and Mrs. Dale F. Dorn

Looking westward from the Dogana at the mouth of the
Grand Canal, Moran centers his composition on the
church and campanile of San Giorgio Maggiore. The
serene masterpiece of Renaissance architect Andrea Palladio, San Giorgio was built late in the sixteenth century
on a small but prominent island which faces the Salute
and Dogana to the west and the Doge's Palace to the
north. Its almost waterborne character is captured in
Moran's image, the vertical tower bracketed and mimicked by sails and masts on either side, and the horizontal
mass of the church echoed in a broad expanse of sky
above and water below. This contrast of vertical and
horizontal forms, the broad cone of vision permitting an
expansive sweep of the scene, the horizontal canvas format, and the location of the horizon line in the lower half
of the canvas all suggest the seriousness with which
Moran treats his monumental subject. A tone of clarity,
order, and heroic poise, overlaid with a rich dramatic
effect, is characteristic of Moran's Venice and reminds us
of seventeenth- and eighteenth-century pictorial conventions, contrasting sharply with the interpretation
of the city by such contemporaries as Prendergast and
Sargent. Moran's manner of seeing and portraying landscapes is, in fact, almost anachronistic in 1903.

Moran is better known today for his views of the geological wonders of the American West, but to his
contemporaries, these architectural wonders of Europe
were equally moving, equally remote, and equally desirable. The taste for Venice in general, and for Moran in
particular, was not limited to urbane travelers; the subject was a popular one, as the reproduction of a Venetian
view by Moran on twenty-two million calendar pictures
in 1898 by the Brown and Bigelow firm attests.[1]

To a certain degree, Moran treated the dramatic monuments of natural history and the great monuments of
human history similarly. The same formatting and framing devices are employed, the same heightened
chromaticism is invoked, and, perhaps more surprisingly,
similar motifs are employed: the rainbow that sets off the
Grand Canyon (*Grand Canyon with Rainbow*, 1912, The
Fine Arts Museums of San Francisco), promising a be-
nevolent custodianship and western future for the
American people, occasionally is also to be seen arching
over the Doge's Palace (*Venice*, 1903, Yale University Art
Gallery).

In such paintings as *View of Venice* Moran is making a
portrait of a building, but he is simultaneously interpreting the painterly tradition and the historic past while
giving us a glimpse of his and his patrons' melancholic,
but not uncomfortable, view of the world.

1. "Sunsets," undated clippings from *Life*, Moran Papers, The Thomas
Gilcrease Institute of American History and Art, Tulsa, Oklahoma,
quoted in Wilkins, p. 195.

Provenance: Pirtle House, Bedford, Texas; Ira Spanierman Gallery,
New York, 1983

Exhibition History and Bibliography: Phyllis Braff, *Thomas Moran: A
Search for the Scenic*, East Hampton, N. Y., Guildhall Museum, 29 November 1980-25 January 1981, p. 41

David Dalhoff Neal
1838 – 1915

During a brief career as a young draftsman for San Francisco wood engravers, Neal won the friendship of émigré
German artist Charles Christian Nahl and the support of
a California patron, S. P. Dewey, who agreed to send him
abroad for training.[1] He arrived in Munich in 1862 and
so thoroughly acquired the marks of the school that he
was spoken of as a "German painter born in America."[2]
During the 1860s, he studied figure and history painting

with Karl Piloty. In a move to be repeated some years later by Frank Duveneck and his pupils, Piloty made an accompanied excursion to Venice which was reported in *The Aldine*:

Piloty's students are attached to him by the strongest ties of love and reverence. He seeks opportunity to give them every advantage in his power, and whenever he makes journeys to picturesque localities for artistic study, he is always accompanied by some of his favorite pupils. Some years since, David Neal and young Kaulbach were his companions on a journey to Venice, where Neal made studies which have already proved of service to him.[3]

It is probable that this sojourn early in his career was the only painting expedition Neal made to Venice. Five known works are associated with this trip, three of which were exhibited at the National Academy of Design in 1866, 1867, and 1871.[4] One of these, *Interior of St. Mark's, Venice* (ca. 1865), was owned by Le Grand Lockwood, a Connecticut tycoon whose Norwalk mansion was the showpiece of the state and remains today an impressive document of the mid-century era.

1. S. G. W. Benjamin, *Our American Artists: Second Series* (Boston: D. Lothrop & Co., 1879), n. p.; John R. Tait, "David Neal," *The Magazine of Art* (1886), p. 95.

2. Tait, p. 95.

3. "Art: David Neal," *The Aldine* 7, no. 7 (July 1874), p. 147.

4. *NAD*, p. 678; *Who Was Who in America*, vol. 1, 1897-1942 (Chicago: A. N. Marquis Co., 1942), p. 888.

29 Interior of St. Mark's, Venice, 1869
Oil on canvas, 72½ × 58½ in. (184.2 × 148.6 cm)
Signed and dated, lower left: *David Neal. München. 1869*
The Art Institute of Chicago. Gift of Samuel Nickerson

The ancient church of San Marco provided one of the few interior Venetian sites popular with artists. In his memoirs, Maitland Armstrong recalled,

In San Marco the artists were privileged, we could sit and paint wherever we pleased, no one ever interfering with us; we were allowed to store our easels and canvases in the sacristy — there were so many of them that it looked more like a studio than the robing-room of a church — and liberal fees for caring for our things made the sacristans our good friends. Never was there a more delightful place to work in.[1]

One of the first Americans to enjoy this hospitality was the young David D. Neal, who visited Venice in the late 1860s and made minute studies of the interior of the great Byzantine church in preparation for at least one large-scale work. In 1866, *Interior of San Marco, Venice* (present location unknown) was bought by a Connecticut collector, while this painting — which may or may not represent the same subject — was painted in 1869 and entered a Chicago collection.[2] Executed back in his Munich studio, the ambitious painting shows the full range of Neal's newly acquired technique. From the invisible brushwork of the floor through the tactile strokes in the marble panels and the roughly textured paint in the pendentive overhead, he suggests not only the visible characteristics but also the nature of the objects portrayed. Ably depicting the haunting cavernous structure, Neal also introduces a romantic historical pantomime: a

sixteenth-century wedding. He may have had a specific text in mind, but it is likely he intended only a generalized aristocratic costume piece.[3] Even more impressive than the processional groups are the still-life elements: the casually draped tapestry on the right, the seating furniture at lower right, and the presiding apostles above the marble screen. These are rendered with exquisite verisimilitude.

Neal's interpretation of Venice is unusual, for it does not seek to interpret and juxtapose the present population and physical condition of Venice with the past; rather, he fully embraces the historical perspective, steeping the viewer in a recaptured fiction. Few artists saw Venice so wholly as the fiefdom of the past, omitting completely the irony of necessary hindsight.

1. Maitland Armstrong, *Day Before Yesterday: Reminiscences of a Varied Life* (New York: Scribner's, 1920), p. 244.

2. This, the Chicago painting, was referred to as *St Mark's, Venice* at the same time (Tait, p. 98; Clement and Hutton, vol. 2, p. 144; David Dalhoff Neal Papers, roll N58, frames 333-334, AAA: an undated, unidentified, printed text on Neal).

3. The pentimento suggests that the cavalier in the left foreground was originally taller. This shift may have been accomplished for reasons of balance, or perhaps it was intended to suppress this figure for the benefit of the brightly lit matron behind, an interpretation that suggests there is an associated tale.

Provenance: The artist, Munich, 1869-1871; Old Crosby Opera House Collection, Chicago, 1871-ca. 1876; Samuel M. Nickerson, Chicago, ca. 1876-1887; The Art Institute of Chicago, 1887

29

Exhibition History and Bibliography: Royal Bavarian Academy, Munich, *Internationale Kunstausstellung*, 1869; National Academy of Design, New York, *Third Annual Winter Exhibition, 1869-1870*, no. 479; idem, *Catalogue of the First Summer Exhibition* [1870], no. 480; Chicago Academy of Design, *Fifth Annual Exhibition*, May 1871, no. 62; idem, *Permanent Exhibition*, February 1871, no. 6, lent by the artist; Yale School of the Fine Arts, New Haven, *Third Annual Exhibition*, 1871, no. 98; *Chicago Inter-State Industrial Exposition*, 7 September-9 October 1876, no. 253; John R. Tait, "David Neal," *Magazine of Art* (1886), p. 98; The Art Institute of Chicago, *Loan Collection of Paintings Exhibited at the Opening of the New Art Museum Together with Other Permanent and Loan Collections*, 1887, no. 122; idem, *Catalogue of the Reid Collection of Drawings and Etchings Exhibited by the Art Institute of Chicago Together with Other Permanent and Loan Collections*, 1888 [?], no. 26; idem, *Catalogue of Paintings Exhibited in the New Galleries*, 1890, no. 10; idem, *Collection of Paintings from Various Sources*, August 1890, no. 56; Clement and Hutton, vol. 2, p. 144; *The National Cyclopaedia of American Biography*, New York: James T. White & Company, 1907, p. 53; Charles Deering Library, Northwestern University, Evanston, Ill., December 1932.

Elizabeth Nourse
1859 – 1938

A native of Cincinnati, Elizabeth Nourse was one of a small group of successful, expatriate women artists based in Paris late in the nineteenth century and early in the twentieth. She made one long painting trip to Italy in 1890, pausing briefly in Venice during the month of April.[1] In Sketchbook No. 10, inscribed "1890 – Italie/ Florence/1891 Boist – Austria/& Nuremburg," preserved in a private collection in Cincinnati, she recorded in nine pencil, chalk, and watercolor drawings her impressions of Venice.[2] The finished paintings that grew out of these sketches include two watercolors and two oils, all very different in character from the large-scale records of peasant life for which she is better known.[3]

1. Mary A. H. Burke, *Elizabeth Nourse, 1859-1938: A Salon Career*, exh. cat. (Washington, D.C.: Smithsonian Institution Press, 1983), pp. 38-41; Charlotte Streifer Rubinstein, *American Women Artists* (Boston: G. K. Hall & Co., 1982) pp. 119-122.

2. Burke, p. 250; Elizabeth Nourse Papers, roll 2758, frames 251-285, AAA.

3. Burke, p. 225.

30 Venetian Scene, 1890
Oil on canvas, 14 × 19½ in. (35.6 × 49.5 cm)
Signed and dated, lower left: *E. Nourse '90*
Mr. and Mrs. Harry A. Lockwood, Cincinnati, Ohio

Depicting the mouth of the Grand Canal, the curve of the Riva, and a glimpse of the Campanile, Nourse's loosely rendered painting captures the vacancy of an overcast April day. A monochromatic grayness tints the pink of the palaces and blue-green of the water, punctuated by opaque black touches in the gondolas and pilings.

Although two preparatory sketches for this painting are known, the immediacy and freshness of the brushstroke suggest that it was painted on the spot, perhaps from Nourse's hotel room balcony, rather than later in the year when she established a studio in Rome.[1] Avoiding both the celebrated monuments and the picturesque inhabitants, she sees Venice with a frankness and directness that makes us wish that Nourse, one of the few professional women artists to depict the city, had stayed longer.

1. Elizabeth Nourse Papers, roll 2758, frames 251-252, AAA; Burke, pp. 39-41.

Exhibition History and Bibliography: Indian Hill Historical Museum Association, Cincinnati, *Cincinnati's Artists in Paris*, May 1983, no. 359.

30

F. Maxfield Parrish
1870 – 1966

Maxfield Parrish visited Europe with his parents in 1877 and 1884/85; he returned in 1895 with his bride and may have visited Venice during these early excursions.[1] His work first came to public attention in 1897, when he won second place in a *Century Magazine* poster competition judged by F. Hopkinson Smith and Elihu Vedder.[2] During the spring of 1903, he traveled throughout Italy making preparatory sketches for illustrations to be included in Edith Wharton's *Italian Villas and Their Gardens*.[3]

Throughout his long and varied career, Parrish used Venetian subjects in his paintings for book and magazine illustrations (such as *Venetian Twilight*, 1904, for *Scribner's Magazine*, April 1906), murals (Curtis Publishing Co., Philadelphia, project, 1911), and paintings for calendar advertisements (such as *Venetian Lamplighter* for General Electric Mazda lamps, 1924). In each case, the city, its boats, and its inhabitants are painted with meticulous precision against ombre skies in a tableau suffused with romantic expression and light. For Parrish, Venice was clearly a state of mind, as real to him as a state of being, infusing much of the enchanted world of his art. It seems no accident in retrospect that Hop Smith (who was enchanted by Venice) and Elihu Vedder (for whom inner spiritual realities and outer Italian topographical realities were central) were the 'discoverers' of Maxfield Parrish on the threshold of his career.

1. *Maxfield Parrish: A Retrospect*, exh. cat. (Springfield, Mass.: The George Walter Vincent Smith Art Museum, 1966), n. p.; Homer Saint-Gaudens, "Maxfield Parrish," *The Critic and Literary World* 46, no. 6 (June 1905), p. 512.
   2. Saint-Gaudens, p. 515.
   3. Coy Ludwig, *Maxfield Parrish* (New York: Watson-Guptill Publications, 1973), p. 32.

31

31 The Cardinal Archbishop Sat on His Shaded Balcony, 1901
Oil on board, 14⅜ × 9¼ in. (36.5 × 23.5 cm)
Signed, lower right: *M.P.*
Mrs. Mary Bell

In his frontispiece for Arthur Cosslett Smith's tale "The Turquoise Cup" (*Scribner's Magazine*, December 1901), Parrish has chosen the first line of the text for illustration. In the story, a venerable clergyman sits in the shade watching his pigeons, musing on their coquetry and their conjugal life. Although Smith speaks of "the blue sky that silhouetted the trees in the garden," Parrish elects to establish the Venetian setting more explicitly by depicting the wide reflective Bacino di San Marco and distant structures reminiscent of the island of San Giorgio. A single pigeon rests on the balcony, his profile echoing those of the carved lion (reminding us once again of Saint Mark and of Venice) and of the prelate himself. Large cumulus clouds punctuate a sky whose blues shade from deepest royal overhead to palest silver at the horizon. Parrish has confined his palette very effectively to variants on these blues and a wide range of browns.

While clearly a specific illustration of a specific fictive episode, *The Cardinal Archbishop* also includes numerous elements personal to Parrish. The archbishop's balcony with its built-in seat and arching aperture is based on his own New Hampshire porch, and the Archbishop himself is a self-portrait. More incongruous is the tea equipage (the Cardinal was educated at Oxford and picked up the habit of afternoon tea, we are told), a miscellaneous group of American Brittania-ware vessels from the early nineteenth century, perched on a late eighteenth-century New England, tilt-top tea table. Despite their eccentric position in this context, these still-life elements are painted with a vivid concreteness that helps us imagine the reality of the extraordinarily precious turquoise cup which is the primary subject of this little adventure. Guarded by the wary but sympathetic Archbishop, the cup is coveted as a love-token by an Irish heiress and her English suitor. Preserved through the prelate's shrewdness and the couple's basic honesty, the priceless cup has much in common with both the natural beauty of the Irish woman and the man-made splendor of Venice itself which Parrish suggests so tellingly in this image.

Provenance: Purchased from La Galeria, San Mateo

Exhibition History and Bibliography: Arthur Cosslett Smith, "The Turquoise Cup," *Scribner's Magazine* 30 (December 1901), frontispiece;

idem, *The Turquoise Cup and the Desert*, New York: Scribner's, 1903, reprinted 1910, frontispiece; Coy Ludwig, *Maxfield Parrish*, New York: Watson-Guptill Publications, 1973, pp. 207, 212; Paul W. Skeeters, *Maxfield Parrish, Early Years 1893-1930*, New York: Chartwell House, Inc., 1973, p. 30; Virginia Reed Colby, "Stephen and Maxfield Parrish in New Hampshire," *Antiques* (June 1979), pp. 1290, 1293.

32   A Venetian Night's Entertainment, 1903
Oil on paper, 17¼ × 11¾ in. (43.8 × 29.9 cm)
Signed, lower left: *M.P*
Judy Goffman Fine Art, New York, and Blue Bell, Pennsylvania

A frontispiece for Edith Wharton's tale of the same name in the December 1903 issue of *Scribner's Magazine*, this painting compresses the whole cast of characters into a single tableau, avoiding the literal illustration of any single fictional event. The press of thirteen figures surrounding and observing "young Tony, newly of age," suggests the artful, labyrinthine web they weave around the protagonist. As so many other Edith Wharton fictions, *A Venetian Night's Entertainment* is a tale of entrapment; but unlike most, in which women are entrapped by men, here it is the emissary of one culture entrapped by denizens of an alien culture. In the person of Tony Bracknell, we observe the confrontation between the young, innocent New World with the experienced, beautiful, treacherous Old.

Set in 1760, the story recapitulates Venice's popular reputation and juxtaposes it with the cultural values of eighteenth-century Salem, Massachusetts. Popular wisdom agreed:

Venice was one of the gayest and most splendid cities in the world – a city of mirth and music, of ball, fête, and carnival, and as renowned for its delights of love and masking as for its mystery and crime. It was the most dissolute capital in Europe, and attracted thus, even as Paris does now [1858], in quest of mere pleasure and excitement, a vast throng of rich nobles and fascinating adventurers, mountebanks, actors, singers, artists, sculptors, poets, scholars, men of science, as well as gamblers, assassins, and courtesans.[1]

And Edith Wharton plays on that opinion in her tale. Parrish pictorializes the situation by placing blond Tony in his tri-cornered hat and deep green coat at the center of the composition. Facing him, in swashbuckling, befeathered headgear, is "the Count" who gestures toward the lure, Polixena Cador. The other seductions of music, wine, and theater surround the young American and collaborate with the primary adventurer.

Although the figures are depicted in fully realistic detail, the image as a whole has an abstract, flattened quality which we associate with much of Parrish's work; more than half the characters appear in profile and they arrange themselves in vertical, but non-recessive, tiers. This stylized pantomime is lit by a violet evening sky without, and buoyant, luminous globes within. A superb piece of artifice itself, Parrish's painting amply suggests the attractive, but dangerous and deceitful, world of Edith Wharton's fiction and Venice's popular reputation.

As this instance suggests, Venice was not just of interest to American artists and their wealthy patrons during the nineteenth century. Through magazine articles and

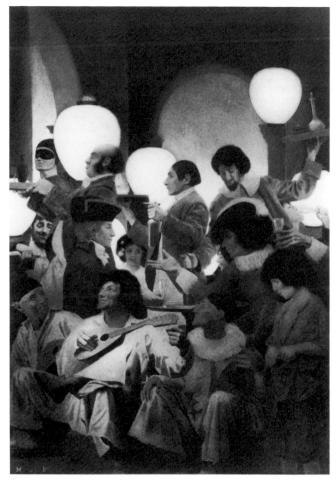

32

pictorial reproductions Venice was well known to Americans who never traveled. Their knowledge of the city was necessarily partial and infused with suggestive stereotypes, as was Tony's acquaintance with the city from a print hanging in his hall in Salem, "a busy, merry, populous scene entitled *St Mark's Square in Venice*," but these familiar images of the city provided a preknowledge, a fiction against which fact might be tested for those able to experience, by travel as well as by imagination, the confusing reality of Venice.

1. Untitled, unsigned review of books on Venice of interest to Americans, *North American Review* (January 1858), p. 114.

Exhibition History and Bibliography: Edith Wharton, "A Venetian Night's Entertainment," *Scribner's Magazine* 34 (December 1903), frontispiece; Coy Ludwig, *Maxfield Parrish*, New York: Watson-Guptill Publications, 1973, p. 212.

Joseph Pennell
1860 – 1926

Joseph Pennell's acquaintance with Venice began when, as a young art student, he saw the exhibition of Whistler's First Venice Set of etchings at the Pennsylvania Academy in 1881.[1] Firmly concentrating on the black and white media (he apparently resisted Thomas Eakins's urging to *paint*), he determined to become an illustrator. He won his first important commission and an opportunity to go to Italy in 1883 to prepare etchings for William Dean Howells's "Tuscan Cities" for *Century Magazine*.[2] After touring northern Italy he arrived in Venice in early June and enjoyed the camaraderie of William Gedney Bunce, Frank Duveneck, and Duveneck's "boys" for almost a month.[3] In a letter of 13 June to his future wife and collaborator, Elizabeth Robins, he described his first impressions of the city:

Oh what an awful sell it is . . . and that beastly black hearse to get into – which rocks like a hammock (I hate hammocks) and smelly canals – and howling women and St. Mark's all polished up and looking like a new town house . . . those were my first impressions of Venice – and I carried them for several days. . . . In short another attack of blues. But one morning I woke up and it all came – lovely – lovely light and everything. . . .

Now I have a gondola and a faithful creature who shrieks in unknown tongues whenever a gentleman in an upper window empties a pan of pea pods upon my head – as fell out the other day – and he rows me – lolling back in cushions – through rippling quivering blue and gold kissed [canals]. . . . To be in piazza *on a June evening is not to be described – only let me say we all go there to drink coffee – we go when it rains to be dry – when hot to be cool – and – we do it all the time – and here is the place to learn to loaf and invite one's soul. But you will see it all before long.*[4]

He concludes his letter with the note that "Hamerton has just accepted an article for *The Portfolio* on San Gimignano and I am going to try to get something out of him on this place." Clearly he did "get something out of him" on Venice as the next year a three-part article by Julia Cartwright entitled "The Artist in Venice" appeared in *Portfolio* with ten handsome illustrations by Pennell. The Venice letter of 13 June is not remarkably long, but in the course of its text Pennell finds opportunity to make reference to five literary giants – John Ruskin, William Dean Howells, Oscar Wilde, Dante Gabriel Rossetti, and Mark Twain – suggesting not only the range of his reading, but also the literary turn of his mind.

Pennell married Elizabeth the next year, and in 1885 they embarked on a European bicycle tour (the newlyweds sharing a tandem tricycle) which brought them to Venice for an extended visit.[5] They stayed at the Casa Kirsch and once more Pennell enjoyed the lively company of the Duveneck circle. It was the Pennells' intention to stay in Europe until their money ran out; her talents as a writer and his as an illustrator served them well, and the couple stayed on until the First World War drove them back to America.[6] Based in London for three decades, the Pennells wrote and/or illustrated more than 100 books, projects that often brought them to the continent and to Italy.[7] Notable among these ventures were the summers of 1901 and 1902, which brought Pennell back to Venice to prepare drawings for Marion Crawford's *Gleanings from Venetian History* and to serve as Commissioner of the newly established Biennale exhibition of contemporary art.[8]

Pennell is best known for his published drawings and etchings, but he also produced lithographs and delicate pastels.[9] Profoundly influenced by Whistler, Pennell's work in black and white is noted for its delicacy of line and tone. Picking up on a minor note in the master's oeuvre, Pennell produced impressive compositions recording industrial scenes and construction projects, including the rebuilding of St. Mark's Campanile.[10]

1. Robert H. Getscher, *The Stamp of Whistler*, exh. cat. (Oberlin, Ohio: Allen Memorial Art Museum, Oberlin College, 1977), p. 185.

2. Mahonri Sharp Young, "The Remarkable Joseph Pennell," *The American Art Journal* 2, no. 1 (Spring 1970), pp. 83-85; Adeline Lee Karpiscak, *Whistler and His Contemporaries: Prints from the University Art Collections, Arizona State University*, exh. cat. (Tucson: University of Arizona Museum of Art, 1982), p. 20; Soria, *Dictionary*, p. 247.

3. Young, p. 85; Getscher, p. 185; Joseph Pennell, *The Adventures of an Illustrator: Mostly in Following His Authors in America and Europe* (Boston: Little, Brown, 1925), p. 141.

4. Elizabeth Robins Pennell, *The Life and Letters of Joseph Pennell*, vol. 1 (Boston: Little, Brown, 1929), pp. 93-94.

5. Young, p. 86; Getscher, p. 185.

6. Young, p. 90.

7. Matthew Baigell, *Dictionary of American Art* (New York: Icon Editions, Harper & Row, 1979), p. 271.

8. Pennell, *Adventures*, pp. 144, 280-286; Elizabeth Robins Pennell, *Joseph Pennell*, exh. cat. (New York: The Metropolitan Museum of Art, 1926), p. 27.

9. Louis A. Wuerth, *Catalogue of the Etchings of Joseph Pennell* (Boston: Little, Brown, 1928); *Memorial Exhibition of the Works of the Late Joseph Pennell* (Philadelphia: The Print Club of Philadelphia, 1926); E. Pennell, *Joseph Pennell*, pp. 27-28, 47.

10. Karpiscak, p. 36; Joseph Pennell, *Venice, the City of the Sea* (Boston: Le Roy Phillips, 1913) n. p., fig. 24.

33 A Water Gate in Venice, 1883
Etching (black ink on oriental paper), plate 8 × 11⅝ in. (20.3 × 29.5 cm), sheet 10⅞ × 15¾ in. (27.6 × 40 cm)
Signed and dated in plate, center left: *Jo. Pennell/3 1883*
The Fine Arts Museums of San Francisco, Achenbach Foundation for Graphic Arts

Executed during his first trip to Venice, this etching appeared as the largest of Pennell's illustrations in Julia Cartwright's three *Portfolio* articles entitled "The Artist in Venice."[1] The young artist's mastery of his medium is evident in the quality of his technique, his selected subject, and his carefully vignetted composition. He has chosen to depict the lower façade of an elegant, but ill-repaired, Renaissance palace, its details crisply spotlit by the noontime sun. As in many of his Venetian works, he sees the building as a series of aperture episodes with a dark water gate the focus of the image's interest. Ajar, this door with its central position and intense blackness contrasted to the tapestried delicacy of the grillwork and façade marbles suggests entry, mystery, and disclosure.

Julia Cartwright tells us in the first section of "The Artist in Venice,"

There are two classes of artists . . . who will always find a wide field in Venice. . . . There are those who . . . devote their

33

powers to the faithful reproduction of the great monuments of the past. . . .

And then there is the artist of a different type. The man who delights in passing impressions and changing effects, who, sensitive to each new loveliness of shape and hue, knows how to seize the quickly shifting scene.[2]
For her, there are chroniclers of the stately, well-known buildings in Venice and chroniclers of glimpses, of corners unknown and undiscovered. Clearly, her sympathies lie with the latter, and both her text and Pennell's illustrations carefully describe their discovered bits of uncelebrated wall and canal. *A Water Gate in Venice* is no exception, with its deliberately partial, seemingly accidental rendition of an unfamiliar façade. The canal is a narrow one, for the horizon level suggests that the artist is seated on a landing or *fondamenta* opposite the palace. As is the case for many artists in Venice, Pennell erases all evidence that he is *not* in a gondola, even encouraging the suggestion that he is waterborne. Even a quiet canal rocks a moored vessel, making exacting work difficult. As Pennell tells us himself in his memoirs, "No one . . . ever takes a gondola in Venice to work from."[3]

The year that this image was executed, Pennell described his working method:
I either work from light to dark, or in the [acid] bath, or make the whole drawing in the old-fashioned way and use stopping-out varnish. In fact, all my work thus far has been merely a series of experiments – most of my plates . . . have been done in a day – and most of them in half of one. About half were done out-of-doors and the rest from sketches. In the future, I intend to do everything from nature direct on the plate.[4]
Like Whistler, whose etched Venetian images had made a deep impression on him when he saw them two years earlier, Pennell strove to preserve the effect of spontaneity, and – despite the destiny of these works to

appear as journal illustrations – to stress the artistic, rather than the mechanically reproductive, dimension of the medium.

1. Julia Cartwright, "The Artist in Venice," *Portfolio* 15 (1884), pp. 17-22, 37-42, 45-48.
2. Cartwright, p. 18.
3. Pennell, *Adventures*, pp. 286-287.
4. Quoted in Karpiscak, p. 29.

Exhibition History and Bibliography: Not in Louis Wuerth, *Catalogue of the Etchings of Joseph Pennell*, Boston: Little, Brown, 1928.

Maurice Brazil Prendergast
1859 – 1924

Maurice Prendergast made six trips abroad, and at least three mark significant watersheds in his career as an artist. In 1886, and again in 1891 to 1895, he visited England and France, pursuing his art studies.[1] However, it was not until his eighteen-month expedition abroad in 1898/99 (financed by Sarah Choate Sears, artist and patron of artists) that he visited Italy, spending the better part of his sojourn very productively in Venice.[2] Staying on the outlying island, the Giudecca, Prendergast spent his time in the center of the city, studying its major art collections, especially, as one early critic put it, the "'primitive' glories in the art of Carpaccio [in the]... little dark Scuola of San Giorgio dei Schiavoni," and painting Venice's major architectural monuments, focusing on the area of the Piazza San Marco.[3] During his stay he associated with other artists including the American William Gedney Bunce (who never tired of painting Venice's bright fishing boats, and who bought one of Prendergast's early monotypes) and his younger brother, Charles Prendergast, a noted frame-maker and naive or 'folk' artist.[4]

Despite one episode of prolonged illness in Venice, Prendergast was able to produce a body of consistently accomplished, mature work which brought him, at exhibitions in Boston and Chicago late in 1899, his first significant recognition as an artist.[5] Toward the end of his stay in Venice he wrote to his brother, who had returned to Boston, concerning the paintings he had studied: "It has been the visit of my life. I have been here almost a year and have seen so many beautiful things it almost makes me ashamed of my profession today."[6] And yet, by 1899 he was very much part of the vanguard of that profession.

For the next decade he sent his Venetian paintings to exhibitions in New York, Philadelphia, Cincinnati, Boston, and other cities around the country.[7] Eager for another look at the contemporary avant-garde, he returned to Paris in 1909/10, and seeking another infusion of Venetian experience, he returned to Italy in 1911/12. This latter trip was, with the exception of an abortive trip to Paris on the eve of World War I, his last trip to Europe.[8] He arrived in Venice in September of 1911 and took rooms at the Casa Frollo on the Zattere (Fondamenta Galoni), a pensione in an inexpensive but not inconvenient part of the city.[9] Again, he was ill and, complaining of his inability to accomplish any painting, he reported in a letter of 18 December 1911 that he had "not touched paint since last August.... My sketching experience this time has been disasterous."[10] Very different in character from the works produced during the first Venetian episode, the later paintings show a shift in temperament as well as in style. In the same discouraged missive, Prendergast wrote, "With all [Venice's] beauty I am never going to do my best work here."[11]

Many would disagree with Prendergast on the relationship of Venice to his best work. The more than fifty watercolors, monotypes, and oil paintings that he produced during his two Venetian sojourns show, at their best, his superb mastery of technique and originality of composition, as well as the complete novelty of his approach to painting. And this is not surprising in an artist for whom (like the French Impressionists in the 1870s) the urban environment and the urbanite at leisure were central concerns. Most of Prendergast's paintings of Venice, unlike those of most of his contemporaries, include both architectural and figurative subject matter. The ancient city and its modern population receive equally enthusiastic attention, usually from a high prospect, often from an eccentric point of view. Although most writers speak of the sunny "sparkle" of his paintings, some of the most interesting are night, evening, or rainy views (cat. nos. 38, 39, 43, 48). And although it is often assumed that his watercolors were executed rapidly and completely *en plein air*, there is reason to believe that they were painted slowly and finished in the studio from sketches and beginnings made on site.

Although quite modest about his achievements and his position in the art world, Prendergast was not unknown to such notables as Whistler, and he was able to secure the patronage of such keen-eyed, prominent collectors as Sarah Sears and Duncan Phillips.[12] As early as 1921, he was enthusiastically embraced as the "first American modernist," and Venice was a central element in that achievement and that recognition.[13]

1. Gwendolyn Owens, *Watercolors by Maurice Prendergast from New England Collections*, exh. cat. (Williamstown, Mass.: Sterling and Francine Clark Art Institute, 1978), p. 9; Eleanor Green, "Maurice Prendergast, Myth and Reality," *American Art Review* 4, no. 1 (July 1977), pp. 89-91.

2. Hedley Howell Rhys, *Maurice Prendergast, 1859-1924*, exh. cat. (Boston: Museum of Fine Arts, 1960), pp. 28-30; Van Wyck Brooks, "Anecdotes of Maurice Prendergast" in *The Prendergasts: Retrospective Exhibition of the Work of Maurice and Charles Prendergast*, exh. cat. (Andover, Mass.: Addison Gallery of American Art, Phillips Academy, 1938), p. 38; Eleanor Green, *Maurice Prendergast: Art of Impulse and Color*, exh. cat. (College Park, Md.: The Art Gallery at the University of Maryland, 1976), p. 38.

3. Brooks, p. 43; William M. Milliken in *The Arts* (April 1926), p. 181, cited in Brooks, pp. 49-50.

4. Rhys, p. 28; Green, p. 40.

5. Rhys, p. 30; Green, p. 40.

6. Cited in Green, p. 40.

7. Green, pp. 40-62.

8. Charles H. Sawyer, "The Prendergasts," *Parnassus* 10, no. 5 (October 1938), p. 11.

9. Green, p. 62.

10. Cited in Green, p. 62.   12. Brooks, pp. 35-36; Green, p. 18.

11. Cited in Green, p. 70.   13. Owens, p. 10

34 Square of S. Marco, Venice (Splash of Sunshine and Rain), 1899
Watercolor on paper, 19⅜ × 14¼ in. (49.2 × 36.2 cm)
Signed and dated, lower left: *Prendergast/Venice 1899*; signed, titled, and dated on label affixed to reverse: *"Splash of Sunshine and Rain"/Chiesa St. Marco/ Venezia/Maurice B. Prendergast/1904*
Alice M. Kaplan
Color plate

On 5 April 1857, Herman Melville noted emphatically, but cryptically, in his journal:
Breakfast on St. Mark's [Square], Austrian flags flying from three masts. Glorious aspect of the Balsulica [basilica] in the sunshine. The charm of the square. The snug little breakfast there. Ladies, flowers, girls – musicians, pedlers of Adriatic

34

shells. *Cigar stores & – Sat in a chair by the arcade at Mindel's some time in the sun looking at the flags, the sun, & the church.*[1]

The same scene, almost unchanged, was exuberantly recorded by Maurice Prendergast decades later in *Square of S. Marco, Venice* when he, too, observed and enjoyed "the flags, the sun, & the church." For centuries, in fact, the elaborate façade of San Marco had presided over the great civic enclosure, the piazza's flat, rectangular blocks of trachyte and marble contrasting with the curving arches and domes of the church. The scene was familiar to everyone who inhabited or visited Venice. It was also known to many who never traveled but who saw Canaletto's widely exported views of the Piazza or the many prints sold throughout Europe and America from the eighteenth century. It is this very fact of the recognizability of the subject that makes Prendergast's work so interesting, for he is able simultaneously to capture the vibrant image of the sunlit piazza while he jolts our complacent recognition with novel elements. The ancient church – essentially Byzantine in structure and fifteenth-century in elaboration – is pressed high on the page, its highest lightning rod intercepted by the paper's edge, its glass panes, bronze horses, and gold mosaics glittering in the sun. A passing shower has left the pavement wet and reflective, a fact seized upon by Prendergast as an opportunity to mirror the elaborate façade and to suggest, in passing, the aquatic nature of the city.

Prendergast has peopled the piazza not with the pro-

cessional clerics of Gentile Bellini's well-known view or the sober senators and bravos of Canaletto's scenes, but with brightly parasoled ladies and girls, their white dresses islands of untouched paper in the tinted medium.[2] As in most Prendergast images, these women occupy the foreground while male figures cluster in the back. These scattered human forms punctuate the strict and compressed geometry of the architectural setting, adding life and contemporaneity without denying the monumental character of this venerable religious and civic place.

The celebratory note of the figures is picked up in the enormous flags, playing in the breeze and casting dark shadows on the church's façade. Until the fall of Venice to Napoleon in 1797, the flagstaffs displayed the standards of Venice's important dependencies Candia, Cyprus, and Morea. When Melville surveyed the scene, the masts flew Austrian flags, for the city had been ceded to that country by France and was occupied (causing a bitterness among the Venetians, eloquently recorded by William Dean Howells in *Venetian Life*) until 1866, when Venice became part of the Kingdom of Italy. Thus, in heraldic form, Prendergast records here the old identity of Venice as an independent republic (in the lesser crimson banners emblazoned with the winged lion of Saint Mark) and its new political identity as a unit in the states of United Italy (in the three green-white-red central flags). The microcosm embraced by this patterned heraldic display and its shimmering reflection includes peddlers, sailors, ladies, and children, as well as the lessons of history, and a celebration of the present. Better than any contemporary, Prendergast has helped us re-see the "glorious aspect of the basilica in the sunshine" and "the charm of the square."

1. Herman Melville, *Journal of a Visit to Europe and the Levant, October 11, 1856-May 6, 1857*, Howard C. Horsford, ed. (Princeton: Princeton University Press, 1955), pp. 231-232.

2. Gentile Bellini, *Procession in the Piazza S. Marco*, 1470s, Accademia, Venice.

Provenance: Sotheby Parke Bernet, New York, 13-14 December 1973, no. 43; Byron Goldman, New York, 1973-1974

Exhibition History and Bibliography: *The Connoisseur* 84 (December 1973), p. 128, illus.; *Impressionism and Modern Art: The Season at Sotheby Parke-Bernet*, London and New York, 1974, p. 247, illus.; *Art at Auction 1973-1974*, New York: Viking Press, 1974, p. 173, illus.; Andrew Crispo Gallery, New York, *Ten Americans*, 16 May-30 June 1974, no. 121; Theodore E. Stebbins, Jr., *American Master Drawings and Watercolors: A History of Works on Paper from Colonial Times to the Present*, New York: Whitney Museum of American Art, 1976, pp. 14, 248, 250, 429; Cecily Langdale, "Maurice Prendergast, An American Post-Impressionist," *Connoisseur* 202, no. 814 (December 1979), pp. 248-253, illus. p. 252; Linda Bantel, *Alice M. Kaplan Collection: Catalogue*, New York: Columbia University Press, 1981; Coe Kerr Gallery, New York, *Americans in Venice: 1879-1913*, 1983, no. 53.

35 St. Mark's, Venice (The Clock Tower), 1898/99
Watercolor over graphite on paper, 23½ × 5¾ in.
(59.7 × 14.6 cm)
Signed, lower left: *Prendergast*
Lent by the William A. Farnsworth Library and Art Museum, Rockland, Maine
Color illustration back cover

35

On an axis perpendicular to that of the façade of San Marco, which faces west to the Piazza, the clock tower (or Torre dell' Orologio) faces south to the lagoon and the open sea. Its richly emblazoned and carefully proportioned Renaissance surface was a well-known landmark, and it is not surprising to read in Van Wyck Brooks's early account of the artist that Prendergast was commissioned to paint it.[1] Although there are two known versions of the work, it seems likely that this, the earlier version, was the one Brooks had in mind.[2] According to museum records, it was acquired directly from the artist by Prendergast's patroness, Sarah Choate Sears, and the commission or purchase was prompted by Mary Cassatt, the noted American expatriate Impressionist, who is better known for her mediating role in promoting and popularizing the work of her French colleagues in America.

In undertaking the 'portrait' of this late fifteenth-century monument, Prendergast seizes upon a subject most appropriate to his talents and ingenuity. In designing his format, he mimics the narrow façade of the building, compressing and isolating its gold, lapis lazuli blue, and white marble splendor in a startlingly vertical treatment. In a very different mode from the eccentric contextualization of the tower in Charles Coleman's *The Bronze Horses of San Marco* (cat. no. 12), Prendergast's movement toward isolation is, nevertheless, equally abrupt, intriguing, and modern in tone.

Beneath the venerable tower with its magically intense, fully saturated blues and golds, figures with bright red umbrellas and brilliantly white dresses spread themselves down the narrow sheet. They cluster here at the junction of the great, open Piazza and the narrow, busy Merceria, Venice's primary shopping street, offering Prendergast an opportunity to complete his palette of primaries and to juxtapose the movement and impermanence of the figures with the more enduring monument above.

A half-century before, Charles Dickens had visited Venice and described his first encounter with the Piazza in terms of a dream: "It was a great Piazza, as I thought; anchored, like all the rest, in the deep ocean. On its broad bosom, was a Palace." His vision continues with a survey of the major civic structures, ending with:

Not far from these again, a . . . tower: richest of the rich in all its decorations: even here, where all was rich: sustained aloft, a great orb, gleaming with gold and deepest blue: the Twelve Signs [of the zodiac] *painted on it, and a mimic sun revolving in its course around them: while above, two bronze giants hammered out the hours upon a sounding bell.*[3]

More than any other artist, Prendergast has succeeded in capturing the otherworldly intensity of the tower "gleaming with gold and deepest blue" without losing the note of contemporaneity by which we know his greatest works.

1. Van Wyck Brooks, "Anecdotes of Maurice Prendergast," in *The Prendergasts: Retrospective Exhibition of the Work of Maurice and Charles Prendergast*, exh. cat. (Andover, Mass.: Addison Gallery of American Art, Phillips Academy, 1938), pp. 38-39.

2. The other version of *The Clock Tower*, 1911, is in the Stanford University Museum of Art; it is illustrated and discussed in Green, pp. 32-34.

3. Charles Dickens, *Pictures from Italy*, David Paroissien, ed. (New York: Coward, McCann & Geoghegan, 1974), p. 121.

Exhibition History and Bibliography: Van Wyck Brooks, *The Prendergasts: Retrospective Exhibition of the Work of Maurice and Charles Prendergast*, Andover, Mass., Addison Gallery of American Art, Phillips Academy, 1938, pp. 38-39 (perhaps this version); Gwendolyn Owens, *Watercolors by Maurice Prendergast from New England Collections*, Sterling and Francine Clark Art Institute, Williamstown, Mass., 11 November-17 December 1978, no. 21; Coe Kerr Gallery, New York, *Americans in Venice, 1879-1913*, 19 October-16 November 1983, no. 54.

36   Piazza di San Marco, 1898/99

Watercolor and pencil on paper, 16⅛ × 15 in.
(41 × 38.1 cm)
Signed in pencil, lower left: *Prendergast*
The Metropolitan Museum of Art. Gift of the Estate of Mrs. Edward Robinson, 1952

Piazza di San Marco, with its radically cropped buildings and precipitous point of view, is as unusual and startling as Prendergast's very different portraits of celebrated monuments utilizing a compressed format (cat. nos. 34 and 35). In this watercolor Prendergast focuses on the three triumphal flags which are also visible in his *Square of S. Marco, Venice* (cat. no. 34) executed during the same trip. To the right, the viewer confronts a fragment of the Renaissance Procuratie Nuove, juxtaposed to a fragment of the Campanile. To the left, a deep, plummeting recession toward the Bacino and lagoon is punctuated by the staccato colonnade of the Libreria Vecchia and silhouetted column of St. Theodore. In the distance, a part of the Benedictine monastery next to San Giorgio is visible. This painting, composed as it is of fractions and nearly

36

37

unrecognizable parts of well-known buildings, takes on the character of a conundrum.

From a vantage point on the narrow roof of the clock tower, perched beside the great bronze bellringers, Prendergast observes the life in the cool, shaded Piazzetta and the sunlit Piazza below. It is late afternoon, and the square is peopled with pigeon-feeders, tourists, loungers, matrons, and girls, minute figures executed with a summary deftness.

In the leaps of scale from giant flag to tiny stroller, in his seemingly arbitrary slicing of the architectural elements, and in his use of a square format, Prendergast demonstrates his modernity. Although to all appearances spontaneous and fragmented, the work is carefully executed and artfully plotted.

Exhibition History and Bibliography: Hedley Howell Rhys, *Maurice Prendergast, 1859-1924*, Museum of Fine Arts, Boston, 26 October-4 December 1960, cat. no. 68, illus. p. 81; Henry Geldzahler, *American Painting in the Twentieth Century*, The Metropolitan Musuem of Art, New York, 1965, p. 35; Albert Ten Eyck Gardner, *History of Water Color Painting in America*, New York: Reinhold, 1966, p. 96, pl. 81; The Metropolitan Museum of Art, New York, *Two Hundred Years of Watercolor Painting in America: An Exhibition Commemorating the Centennial of the American Watercolor Society*, 8 December 1966-29 January 1967, no. 129; Larry Curry, *Eight American Masters of Watercolor*, Los Angeles County Museum of Art, 23 April-16 June 1968, no. 31.

37 Sunlight on the Piazzetta, Venice, 1898/99
Watercolor over graphite on paper, 12½ × 20⅝ in.
(31.8 × 52.4 cm)
Signed lower left: *Prendergast / Venice*
Museum of Fine Arts, Boston. Gift of Mr. and Mrs.
William T. Aldrich
Color plate

Dividing his image into two bands, a section of the ancient Doge's Palace with its rhythmic colonnades above and a slice of the vibrant life on the Piazzetta below, Prendergast creates one of his most memorable tableaux. As is usually the case, he has selected a high vantage point – one several feet higher than a normal standing posture. One imagines him perched on a ladder, or taking advantage of a temporary staging among the tables of the cafe that borders the Piazzetta on the west. This slight elevation allows the pedestrian figures to spread down the page in a clearer, larger pattern than would be the case from an eye-level prospect.

The look of the crowd against what Herman Melville terms "the Ducal palace's colonnade-like hedge of architecture" is Prendergast's subject, and he treats it here with extraordinary success.[1] Children feeding pigeons, solicitous nannies, ladies of fashion with their elaborate millinery, gondoliers, and bareheaded working women constitute this microcosm of fin de siècle Venice. The telling gesture, the characteristic stride, the stiff breeze blowing from the sea are caught and frozen with a permanence akin to that of the venerable Gothic façade behind.

As in other of his Venetian works of this period, there are few clusters of figures composed of both men and women, the children move prominently to the foreground, and a solitary Venetian woman emerges as a subtle, sympathetic protagonist in the pantomime. The slender, auburn-haired, Venetian woman fixed in the deep shadow of the Libreria in the lower left is such a figure. She is a personage, or more precisely, an archetype, observed by many but recorded most eloquently in paint by Sargent and Prendergast. She wears the characteristic long, black shawl and pauses to adjust her garments. As one Venice observer put it,

[The] *women are never at rest in their shawls; they are always unwinding them, resettling their folds, shifting them from head to shoulders, and back again, slipping out a ringed hand to sketch a whole series of gestures.* [2]

For many, she was an ambivalent figure; an American authoress of the period describes her 'type' with the distinct, but unconscious, voice of cultural otherness:

The Venetian women, as seen on the streets of their city, are untidy, dirty, although picturesque, often slight in youth, but dumpy and shapeless in middle life. Almost all of them wear black shawls, thrown over their heads, if the weather be cool, if warm, merely draped with careless grace over their shoulders. The beautiful red-gold hair one does sometimes find, however, but so untidily arranged. [3]

Prendergast clearly finds her one of the most intriguing aspects of Venice. For him, the social facts of the city are as paintable as the architectural facts, and he finds this wind-blown, Titian-haired contemporary as interesting as the quatrefoils of sunlight projected with such precision and regularity on the Palace wall behind.

1. Melville, p. 234.
2. Arthur Symons, *Cities of Italy* (New York: E. P. Dutton & Co., 1907), p. 88.
3. Elise Lathrop, *Sunny Days in Italy* (New York: James Pott & Co., 1907), p. 296.

Provenance: Gift of Mr. and Mrs. William T. Aldrich, 1961

Exhibition History and Bibliography: Hedley Howell Rhys, *Maurice Prendergast, 1859-1924*, Museum of Fine Arts, Boston, 26 October-4 December 1960, no. 80; Gwendolyn Owens, *Watercolors by Maurice Prendergast from New England Collections*, Sterling and Francine Clark Art Institute, Williamstown, Mass., 11 November-17 December 1978, no. 19.

38 Festival Day, Venice, 1898/99
Watercolor and pencil on paper, 12⅝ × 20 in.
(32.1 × 50.8 cm)
Signed in pencil, lower left: *Prendergast*
Mount Holyoke College Art Museum. Museum purchase, Gertrude Jewett Hunt Fund, in memory of Louise R. Jewett, 1951

As in *Sunlight on the Piazzetta* (cat. no. 37), Prendergast has selected for his subject a colorful crowd in front of the Piazzetta façade of the Doge's Palace. However, there he organized the architectural and human elements in frieze-like bands parallel to the picture plane. Here the pattern of space and figures is more complex. The elaborate arches of the early fifteenth-century palace recede on a diagonal, and the movement of processional figures traces a wide loop from the Baptistry of San Marco (a corner of which is just visible on the left), across the image, turning toward the observer on the far right. Marked by the banners, tapers, torchères, and lanterns they carry, the brightly robed clerics are the object of attention both for the crowd on the square and for ourselves. The most distant members of the procession – those whose presence is noted only by the tall candles they bear – are completely invisible, but significantly felt.

As in most Prendergast watercolors of this period, a nervous, descriptive pencil line is visible below the washes of pigment. These are applied in a rather wet and fluid state as he eschews the fine detail achievable with a drier, more Ruskinian brush. By deliberately avoiding particularity of faces and such architectural features as

38

39

the intricate and celebrated capitals, Prendergast forces
our attention on the overall scene and the tone of the
event, rather than on the character of its individual parts.

Venice was famous for extravagant festivals and pro-
cessions at the height of its glory, and Prendergast
carefully scrutinizes the modest relics of those public displays that survived to the eve of the twentieth century.[1]
Elizabeth Pennell, wife of the artist Joseph Pennell,
looked back from the perspective of 1917 on her experience of such events in 1884:

There was never a festa *in the Piazza that we were not there,
watching or walking with the bewildering procession of elegant young Venetians, and peasants from the mainland, and
officers, and soldiers, and gondoliers with big caps set jauntily
on their curls, and beautiful girls in the gay fringed shawls
that have disappeared from Venice and the wooden shoes that
once made an endless clatter along the* Riva *but are heard no
more.*[2]

Archaic even in its day, and particularly so from the perspective of the cataclysmic period of World War I, this
scene preserves a certain innocence. Prendergast, with
his very modern eyes, fixes for us in this image a glimpse
of the gestures, colors, and tone of Venice's pre-modern
rites and populace.

1. For a period description of these ancient civic events, see William
Roscoe Thayer, "Legends and Pageants of Venice," *Lippincott's Monthly
Magazine* 74 (November 1904), pp. 637-649.
2. Elizabeth Robins Pennell, *Nights: Rome, Venice in the Aesthetic
Eighties: London, Paris in the Fighting Nineties* (Philadelphia: J. B.
Lippincott Co., 1916), p. 109.

Exhibition History and Bibliography: Cleveland Museum of Art,
Maurice Prendergast Memorial Exhibition, 1926; William M. Milliken,
"Maurice Prendergast, American Artist," *The Arts* 9, no. 4 (April 1926),
p. 184, ill. p. 183; Whitney Museum of American Art, New York, *Maurice
Prendergast Memorial Exhibition*, 1934, no. 27; idem, *A History of Ameri-
can Watercolor Painting*, 1942, no. 149; Lloyd Goodrich, "American
Watercolor and Winslow Homer," Minneapolis: Walker Art Center,

1945, p. 52; Allen Memorial Art Museum, Oberlin College, Ohio, *An
Exhibition of Paintings from College and University Collections*, 20 Janu-
ary-15 February 1953, no. 10; "Exhibition of Paintings from College and
University Collections," *Allen Memorial Art Museum Bulletin* 10 (Winter
1953); Mount Holyoke College Art Museum, South Hadley, Mass., *An
Exhibition of Works by Bellows, Davies, Henri, Lawson, Luks, Prendergast,
Shinn, and Sloan*, 11 April-3 May 1955, no. 37; idem, *French and Ameri-
can Impressionism*, 5 October-4 November 1956, no. 42; Dorothy
Cogswell, "Friends of Art at the 25 Mark," *Mount Holyoke College Alum-
nae Quarterly* 40, no. 4 (1957), pp. 149-153; Springfield Museum of Fine
Arts, Springfield, Mass., *An Exhibition in Honor of the 125th Anniversary of
the Springfield Mount Holyoke Alumnae Club*, 1-15 October 1961; Hedley
Howell Rhys, *Maurice Prendergast, 1859-1924*, Museum of Fine Arts,
Boston, 26 October-4 December 1960, no. 79; Andrew Crispo Gallery,
New York, *Ten Americans: Masters of Watercolor*, 16 May-30 June 1974,
no. 120; Gwendolyn Owens, *Watercolors by Maurice Prendergast from New
England Collections*, Sterling and Francine Clark Art Institute, Williams-
town, Mass., 11 November-17 December 1978, no. 17; Cecily Langdale,
"Maurice Prendergast, An American Post-Impressionist," *Connoisseur*
202, no. 814 (December 1979), p. 2511; Coe Kerr Gallery, New York,
Americans in Venice, 1879-1913, 19 October-16 November 1983, no. 57.

39   **Umbrellas in the Rain,** 1899
Watercolor on paper, 13⅝ × 20½ in. (34.6 × 52.7 cm)
Signed, titled, and dated in pen, lower left:
Prendergast / Maurice B. Prendergast Venice / 1899
Museum of Fine Arts, Boston. The Hayden Collection
Color plate

One traveler to Venice at the turn of the century remarked,
*Rain in autumn brings a new, fierce beauty into Venice, as it
falls hammering on the water and rattles on the wood of the
boats and settles in pools in all the hollows of the stones. . . .
Venice is as if veiled, and all its colours take on a fine, deep
richness, seen through water, like polished stones in sea-pools.*[1]

Although we think of Prendergast as an artist particularly gifted in recording vibrating sunshine, some of his best Venetian images describe the effects of deeply shadowed evening light (cat. nos. 38 and 48) and drizzling rain (cat. no. 43). In this, one of his most arresting paintings, he executes the entire work in pale browns and grays, punctuating this monochrome palette with bright red, blue, and yellow umbrellas that glow "like polished stones in sea-pools."

As in *Square of S. Marco, Venice* (cat. no. 34), Prendergast has lifted his architectural subject inordinately high on the page, devoting the lower half of the image to reflective pools of transparent pigment. The taut arch of the Ponte della Paglia serves as the picture's basic armature and establishes its lateral boundaries. Behind, the decorative colonnade of the Doge's Palace recedes to the west, and on the right we glimpse the notorious Carceri, or prisons. The central energy and vibrancy of the picture is concentrated, however, in the random, ballooning umbrellas which mark human progress over the bridge and in the marvelously captured posture and movement of the women and children in the foreground.

A related watercolor, also entitled *Umbrellas in the Rain* (The Metropolitan Museum of Art) records this same view in an unfinished, almost certainly earlier, state. Islands of flat color float on the half-empty sheet and suggest much about Prendergast's working methods and compositional revisions. In the finished version, the entire sheet is covered with pigment, reserving only the areas of highest value, while layered washes articulate detail and depth. In terms of composition, the finished watercolor makes two significant changes: the inclusion of the entire left-hand side of the bridge, and the shift of a lamppost from its position beside the dark void of the underbridge hemicycle to a fulcrum-like midpoint. Seemingly unerring in both his sense of composition and his description of human and architectural gesture, Prendergast, in such a work, belies his modest, even discouraged, appraisal of his Venetian achievement in an oft-quoted letter to his brother: "With all [Venice's] beauty I am never going to do my best work here."[2]

1. Symons, p. 101.
2. Cited in Green, p. 70.

Provenance: Purchased from Victor Spark, 1959

Exhibition History and Bibliography: Hedley Howell Rhys, *Maurice Prendergast, 1859-1924*, Museum of Fine Arts, Boston, 26 October-4 December 1960, no. 77; Meredith, Long & Co., Houston, "Americans at Home and Abroad," 26 March-9 April 1971, no. 28; Eleanor Green, *Maurice Prendergast: Art of Impulse and Color*, College Park, Md.: The Art Gallery at the University of Maryland, 1976, p. 16; Gwendolyn Owens, *Watercolors by Maurice Prendergast from New England Collections*, Sterling and Francine Clark Art Institute, Williamstown, Mass., 11 November-17 December 1978, no. 20.

40

40   **Ponte della Paglia (Marble Bridge),** 1898/99
Watercolor on paper, 17¾ × 14⅛ in. (45.1 × 36 cm)
Signed, lower right: *Prendergast/Prendergast*
Mr. and Mrs. Arthur G. Altschul

In this sun-soaked view of the stately marble bridge that connects the Molo and the area of the Piazza with the Riva – a long quay that stretches the length of the Bacino – Prendergast captures throngs of strollers. Prominent in the crowd are fashionable women, gaily parasoled and dressed in summer white. A second version of this view executed in oil (cat. no. 41) repeats the composition almost verbatim. The same bridge, viewed from ground level on the opposite side of the narrow Rio di Palazzo della Paglia, is the subject of the very different watercolor, *Umbrellas in the Rain* (cat. no. 39). More so than many other artists, Prendergast seemed inclined to paint radically different interpretations of the same Venetian monument. Other instances include multiple views of the flags on the Piazza San Marco (cat. nos. 34 and 36) and the Rialto bridge (cat. nos. 46 and 47).

From a vantage point in the upper colonnade of the Doge's Palace, Prendergast looks down at the landmark bridge and across to the further bridges and buildings that mark the impressive sweep of the Riva as it curves toward the Public Gardens on the easternmost tip of Venice. Unlike the artists who painted what could be called the opposite view – the central buildings of Venice from sites along the Riva – such as Robert Salmon (cat. no. 51), Sanford R. Gifford (cat. no. 16), William S. Haseltine (cat. no. 19), and Thomas Moran (cat. nos.

25-28), Prendergast suppresses the sea and sky, pressing the buildings to the top of a vertical page. The effect, combined with his favored precipitous prospect on the scene, is startling. The viewer is presented with a chromatically brilliant field of carefully undetailed, visual events. No mere record of topographical fact, the image reads as a series of visual suggestions that knit themselves into a vibrant, contemporary tapestry. In the distance we see a familiar group of red- and yellow-sailed fishing vessels, but Prendergast has contextualized their trapezoidal sails within a panorama marked by a tourist restaurant, a vaporetto (or steampowered waterbus) pier, and a parade of contemporary fashion. The elegiac mood these sails evoke in paintings by Haseltine or Moran is entirely absent, consumed in the bright panorama of juxtaposed cultural and color facts.

41

Exhibition History and Bibliography: Boston Watercolor Club exhibition, 2-15 March 1899, no. 105 (possibly this version); Macbeth Gallery, New York, 9-24 March 1900, no. 1a; *Buffalo Third Annual Exhibition of Selected Watercolor Paintings by American Artists*, 12 December 1907-12 January 1908, no. 118 (possibly this version); Detroit Institute of Arts, *Third Exhibition of Watercolors by American Artists*, March 1908, no. 118; Whitney Museum of American Art, New York, 1934, no. 5 (under the title *Venice, 1898*); Eleanor Green, *Maurice Prendergast: Art of Impulse and Color*, College Park, Md.: The Art Gallery at the University of Maryland, 1976.

41   Ponte della Paglia, 1899 and 1922
Oil on canvas, 28 × 23 in. (71.1 × 58.4 cm)
Signed, lower left: *Prendergast*
The Phillips Collection, Washington, D.C.

A unique instance in Prendergast's oeuvre of nearly identical oil and watercolor compositions (cat. no. 40), these two versions of the *Ponte della Paglia* present us with two distinct artistic personalities. The watercolor, although signed twice, is clearly the result of a single campaign. It is both internally consistent and consistent with the artist's handling of the medium in other works from 1898/99. The work in oil is very different. This *Ponte della Paglia* is almost certainly based on the watercolor (or both could be based on a lost preparatory work), but its departures are significant. Its composition reflects Prendergast's early interest in deep, complex space, while its technique is one he used decades later. As we know that the watercolor was painted in 1899 and sold in 1912, and that the oil was still being worked on (or possibly completely reworked after long absence from the project) in 1922, the puzzle of the incongruity of technique and composition is at least partially solved.[1] In any event, the oil clearly took on a life of its own after the watercolor left the studio.

In the watercolor the brushwork is delicate and invisible, the medium wet and thin, the color crystalline and transparent. The oil painting, on the other hand, is rendered with a larger, drier brush. The colors are opaque and emphatic. To the already busy composition Prendergast adds more boats, creating incident in the two small plots of open water. And he begins to add a figure to the partial void of the lower right, fitting her outline quite precisely between two extant figures. There seems to be a movement here not only towards larger, more summary brushstrokes and denser colors, but also to-

ward a field completely filled with tangential and overlapping visual incident. More important, the earlier emphasis on gesture is replaced with a new overriding enthusiasm for pattern.

As an oil, this painting is very rare among Prendergast's Venetian works. But it is one of several to directly enter distinguished collections during the artist's lifetime. Prendergast's eleventh-hour work on the painting (it had been exhibited in 1920, so it had, to that degree, reached a finished state before its sale to Duncan Phillips in 1922) may have been the result of many factors, but it is not impossible that the artist, once aware that the painting would enter Phillips's remarkable contemporary collection, felt impelled to 'modernize' the image. The hurried post-sale, pre-delivery work on the painting is recorded in a series of letters in which Prendergast insists, "I must be thoroughly satisfied with it before I let it go."[2]

1. Green, pp. 26, 98.
2. Green, pp. 26, 98.

Provenance: The artist, through C. W. Kraushaar, New York, to the Phillips Memorial Gallery (now The Phillips Collection), 1922

Exhibition History and Bibliography: St. Louis Art Museum, *15th Annual Exhibition*, 15 September-31 October 1920, no. 130; Venice, *Biennale: Exhibition of American Paintings*, 25 April-30 October 1924; Phillips Memorial Gallery, Washington, D.C., *Intimate Impressionists*, 8-13 May 1925; Cleveland Museum of Art, *Maurice Prendergast Memorial Exhibition*, 16 January-15 February 1926; Duncan Phillips, *A Collection in the Making*, Cambridge, 1926, pl. LXV; William M. Milliken, "Maurice Prendergast, American Artist," *The Arts* 9, no. 4 (April 1926), p. 187; Harvard Society for Contemporary Art, *Maurice Prendergast*, 1-30 May 1929, no. 2; Phillips Memorial Gallery, Washington, D.C., *First Exhibi-

tions 1930-1931, 5 October 1930-25 January 1931, no. 12; Margaret Breuning, *Maurice Prendergast*, New York: Whitney Museum of American Art, 1931, pp. 11, 56, 57; The Museum of Modern Art, New York, *American Painting and Sculpture 1862-1932*, 31 October 1932-31 January 1933, no. 80; Baltimore Museum of Art, *Survey of American Painting*, 10 January-28 February 1934, no. 25; Virginia Museum of Fine Arts, Richmond, *Main Currents in the Development of American Painting*, 16 January-1 March 1936, no. 91; Telfair Academy of Arts and Sciences, Savannah, *Survey of American Art*, 7-28 March 1937, no. 28; Musée du Jeu de Paume, Paris, *Trois Siècles d'art aux Etats-Unis*, 24 May-30 July 1938, no. 135; Addison Gallery of American Art, Phillips Academy, Andover, Mass., *The Prendergasts: Retrospective Exhibition of the Work of Maurice and Charles Prendergast*, 1938, no. 67; Carnegie Institute, Pittsburgh, *Survey of American Painting*, 24 October-15 December 1940, no. 224; Brooklyn Museum, *The Eight*, November 1943-January 1944, no. 45; Tate Gallery, London, *American Paintings from the 18th Century to the Present Day*, Summer 1946; Corcoran Gallery of Art, Washington, D.C., *De Gustibus*, 9 January-20 February 1949, no. 34; Society of the Four Arts, Palm Beach, Fla., *From Plymouth Rock to the Armory*, 9 February-5 March 1950, no. 46; The Phillips Collection, Washington, D.C., *The Phillips Collection: A Museum of Modern Art and Its Resources*, New York and London: Thames and Hudson, 1952, p. 82, pl. 83; Syracuse Museum of Fine Arts, *Eight*, 3-24 February 1958, no. 18; American Academy of Arts and Letters, New York, *Impressionist Mood in American Painting*, January-February 1959; Jewett Arts Center, Wellesley College, *Four Boston Masters*, 10 April-11 May 1959, no. 35; Hedley Howell Rhys, *Maurice Prendergast, 1859-1924*, Museum of Fine Arts, Boston, 26 October-4 December 1960, no. 9; Meredith Long and Co., Houston, *Americans at Home and Abroad*, 26 March-9 April 1971, no. 27; Eleanor Green, *Maurice Prendergast: Art of Impulse and Color*, College Park, Md.: The Art Gallery at the University of Maryland, 1976, no. 25; P. Courthion, *Impressionism*, New York, 1972, pp. 198, 199; Smithsonian Institution Traveling Exhibition Service, Washington, D.C., *The Phillips Collection in the Making*, May 1979-January 1981, no. 27; D. Scott, *Maurice Prendergast*, Mt. Vernon, N.Y., 1980, p. 7, pl. 3; The Phillips Collection, Washington, D.C., *Impressionism and the Modern Vision: Master Paintings from The Phillips Collection*, circulated July 1981-January 1984.

42 Riva degli Schiavoni, Castello, 1898

Watercolor on paper, 14½ × 19 in. (36.8 × 48.3 cm)
Signed, lower left: *Prendergast*
David Nisinson Fine Art
Color plate

East of the Ponte della Paglia, the broad, paved Riva bordering on the Bacino continues for almost a third of a mile in a gentle crescent. The quay is wide and busy with local foot traffic. Representing one of Prendergast's very few ventures into this section of Venice, this watercolor records a site along the Riva familiar to us, and to Prendergast no doubt, from Whistler's etching of 1879/80, *San Biagio* (cat. no. 110). As in Whistler's images, the enormous arched gateway is festooned with laundry, and the courtyard beyond is busy with gossip and activity.

Whistler, Duveneck, Pennell, and other American artists stayed out in this section of the Riva, near the church of San Biagio, their windows overlooking the broad Bacino and their rents considerably lower than those of artists closer to the Piazza or the Grand Canal. Prendergast lived in even less expensive lodgings on the Giudecca and the Zattere, far to the southwest of this site.

Against a pale, neutral palette in the architectural elements – brick wall, buff stucco, and faded green shutters – Prendergast plants the strong reds, blues, and violets of Venetian fabrics, both those worn and those

42

hung to dry. The visual inventory is evidently true to life, for at least one contemporary was greatly taken with *the vivid colours of shawls, and dresses, and stockings, which would be gaudy elsewhere, but which here, in the heat and glitter of such an atmosphere, are always in place, never immoderate; they are all part of the picture, the great genre picture which is Venice.*[1]
Among the bits of laundry hanging like so many nautical signal flags, three narrow streamers hang from the window above the arch. Blue, red, and yellow, these bright primaries seem to set the tone for the whole work.

1. Symons, p. 92.

Provenance: Richard Bissell to son, William Bissell; Christie's, New York, 11 December 1981, no. 199

43 Rainy Day, Venice, 1898

Watercolor on paper, 16½ × 12½ in. (41.9 × 31.7 cm)
Signed twice, lower left: *Maurice Prendergast* and *Prendergast*
Courtesy Wichita Art Museum. The Roland P. Murdock Collection

In *Piazza di San Marco* (cat. no. 36), the two *Ponte della Paglia* works (cat. nos. 40 and 41), *Festival, Venice* (cat. no. 48), and this painting, Prendergast displays a keen interest in deep, complex pictorial space and an extraordinary mastery of the problems involved. Ever inventive, he discards the familiar horizontal cityscape and landscape format, which allows the traditional artist to establish deep, three-dimensional spatial relationships. Prendergast's vertical sheet gives his images a very different, more condensed appearance. Visual episodes look discontinuous, sliced, and abrupt, an effect further emphasized by Prendergast's introduction of emphatic architectural diagonals which establish a geometry unrelated to that of the picture plane. Lastly, all of these works place the viewer high above the subject, and Prendergast avoids establishing any grounding underfoot to help us measure our own position or relationship to the

43

imaged world. Deliberately baffling, these views are nonetheless topographically accurate. In this case we are perched high above the small canal that borders the great Baroque church Santa Maria della Salute, which faces the Piazza and marks the entrance to the Grand Canal. We see the steps of the church and the patterned pavement of its landing, but the building itself is invisible.

Of this set of radical vertical views, *Rainy Day, Venice* has the subtlest color harmony. Steel-blue water and tan-pink pavement and palaces are relieved only by black boats and soberly dressed pedestrian figures. It is winter: the gondolas wear their *felzi*, or rounded hoods, and the Venetians have abandoned their gay summer garb. The tone is gentle, pensive, but not forlorn. The soft rain only gives the city a new type of visual sensuality. The warmly evocative image clarifies for us Herman Melville's diary notation that he would "rather be in Venice on [a] rainy day, than in . . . [a] capital on [a] fine one."[1]

1. Melville, p. 235.

Provenance: John F. Kraushaar, New York; purchased from Mrs. John F. Kraushaar, New York, 1942

Exhibition History and Bibliography: William M. Milliken, "Maurice Prendergast, American Artist," *The Arts* 9, no. 4 (April 1926), pp. 182, 184, 185; Suzanne La Follette, *Art in America*, New York and London: Harper and Brothers, 1929, p. 267; Margaret Breuning, *Maurice Prendergast*, New York: Whitney Museum of American Art, 1931, pp. 9, 11, 58, 59; Addison Gallery of American Art, Phillips Academy, Andover, Mass., *The Prendergasts: Retrospective Exhibition of the Work of Maurice and Charles Prendergast*, 1938, no. 12; Charles H. Sawyer, "The Prendergasts," *Parnassus* 10 (October 1938), p. 10; "The Murdock Collection," *Arts* 30 (July 1956), p. 15; George P. Tomko, *Catalogue of the Roland P. Murdock Collection*, Wichita Art Museum, 1972, p. 166.

44 Venetian Palaces on the Grand Canal, 1899

Watercolor on paper, 14 × 20¾ in. (35.6 × 52.7 cm)
Signed and dated, lower left: *Maurice Prendergast 1899*
Mr. and Mrs. Arthur G. Altschul

While one group of Prendergast's watercolors of 1898/99 is notable for emphasizing a complex pattern of diagonals receding abruptly into deep space (cat. nos. 36, 40, 41, 43, and 48), another set deals with a rather different compositional problem. These works include this watercolor, as well as *Square of S. Marco, Venice* (cat. no. 34), and *St. Mark's, Venice (The Clock Tower)* (cat. no. 35), and, to a lesser extent, *Sunlight on the Piazzetta, Venice* (cat. no. 37); in each case the subject is a well-known monument presented absolutely parallel to the picture plane. The buildings are raised high on the picture surface and press the edges of the composition. The effect is very formal, emphasizing the two-dimensional aspect of the façades and reducing our experience of the building to a rich pattern of linear voids and visual episodes. Less symmetrical than the façades of San Marco, the clock tower, or the Doge's Palace in the other works in the set, this group of palace fronts is leveled and regularized by the abrupt deletion of a fourth story from the largest and oldest building, the thirteenth-century Ca' da Mosto. By establishing this even, flat skyline, Prendergast emphasizes and unifies his disparate subjects.

These abutting palaces – the group also includes the fifteenth-century Palazzo Dolfin with its Gothic arched windows and the sixteenth-century Palazzo Bolani on the right – occupy a prominent position on the Grand Canal just north of the Rialto Bridge. Although it appears that Prendergast observed and recorded this scene from a boat, he in fact stood on the open square near Venice's food markets across the Grand Canal. In this and several other instances he is careful to omit any reference to his footing, but it is clear from an inspection of his paintings and their sites that Prendergast never painted in a gondola. Although we might be tempted to attribute this fact to his relative poverty and consequent unwillingness to incur expense, it should be noted that very few artists executed finished work while waterborne. Although they often found sites and composed their works (as in *Venetian Palaces*) to give the viewer the effect of an aquatic viewpoint, it is surprisingly seldom actually the case. Even had gondola-hire been free and the difficulty of executing exacting work in a rocking boat been solved, Prendergast would almost certainly have avoided a boat-prospect on his subjects, for his finished works make it clear that he infinitely preferred to be above his subjects, often radically so. He usually avoided even such a pedestrian-level prospect as he has here executed with such success.

Exhibition History and Bibliography: Robert Schoelkopf Gallery, New York, 1964; The Metropolitan Museum of Art, New York, *200 Years of Watercolor Paintings in America*, 8 December 1966-29 January 1967, no. 131, p. 24; William H. Gerdts, *American Impressionism*, Seattle: The Henry Art Gallery, University of Washington, 1980, p. 118.

44

45

45 The Rialto Bridge, Venice, 1911/12

Watercolor on paper, 15¼ × 22⅛ in. (38.7 × 56.2 cm)
Signed, lower left: *Prendergast*
The Metropolitan Museum of Art. The Lesley and Emma Sheafer Collection, Bequest of Emma A. Sheafer, 1974

The only work in this exhibition from Prendergast's second expedition to Venice, *The Rialto Bridge, Venice* (formerly known as *Covered Bridge, Venice*) illustrates his later manner as well as his continued interest in well-known architectural subjects. Next to the monuments of the Piazza San Marco, the celebrated Renaissance Rialto Bridge provided him with more subjects than any other site in Venice. In this case he observes the bridge from a site several feet above pedestrian eye level on the Fondamenta del Vino, one of the few walkways along the whole length of the Grand Canal. In 1898/99 he had painted this same pavement from the opposite direction, from the bridge landing, in *The Grand Canal, Venice* (cat. no. 46). A comparison of these two works, painted a decade apart, suggests the intervening substantial evolution in his technique and handling of form. His early careful emphasis on the individual gesture and gait of pedestrians and on the sensuous line and form of boats evolved into a more unified, more stylized image. Insistent outlining and the elimination of both shadows and reflections place the later work at a greater remove from the imaged scene and from Renaissance conventions of portrayal of form and space.

The broad parabolic curve of the bridge has been altered to a chunky near-hemicircle in Prendergast's compression of a wide visual field into a shortened rectangle. The basic visual facts of the bridge's design have, however, been described. The bridge is 'covered' not in the manner of covered bridges in Prendergast's native New England, but in a more complicated pattern. Three broad sets of marble stairs – one in the center and one on either side next to the richly balustered railings of the bridge – are open to the sky. Between these stepped walkways, two ranges of lead-roofed shops run the length of the bridge. On the nearest set of steps, pedestrians move in a continuous stream, bending around onto the *fondamenta* in the foreground. Much less particularized than figures in the early works, these Venetians are presented more as stylized episodes of color than as social types or particularized individuals.

Provenance: The artist, to Kraushaar Gallery, New York; purchased from the Gallery by Mr. and Mrs. Lesley Sheafer, 1930; bequeathed to the Museum by Emma A. Sheafer, 1974

Exhibition History and Bibliography: Eleanor Green, *Maurice Prendergast: Art of Impulse and Color*, College Park, Md.: The Art Gallery at the University of Maryland, 1976, no. 64.

46

46 **The Grand Canal, Venice,** 1898/99
Watercolor on paper, 17⅜ × 13¾ in. (44.1 × 34.9 cm)
Signed, lower center: *Prendergast*, and lower right:
Prendergast / Venice
Daniel J. Terra Collection, Terra Museum of American Art, Evanston, Illinois

Few painters could triumph as effectively as Prendergast over the seeming awkwardness of a vertically bisected sheet. One has the sense of the artist here, and in his other Venetian works, relentlessly exploring the full range of 'impossible' pictorial geometries. The potential visual harshness of this radically divided image is softened at every point by Prendergast's delicate, sensuous color and line. His sensitivity to tone and time is evident in the rapidity with which we can read the season and the time of day. It is summer – the gondoliers and girls wear white, many wear straw hats – and it is evening – the Fondamenta del Vino in front of us is already in shadow, the lamps lit, while the façades of the ancient Palazzo Loredan and Palazzo Farsetti on the opposite side of the Grand Canal glow with the golden light of a setting sun. Languidly strolling or pausing to chat, the crowd disposes itself in artful clumps as far as the eye can see.

As is often the case, Prendergast gives no hint to the uninitiated concerning his point of view. No fragment of the Rialto Bridge, on the broad balustered parapet of which he leans to work, is visible. His presence is evident only in the scene itself, and nowhere more artfully than on the left, in the water half of the image. There the

brushstokes are visible; broken swatches of color richly describe blue and yellow reflections while purple shadows echo the gondolas and mooring posts that punctuate the water's surface. Brisk calligraphic ripples of water enliven the scene and contrast boldly with the smoothly applied pigment elsewhere in the painting. A very different work in tone and manner and in devotion to the facts of his subject than the 'opposite' view (cat. no. 45) done ten years later, *The Grand Canal* exemplifies both his extraordinary experimentation with pictorial spaces and geometry and his palpable fondness for his subject.

Provenance: The artist, to Macbeth Gallery, 1900; May Hollowell, Worcester, Mass.; Frank S. Churchill, Bass River, Mass.; Mr. and Mrs. H. Donaldson Jordan, Worcester, Mass.; estate of Lucretia Jordan, Worcester, Mass.; purchased by the Museum from Adams Davidson Galleries, Washington, D.C., 1979

Exhibition History and Bibliography: Macbeth Gallery, New York, *First Annual New Gallery Exhibition of Contemporary American Art*, 21 November-16 December 1900; Whitney Museum of American Art, New York, *Maurice Prendergast Memorial Exhibition*, 21 February-22 March 1934, no. 21; Adams Davidson Galleries, Washington, D.C., *Recent Acquisitions of Important 19th Century American Art*, September-October 1979; William H. Gerdts, *American Impressionism*, Seattle: The Henry Art Gallery, University of Washington, Seattle: 1980, p. 137; Terra Museum of American Art, *Five American Masters of Watercolor*, 5 May-12 July 1981, cover; Coe Kerr Gallery, New York, *Americans in Venice, 1879-1913*, 19 October-16 November 1983, no. 52.

47 Market Place, Venice, 1898
Watercolor on paper, 13⅝ × 10 in. (34.6 × 25.4 cm)
Signed, lower right: *Maurice B. Prendergast*; inscribed on
the reverse, in pencil: *Venice/1898/Street in Venice/no. 13*
Private collection

Market Place, Venice gives us, like *Rainy Day, Venice* (cat.
no. 43), an oblique, almost unrecognizable fragment of a
well-known monument, in this case the Rialto Bridge.
The broadly terraced steps that occupy the lower half of
the picture are the middle set of stairs on the northern
half of the bridge. The mass and width of the Rialto, its
ranged steps and arching profile, are neither portrayed
nor suggested. This very unconventional image of the
familiar Renaissance landmark yokes together several
disparate elements: the almost abstract pattern of steps, a
single female figure poised in the foreground, busy market stalls beyond, the mass of S. Giacomo di Rialto on the
right, and an enormous, spatially ambiguous red banner.
Parallel to the picture plane and to the emphatic horizontal lines of the steps, the flag blocks our visual progress
into the distance. Its bright red surface stands out
vibrantly against the indigo figures and brick-red buildings. But most extraordinary of all, Prendergast has
'hung' it, not from a wire or lamp post within the picture,
but from the top edge of his sheet. The puzzling flag and
the partial bridge give us two supreme instances of Prendergast's inventive pictorial wit.

The site itself was often remarked on by travelers as a
disappointment. Their familiarity with the Rialto of
Canaletto and of Shakespeare's Shylock was inconsistent
with the triviality of the merchandise and the modesty of
the merchants that occupied the Rialto stalls in the late
nineteenth century. As one writer put it, a visitor could
look down the
*broad stairs of the Rialto . . . bright with moving crowds of
colour, winding up and down on each side of the central line
of stalls, between the shops, hung with long coloured stripes
. . . . [Just beyond the bridge] the stalls are but a few boards,
hastily set up on trestles; they are hung with bright rows of
stockings, necklaces, toys, heaped with sweets, and shirts, and
shawls, . . . worthless books in all languages . . . and there are
glittering copper things, pots and pans, lying all over the
ground.*[1]
Prendergast avoids visual specificity but suggests the nature of the trinket wares exchanged here at the foot of the
noble Rialto – once the commercial heart of a great empire – by the miscellaneous and predominately female
nature of his crowd. Muffled against the wintry season,
these graceful figures suggest by their demeanor a trade
focused not on exotic jewels and spices and priceless
Eastern cargoes, but on a diminished commerce, a small
trade in "sweets, and shirts, and shawls."

    1. Symons, p. 85.

Provenance: Acquired by Davis and Long Co., New York (now Davis and
Langdale) from the estate of the artist, 1975

Exhibition History and Bibliography: The Cleveland Museum of Art,
Prendergast Memorial Exhibition, 1926; Whitney Museum of American
Art, New York, *Maurice Prendergast*, 1934, no. 29; Hedley Howell Rhys,
Maurice Prendergast, 1859-1924, Museum of Fine Arts, Boston, 26 Octo-
ber-4 December 1960, no. 78; Eleanor Green, *Maurice Prendergast: Art of
Impulse and Color*, College Park, Md.: The Art Gallery at the University of
Maryland, 1976, no. 17.

47

48 Festival, Venice, 1898/99
Watercolor on paper, 16⅝ × 14 in. (42.2 × 35.6 cm)
Signed, lower left: *Prendergast*; inscribed, on the reverse:
Venetian Festival; *Festival Venice*
The Museum of Modern Art, New York. Gift of Abby
Aldrich Rockefeller

Festival, Venice belongs to a group of Venetian watercolors from 1898/99 in which Prendergast investigates
complex spatial problems. The geometry of the open
square (the little Campo di S. Apollinare near the Rialto
Bridge) creates a series of unresolved diagonals similar to
those observed in *Piazza di San Marco* (cat. no. 36), *Ponte
della Paglia* (cat. nos. 40 and 41), and *Rainy Day, Venice*
(cat. no. 43). These works are very different in character
from those in which the architectural subjects lie parallel
to the picture plane – *Square of S. Marco, Venice* (cat. no.
34), *St. Mark's, Venice* (cat. no. 35), *Sunlight on the Piazzetta, Venice* (cat. no. 37), and *Venetian Palaces on the Grand
Canal* (cat. no. 44) – or perpendicular to it – *The Grand
Canal, Venice* (cat. no. 46) – although they have in common a high vantage point and the artful combination of
figures and structures. In this watercolor, the homely vernacular buildings form a background screen, while
marble lines inset in the pavement establish the oblique
relationship of our position to the principal geometry of
the square, and long wires carry flags and lit globe lights

overhead, marking out yet another, an aerial, geometric pattern. Near the center of the image, beneath the crossing strings of lights and framed by the marble pavement outline, an elaborate Baroque wellhead presides. Its circular form dominates the center of the little square as it does Prendergast's image, and here the geometries of space and picture coincide.

Random figures populate the square. Very different in character from the crowd that Prendergast finds in the areas around the Piazza San Marco – *Sunlight on the Piazzetta, Venice* (cat. no. 37), *Umbrellas in the Rain* (cat. no. 39), and *Ponte della Paglia* (cat. nos. 40 and 41) – the populace of Campo S. Apollinare includes no tourists, nannies, or ladies of fashion. This festival is very much a local affair. Prendergast seems drawn to these people, and, as in the case in several other watercolors from the 1898/99 visit, he singles out a young Venetian woman for particular attention (see cat. nos. 37 and 47). With her characteristic attributes – a black shawl and bright red fan – she pauses in the left foreground observing the observing artist. In the faceless crowd of this picture, indeed in the faceless crowds of all Prendergast's Venetian works, the particularity he bestows upon her features is striking. Pensive, even somewhat wistful, her face belies its holiday context. This slight incongruity seems to suggest not just the particular situation of this individual, but the larger situation of fin de siècle Venice – handsome, festive, yet necessarily reduced in circumstances and melancholic.

Provenance: Montross Gallery, New York; Abby Aldrich Rockefeller, 1927; The Museum of Modern Art, Gift of Abby Aldrich Rockefeller, 1935

Exhibition History and Bibliography: William M. Milliken, "Maurice Prendergast, American Artist," *The Arts* 9, no. 4 (April 1926), pp. 181-192, mentions a watercolor *Festival Day, Venice*, which may well be the same work; The Museum of Modern Art, New York, *The Museum Collection and a Private Collection on Loan*, 4 June-24 September 1935; idem, *New Acquisitions: The Collection of Mrs. John D. Rockefeller, Jr.*, 14 January-16 February 1936; idem, *Twenty-five Watercolors by Six Americans*, circulating November 1935-June 1937; Wadsworth Atheneum, Hartford, exhibition for Connecticut boys' schools, October 1937-June 1938; Addison Gallery of American Art, Phillips Academy, Andover, Mass., *The Prendergasts: Retrospective Exhibition of the Work of Maurice and Charles Prendergast*, 1938, cat. no. 11, p. 11; The Museum of Modern Art, New York, *Our Leading Watercolorists*, circulating September 1942-July 1943; American Federation of Arts, *A History of American Watercolor Painting*, circulating November 1945-December 1946; The Museum of Modern Art, New York, *American Paintings from the Museum Collection*, circulating May 1950-June 1952; idem, *Seven American Watercolorists*, circulating May 1953-January 1954; idem, *The Versatile Medium*, circulating January 1955-June 1956; French and Co., Inc., New York, for exhibition at Emma Willard Alumnae Association, Troy, N.Y., 26 October-5 November 1960; Tennessee Fine Arts Center, Nashville, *People and Places: Watercolors and Drawings from the Museum of Modern Art*, 12 May-15 June 1961; Andrew Crispo Gallery, Inc., New York, *Ten Americans: Masters of Watercolor*, 16 May-15 July 1974; Eleanor Green, *Maurice Prendergast: Art of Impulse and Color*, College Park Md.: The Art Gallery at the University of Maryland, 1976, no. 16, pp. 16, 93.

48

49 **Orange Market**, ca. 1899
Color monotype, oil on oriental paper,
plate 12½ × 9⅛ in. (31.7 × 23.2 cm),
sheet 15⅝ × 11 in. (39.7 × 27.9 cm)
Signed in pencil, in plate, lower left: monogram *MPB*
The Museum of Modern Art, New York. Gift of Abby Aldrich Rockefeller

Although most of the works that resulted from Prendergast's first trip to Venice were watercolors, some of the most experimental were colored monotypes. Between 1892 and 1905 he was very active in this medium and produced some of his most memorable works, including the striking *Orange Market*. His monotype technique is preserved in his instructions to Mrs. Oliver Williams: *Paint on copper in oils, wiping parts to be white. When* [the] *picture suits you, place it on Japanese paper and either press in a press or rub with a spoon till it pleases you. Sometimes the second or third plate* [print?] *is the best.*[1]
But the novelty of his work in this medium lies not in the technique outlined so precisely here, but rather in his composition and execution. As *Orange Market* makes clear, he eschews in his monotypes the level of color differentiation and linear detail we find in the watercolors of 1898/99. The color range narrows radically – in this case to black, brown, and yellow – and the oil-based pigment is applied with a large flat brush. This visible brushwork and the general suppression of detail in favor of impact seems to have more in common with his later oils than with the contemporary watercolors. However, the pictorial organization is familiar: the composition of *Orange Market* echoes that of *Square of S. Marco, Venice* (cat. no. 34) with its radical horizontal division slightly

49

ter, Wellesley College, *4 Boston Masters*, 10 April-11 May 1959, cat. no. 37, p. 69; Museum of Fine Arts, Boston, 15 May-13 June 1959; Hedley Howell Rhys, *Maurice Prendergast, 1859-1924*, Museum of Fine Arts, Boston, 26 October-4 December 1960, p. 34, cat. no. 133, ill. p. 37; Yale University Art Gallery, 10 October 1962-6 January 1963; William Cooper Proctor Art Center, Bard College, Annandale-on-Hudson, New York, *Prendergast Monotypes*, 1-21 May 1967; Guild Hall, Easthampton, New York, *American Printmaking 1670-1968*, 20 July-11 August 1968; Davis and Long, New York, *Prendergast Monotypes*, April 1979, cat. no. 72, p. 107; The Metropolitan Museum of Art, New York, *The Painterly Print*, 15 October-7 December 1980.

50 Venetian Well, ca. 1899

Color monotype, sheet 11 × 13⅝ in. (27.9 × 34.6 cm), plate 9⅛ × 10⅛ in. (23.2 × 25.7 cm)
Signed in crayon over pencil, in plate, lower left: monogram *MBP*
Addison Gallery of American Art, Phillips Academy, Andover, Massachusetts

Venetian Well, with its monochromatic palette and pervasive *japonisme*, is the most Whistlerian of Prendergast's works. The tone is subdued and the coloration is confined to subtle grays and browns accented by sharp white lines and a few pale areas of erased pigment.

The sensitivity to gesture and movement that we are accustomed to find in Prendergast's work is present here, but with a difference. The figures are stylized, their poses formalized and even somewhat hybridized with their counterparts in Japanese prints. In drawing the parallel between the black-shawled women of Venice and their more exotic Asian counterparts, Prendergast is not alone. One contemporary noted in his Venetian travels during the 1890s,

It is not altogether surprising to find among the Venetian types, and not least frequently, one which is almost Japanese. They are singularly charming, these small, dark, cat-like creatures, with their small black eyes . . . their hair, too, sometimes drawn back in the Japanese manner. And they have that look of cat-like comfort and good humour which is also a Japanese habit.[1]

Prendergast, himself, adopted a familiar "Japanese habit" in introducing on the flag post – the same we find in *Festival, Venice* (cat. no. 48) – a vertical series of character-like cyphers.

Despite the oriental character Prendergast has bestowed upon aspects of this scene, the situation is distinctly Venetian. The women gather with their buckets at the center of their community, the wellhead in a small campo, awaiting the opening of the well. Ever-watchful for paintable subjects, Julia Cartwright experienced and recorded the situation:

Out of these crooked and bewildering streets . . . we emerge on to the campi, *or squares, in front of the churches, to which they were originally attached as burial-grounds. Each of these squares is now a little centre of life, and has its farmacia and grocery and fruiterer's shop, perhaps a palazzo with the upper stories to let. . . . Each has its well generally raised on steps, round which the gossips of the place collect and where you may glean many a characteristic and amusing incident of Venetian*

above the center line, its subject – in this case a broad arching umbrella – crowding the upper and lateral limits of the plate. Here a sea of oranges in brilliant, shadowless profusion gives the image a distinctly celebratory tone.

The food markets near the Rialto Bridge and the incoming produce boats were very much part of a visitor's experience in turn-of-the-century Venice. Julia Cartwright remarked in her *Portfolio* articles on Venice, *Everywhere there is a fullness of life and colour. Now [in autumn] . . . it is the artist's time, and you meet them wherever you go, not only round St. Mark's and the Piazza, where they cluster like bees, but in the more remote quarters and distant canals, painting the fruit-laden rafts . . . and marketplaces. . . . Earlier in the year you have had the cherries and the strawberries; all winter there were pyramids of oranges and lemons, and cartloads of chestnuts, but now you have black and white grapes and purple figs, and scarlet tomatoes and pomegranates, and peaches, and apples and pears, in countless profusion.*[2]
More than any other artist, Prendergast has captured the visual effect of this "countless profusion," not by literalizing it but by richly suggesting it.

1. Quoted in Rhys, p. 34.
2. Cartwright, p. 38.

Provenance: Kraushaar Art Galleries, New York, 1945

Exhibition History and Bibliography: The Museum of Modern Art, New York, *Recent Acquisitions in Painting and Sculpture*, 6-24 February 1946; idem, circulating exhibition, 30 March-15 May 1955; Jewett Arts Cen-

50

life. Every morning at eight o'clock the iron lid which closes its mouth is unlocked, and then there is a clanking of heels on the stone pavement and a brisk chattering of tongues, as the water carriers [gather].[2]

Prendergast has imaged this vital ritual in the novel medium of monotype, giving the scene at once a quiet Venetian authenticity and a distinctly oriental note.

1. Symons, p. 90.
2. Cartwright, p. 46.

Provenance: Addison Gallery of American Art since 1939

Exhibition History and Bibliography: Probably Museum of Fine Arts, Boston, no. 59; Cincinnati Museum Association, 1902, no. 53; Kraushaar Galleries, New York, 8-31 December 1936, no. 3; Corcoran Gallery of Art, Washington, D.C., 1937, no. 22; Addison Gallery of American Art, Phillips Academy, Andover, Mass., *The Prendergasts: Retrospective Exhibition of the Work of Maurice and Charles Prendergast*, 1938, no. 110; American Academy of Arts and Letters, New York, 1960; William Cooper Proctor Art Center, Bard College, Annandale-on-Hudson, N.Y., *Maurice Prendergast: The Monotypes*, 1-21 May 1967, cat. no. 18; Eleanor Green, *Maurice Prendergast: Art of Impulse and Color*, College Park, Md.: The Art Gallery at the University of Maryland, 1976.

51

Robert Salmon
1775–ca. 1848/51

Little is known of Salmon's sojourn in Italy; in fact, the only document we have linking him to Venice is the large-scale ambitious painting, signed and dated 1845, that is included in this exhibition. An English artist who had emigrated to America and settled in Boston, Salmon returned to Europe in 1842 and apparently traveled on the continent in his final years.[1]

1. John Wilmerding, *Robert Salmon: Painter of Ship and Shore* (Salem: Peabody Museum and Boston Public Library, 1971), pp. xv-xvi.

51 View of Venice, 1845
Oil on canvas, 25½ × 55 in. (64.8 × 139.7 cm)
Signed, lower left: *R. S. 1845*
Thyssen-Bornemisza Collection, Lugano, Switzerland

A recently discovered pair of large canvases depicting Palermo and Venice links Salmon to Italy and suggests that his productive career extended further into the 1840s than previously had been believed. A sale notice in the *Boston Advertiser* of 16 July 1840 notes that Salmon's doctor had "forbidden him to paint any small work," presumably to save his failing eyesight the strain of minute visual concentration.[1] Shortly afterward he left for England and, possibly, the continent, but it is clear from the *View of Venice* that, however impaired his eyesight, he was in 1845 still a master of his craft.

Larger than most of his better-known views of Boston, Liverpool, and other ports, this panorama of the Bacino San Marco encompasses a broad sweep of sea, sky, and monumental architecture. He chose the archetypical point of view from which to render the Venetian cityscape, delineating its towers, domes, vessels, and buoyant atmosphere with the clarity and precision that we associate with his formidable brush. Evoking at once the early landscapes of J. M. W. Turner, the brilliant 'souvenir' panoramas of Canaletto, and the exuberant French scenic wallpapers of Joseph Dufour and Jean Zuber, Salmon paints the city in a distinctly celebratory mood. Although we should not rule out the possibility that the painting was executed in England from secondary visual sources, it is probable that it was done on site. If so, it is curious that Salmon – who once remarked of a fellow Bostonian bound for a painting expedition abroad, "Can't he find anything to paint here?" – should end his days so far afield.[2] But in another sense, Salmon's life-long preoccupation with ports, coastal waters, and marine matters logically terminates in the marine-urban environment of Venice. In doing so, his career ends with a beginning, for it could fairly be said that (if we invoke his Boston citizenship) this is the first of thousands of paintings of Venice by Americans.

1. John Wilmerding, "A New Look at Robert Salmon," *Antiques* 87, no. 1 (January 1965), p. 92.
2. Wilmerding, "A New Look," p. 89.

Provenance: Ira Spanierman Galleries, New York, 1971; sale, Sotheby Parke Bernet, New York, 19 October 1972, bought in; Ira Spanierman Galleries, New York, 1978

Exhibition History and Bibliography: John Wilmerding, *Robert Salmon: Painter of Ship and Shore*, Salem: Peabody Museum and Boston Public Library, 1971, p. 55 and pl. 27; Spencer Museum of Art, Lawrence, Kansas, *The Arcadian Landscape: Nineteenth-Century American Painters in Italy*, 4 November-3 December 1972, no. 36 (mentioned, not in exhibition); *The Magazine Antiques* 113, no. 2 (February 1978), p. 294.

John Singer Sargent
1856 – 1925

Sargent's paintings of Venice are among his most numerous and his most modern.[1] Again and again he returned to the city, producing, over the course of four decades, distinguished work in both oil and watercolor. Not always critically acclaimed at the time of their production, his haunting Venetian genre scenes and his startlingly sliced architectural views now rival his more celebrated portraits for major importance in his oeuvre.

In February of 1874, at the age of eighteen, Sargent arrived in Venice with his peripatetic family.[2] They stayed on the Grand Canal into the spring (with a brief side trip to Florence), and although no paintings can be dated to this trip, it is clear from a letter of 22 March that Sargent seized the opportunity to further his visual education by studying the works of Tintoretto in Venetian churches and collections.[3] Six years later, during the fall of 1880, Sargent returned to Venice as a precociously accomplished artist and began his serious campaign of chronicling and analyzing the city and its inhabitants. He stayed with his family at the Hôtel d'Italie on the Campo San Moisè, moving after they left the city to lodgings at 290 Piazza San Marco, All' Orologio.[4] So situated beside the clock tower at the heart of the city, he was surrounded by the premier historic buildings and the gay crowds on the Piazza. Yet, surprisingly, he avoided these classic subjects in his paintings. In a studio on an upper floor of the elegant Palazzo Rezzonico – the sumptuous seventeenth-century palace on the Grand Canal rented at the time and purchased a few years later by Robert Browning – Sargent began a group of genre paintings that constitute one of his most memorable achievements.[5] Also ensconced in studios in the Rezzonico that year were a number of other artists; it is probable that Whistler had taken a studio there the previous year.[6]

As Sargent returned to Venice twice during the decade, pursuing the same type of subject each time and omitting to date his work, it is difficult to establish a chronology of the approximately twenty-five early paintings.[7] Yet it is clear that during the initial year, 1880, he produced at least four significant works: he exhibited two watercolors entitled *Vue de Venise* at the Paris Salon in May 1881, and two oils entitled *Venetian Interior* at Grosvenor Gallery in London in May 1882 – both exhibitions occurring before his return to Venice in August that year.[8] Already in 1880, then, the pattern of interior views in oils and architectural views in watercolors was established (although the latter vein was apparently not seriously taken up until after the turn of the century). There has been much speculation concerning which of the interiors were shown at Grosvenor Gallery, but, from Henry James's remarks in his review of 1887 of Sargent's nascent career, it seems probable that *Venetian Women in the Palazzo Rezzonico* (cat. no. 58) was one of the two.[9] James was full of enthusiasm for this "pure gem" and for *The Daughters of Edward Darley Boit* (Museum of Fine Arts, Boston) which Sargent exhibited at the Salon the next year and which the writer perceptively saw as a related work.[10] In the same essay James remarked aptly on the "slightly 'uncanny' spectacle of a talent which on the very threshold of its career has nothing more to learn."[11]

By the time James wrote his milestone essay, Sargent had turned thirty; looking backwards, the man of letters noted that "as he saw and 'rendered' ten years ago, so he sees and renders today."[12] This fact is apparent to those who would rediscover the chronology of the Venetian genre works. Their consistency, in terms of both manner and subject, is apparent, and yet we have reason to believe they were painted during two, possibly three, separate visits. The second stay extended from August 1882 to the early weeks of 1883. Until December he stayed in the Palazzo Barbaro, a fifteenth-century palace on the Grand Canal owned by the Daniel Curtises, an American expatriate family who were distant relatives.[13] Most of the genre works are usually attributed to this visit. Three of which we can be confident are the *Italian Girl with Fan* (Cincinnati Art Museum), *The Sulphur Match* (private collection), which are dated, and *A Street in Venice* (National Gallery of Art, Washington, D.C.), which is pictured in a review of the first exhibition of the Société Internationale de Peintres et Sculpteurs in the *Gazette des Beaux-Arts* the following year.[14] The *Gazette* critic, Arthur Baignères, also makes reference to the two Venetian interior scenes exhibited. He finds Sargent's avoidance of the Grand Canal, San Marco, and the Venetian sunlight completely baffling.[15] Others were equally troubled by these pictures. A trustee of the Museum of Fine Arts, Boston, Martin Brimmer, reported in a letter of 26 October 1882:

Young Sargent has been staying with them [the Curtises] and is an attractive man. The only picture of his I have seen is a portrait of Thornton Lothrop, in which I thought the head a masterly piece of painting. He had besides some half-finished pictures of Venice. They are very clever, but a good deal inspired by the desire of finding what no one else has sought here – unpicturesque subjects, absence of color, absence of sunlight. It seems hardly worthwhile to travel so far for these.

Brimmer, in a move not so much charitable as rightly perceiving the aptness of Sargent's images for his age, adds:

But he has some qualities to an unusual degree – a sense of values and faculty for making his personages move. But it would be unfair to form an opinion of him from what I saw – and when one turns from Bellini and Tintoretto to an artist of his school, one feels painfully the lack of purpose which is more justly to be charged to the painter's environment than to the painter himself.[16]

What Brimmer interprets as "lack of purpose" is more a quality of Sargent's languid Venetians than of his painting. And yet the pictures, like those of Degas, do deliberately avoid overt meaning and purposefulness, do seek to artfully mimic visual accident, and do repeat themselves in series. In announcing their disquieting "lack of purpose" these works announce their modernity. Repeatedly returning to the same tenebrous situation, women in abruptly receding, back-lit hallways, Sargent continued to explore a subject and composition that his critics would call with some puzzlement "four corners and a void."[17]

Although most of these genre oils are attributed to the 1882/83 visit, several have been variously ascribed to 1886, and certainly the sheer number alone makes it difficult to imagine that he could have produced them all in six months. With the important exception of Henry James, most of Sargent's contemporaries seemed to feel that his "desire of finding what no one else has sought here – unpicturesque subjects, absence of color, absence of sunlight" was a quixotic enterprise. He exhibited two Venetian works at the National Academy of Design in 1888 (the National Gallery picture, owned at the time by architect Stanford White, and *Venetian Bead Stringers*, cat. no. 55) and then seems to have abandoned the subject.[18] *An Interior in Venice* (cat. no. 60) of 1899, a view of the *salone* of the Palazzo Barbaro, echoes the eccentric coloring and composition of the genre work of the previous decade and was equally unsettling to its audience (Mrs. Curtis reportedly rejected it), but after that date, Sargent seems to have confined his Venetian work in oils to a few unpeopled, sunlit architectural subjects (see cat. nos. 67 and 79), closer in tone and manner to his watercolors.

Sargent's relative lack of success with his Venetian genre works had a parallel in his less-than-successful early career as a portraitist.[19] Following his move from Paris to London in 1884, however, his portrait patronage improved, and after 1887 it became enthusiastic, eventually consuming almost his entire artistic energy. Perhaps as a reaction to the heavy demand for his work as a portraitist after 1900, Sargent took up watercolor again, recording in this medium – which he had mastered as a child and used intermittently as an adult – glimpses of his far-flung travels.[20] The critic Royal Cortissoz spoke in 1903 of the "studies and sketches with which he amused himself when on his travels, and in the intervals of painting portraits, at home."[21] These paintings were distinctly different from his commissioned portrait work in oils. Although there are a few instances of similar compositions in both media, it is unlikely that the watercolors were intended specifically as preparatory works for the oils (see cat. nos. 66 and 67, 73 and 74).

Sargent's travels took him to Venice in 1895, 1899, 1902, 1904, 1906, 1907, 1909, 1911, and 1913.[22] Although the watercolors are undated, we can assume that they were done over the course of the whole first decade of the twentieth century and into the next. In composition they seem to respond to Ruskin's plea in *The Stones of Venice* for the "abandonment of the impotent feelings of romance so singularly characteristic of this century," which he terms "a mere efflorescence of decay," in favor of a clear view of "the magnificent fragments [of Venice in] . . . their own strength."[23] Radically restricting the field of vision, Sargent concentrates on the seemingly objective qualities of light and substance, deromanticizing, in fact dehistoricizing his subjects. In the genre subjects, he alchemized mundane scenes into "pure gems," or, as another contemporary put it, he gave us "motifs taken from common life . . . lifted at once out of the commonplace."[24] In the watercolors, on the other hand, he seized upon celebrated subjects and lifted them at once out of their preciousness: he fragmentized and completely decontextualized them. Sargent seems to have thought of 'sliced' compositions as even conceivably literally that; his early biographer, Evan Charteris, records,

Sargent used to say that Whistler's use of paint was so exquisite that if a piece of canvas were cut out of one of his pictures one would find that it was in itself a thing of beauty by the very texture and substance into which it had been transformed by his brush.[25]
Some of Sargent's most dramatic watercolors seem to mimic this speculative endeavor, and do so with singular success.

Most of the watercolors are undated and untitled, but many carry inscriptions, suggesting a donative function. While scholars have taken these works to be mere vacation pastimes, private antidotes to an increasingly difficult public career, or simple scraps almost valueless to the artist, it is clear that Sargent actively exhibited and sold them, and developed new arenas of patronage with them.[26] He exhibited his Venetian watercolors regularly during the first decade of the twentieth century: seven at the Carfax Galleries in 1903, two at the Royal Watercolour Society in 1904, nineteen at the Carfax Galleries in April of 1905, six at the Carfax Galleries in the winter of 1908, and two at the Royal Watercolour Society in 1910.[27] More important was an exhibition that included eighty-three of his watercolors at M. Knoedler & Co. in 1909.[28] A. Augustus Healy, President of The Brooklyn Museum, who had commissioned a portrait from Sargent two years earlier, secured the purchase of almost the entire set for Brooklyn.[29] A smaller group was exhibited in New York in 1912 and was purchased by the Museum of Fine Arts, Boston; in 1915 The Metropolitan Museum in New York bought eleven from the artist; and in 1917 both the Worcester Art Museum and Carnegie Institute in Pittsburgh bought groups of watercolors.[30] These purchases by American museums mark a turn in Sargent's sponsorship to solid institutional patronage, but the Americanness of the buyers was not new. From the outset, Americans had provided the key element in his success.[31]

It is relevant to turn to the vexed question of Sargent's own Americanness in the context of these institutional purchases, inspecting the remarks and actions of his contemporaries. One could read the steady stream of American portrait commissions and the competitive museum patronage as a clear sign that Sargent was recognized as a native son. Always a little hesitant to categorize him nationally, contemporary writers such as Henry James, Kenyon Cox, and the French critic Arthur Baignères usually brought up the issue in their essays, deciding in the end that he was to be spoken of as American.[32] For his own part, Sargent was careful to return to the United States to secure his citizenship, refused knighthood with the argument that such honors were inappropriate to American citizens, and spoke warmly of the responsibility of "our" (U.S.) government in the matter of the First World War.[33] Generally speaking, however, the fact that Sargent's Americanness is a question points firmly to the cosmopolitan nature of his background and his art. As the writer Vernon Lee observed of his mastery of European languages and his eccentric cultural identity, "John is . . . [a] completely accentless mongrel."[34] In this ambiguous internationalism we sense the presence of a modernity absolutely congruent with the evidence of his artworks, nowhere more observable than in the stark and "purposeless" paintings that he executed in Venice.

1. James Lomax and Richard Ormond, *John Singer Sargent and the Edwardian Age*, exh. cat. (Leeds: Leeds Art Galleries, 1979), p. 96; *Inventory of American Paintings*.

2. Carter Ratcliff, *John Singer Sargent* (New York: Abbeville Press, 1982), p. 243.

3. Quoted in Evan Charteris, *John Sargent* (New York: Scribner's, 1927), p. 18.

4. Charteris, pp. 53-54.

5. Charles Merrill Mount, *John Singer Sargent: A Biography* (New York: Norton, 1955), pp. 67-68; Ratcliff, p. 61; Lillian Whiting, *Italy: The Magic Land* (Boston: Little, Brown, 1910), p. 406.

6. Richard Ormond, *John Singer Sargent: Paintings, Drawings, Watercolors* (New York and Evanston: Harper & Row, 1970), p. 29.

7. *Inventory of American Paintings*

8. Edward J. Nygren, *John Singer Sargent: Drawings from the Corcoran Gallery of Art*, exh. cat. (Washington, D.C.: Smithsonian Institution Traveling Exhibition Service and Corcoran Gallery of Art, 1983), p. 53; Ormond, p. 238; Ratcliff, p. 244.

9. Henry James, "John S. Sargent," *Harper's New Monthly Magazine* 75, no. 449 (October 1887), p. 689.

10. James, pp. 684, 688, 689.

11. James, p. 684.

12. James, p. 684.

13. Charteris, p. 57; Ratcliff, pp. 73, 244.

14. Arthur Baignères, "Première Exposition de la Société Internationale de Peintres et Sculpteurs," *Gazette des Beaux Arts* 27 (1883), p. 192.

15. Baignères, p. 190; these paintings are listed in the catalogue as: no. 96 *Venetian Interior*, no. 97 *Another Venetian Interior*, and no. 99 *A Street in Venice* (letter 18 May 1979, D. Gazier to Ms. L. Hardenburgh, Art Institute of Chicago files).

16. Correspondence from Martin Brimmer to Sarah Wyman Whitman, Martin Brimmer Papers, Roll D32, frames 184-185, AAA.

17. Quoted in Charteris, p. 57; these same two pictures were exhibited again at the Pan American Exposition in 1901 (Charles H. Caffin, "The Picture Exhibition at the Pan American Exposition, Continued," *International Studio* 14, no. 55, pp. 21-22).

18. *NAD*, p. 822.

19. Charles Mount, "New Discoveries Illumine Sargent's Paris Career," *The Art Quarterly* 20, no. 3 (Autumn 1957), pp. 312-313; Ormond, p. 30.

20. Norman Kent, "The Watercolors of John Singer Sargent (1856-1925): A Brief Estimate," *American Art* 34, no. 10 (November 1970), p. 70.

21. Royal Cortissoz, *Personalities in Art* (New York: Scribner's, 1925), p. 254.

22. Louise Hall Tharp, *Mrs. Jack* (Boston: Little, Brown, 1965), p. 185; Isabella Stewart Gardner Papers, Roll 408, frame 384, AAA; Ratcliff, p. 245; Ormond, pp. 75, 76, 257; Charteris, p. 291.

23. John Ruskin, *The Stones of Venice*, excerpted in "The Approach to Venice," *The Crayon* 2, no. 1 (14 July 1855), p. 7.

24. Cortissoz, p. 520.

25. Charteris, p. 21.

26. Catherine Beach Ely, "Sargent as a Watercolorist," *Art in America* 11, no. 11 (February 1923), p. 98; Ormond, p. 68; Kent, p. 70.

27. Typescript "Exhibited Works by Sargent," Victoria and Albert Museum Records.

28. Donelson F. Hoopes, *Sargent Watercolors* (New York: Watson-Guptill Publications, 1970), p. 19; *Museum of Fine Arts* [Boston] *Bulletin* 10, no. 57 (June 1912), p. 19; Nelson Lansdale, "John Singer Sargent: His Private World," *American Artist* 28, no. 9, issue 279, p. 82.

29. Hoopes, p. 19; Kent, p. 70.

30. Susan E. Strickler, "John Singer Sargent and Worcester," *Worcester Museum Journal* 6 (1982-1983), pp. 31-32; Hoopes, p. 19; *Museum of Fine Arts Bulletin*, p. 19.

31. Mount, "New Discoveries," pp. 312-314.

32. James, p. 683; Kenyon Cox, *Old Masters and New: Essays in Criticism* (New York: Fox, Duffield & Co., 1905), p. 255; Baignères, p. 189.

33. Michael Quick, *American Expatriate Painters of the Late Nineteenth Century*, exh. cat. (Dayton, Ohio: The Dayton Art Institute, 1976), p. 129; Lansdale, p. 59; Percy Lubbock, ed., *The Letters of Henry James* (New York: Scribner's, 1920), p. 493.

34. Ratcliff, p. 65.

52

52 **A Street in Venice**, ca. 1882
Oil on canvas, 27⅝ × 20⅝ in. (70.1 × 52.4 cm)
Signed, lower right: *John S. Sargent/Venise*
Sterling and Francine Clark Art Institute, Williamstown, Massachusetts

Sargent's exterior genre scenes usually include male as well as female figures – as in this painting – and are set in structurally confined and architecturally undistinguished spaces. Works related to this include *A Street in Venice* (National Gallery of Art, Washington, D.C.), *A Street in Venice* (private collection), and *Venetian Street* (private collection).[1] All employ a narrow, dark palette and focus on figures cloaked in wintry black. This painting with its vertical format and precipitous recession is the most concentrated and perhaps the most disquieting of the group. A reviewer of the first exhibition in Paris of Sargent's Venetian views commented tellingly about the paintings:
Nous n'y verrons ni grand Canal ni place Saint-Marc . . . M. Sargent nous conduit dans d'obscurs carrefours et dans des salles basses toutes noires que transperce un rayon de soleil. Où se cachent les belles du Titien? Ce ne sont certes par leurs descendantes que nous apercevons à peine sous leurs chevelure inculte, drapées dans un vieux châle noir comme si elles grelottaient la fièvre. A quoi bon aller en Italie pour y recueillir de pareilles impressions?
(We see neither the Grand Canal, nor the Piazza San Marco . . . Mr. Sargent takes us into gloomy little squares

and mean dark rooms which are pierced by a single ray of sunshine. Where are Titian's beautiful women? These are certainly not their descendants, women we can scarcely see under their unkempt hair, cloaked in an old shawl as though shivering from a fever. Why need one go to Italy to collect such impressions?)[2]

Sargent's deliberate avoidance of the well-known aspects of Venice, of handsome Venice, was only one aspect of these works that gave his audiences difficulty. The paintings are also technically and psychologically abrupt. The areas of highest value, for instance, often describe the furthermost objects, sharply juxtaposing near and far, and the pigment is laid on roughly (as in the lower left here) to simulate spontaneity. But most pointedly, the figures seem confrontational. The viewer is standing and is observed but unrecognized by the protagonists. We feel ourselves, in this narrow place, interlopers; we are not unseen voyeurs, as in most genre works, but intruding participants. In these works Venetian architectural space and inhabitants both seem problematic, even mildly unpleasant.

The pitted stucco crumbling off the brick wall on the left echoes the rumpled pink skirt of the woman. She is wedged uncomfortably between the man who occupies the center of the painting and the tavern doorway on the right, her foot poised on the threshold. A fringed shawl partially covers her salmon-colored skirt, and beneath, a long black underskirt and a corner of white lining sug-

gest the intensity of the cold and the levels of closure and disclosure she is willing to grant us.

Sargent signed the work and then added "Venise," using the French name because, in his polyglot life, he was at the time based in Paris. This will to name the place is noteworthy, as though Sargent were marking the distance between this tableau and one's 'knowledge' of the city. The salient features of the situation could be seen, as the French reviewer cited above notes, in any contemporary city. There is an element of wit in this naming, this insistent conjunction of the remembered value and the perceived reality. Yet, perhaps more important, Sargent's Venetians are not hapless pawns of history or picturesque peasants; they are unpredictable and alive, albeit confined within the cold, dark shell of a formerly glorious city.

1. *Exhibition of Works by John Singer Sargent, R.A.*, exh. cat. (Birmingham, England: Birmingham City Museum and Art Gallery, 1964), p. 9; *Americans in Venice 1879-1913*, exh. cat. (New York: Coe Kerr Gallery, 1983), pl. 31.
2. Baignères, p. 190, author's translation.

Provenance: Presented by the artist to J. Nicolopoulo, Greek Minister to France; Scott and Fowles, New York; R. S. Clark, 2 November 1926; Sterling and Francine Clark Art Institute, 1955

Exhibition History and Bibliography: Charles Merrill Mount, *John Singer Sargent: A Biography*, New York: Norton, 1955, p. 444; Sterling and Francine Clark Art Institute, Williamstown, Mass., *Exhibit Seven: The Regency and Louis XVI Rooms*, 1957, no. 315; idem, *Exhibit Four and Exhibit Seven*, 1958, pl. LXVI; Charles Merrill Mount, "Carolus-Duran and

53

54

the Development of Sargent," *Art Quarterly* 26, no. 4 (Winter 1963), p. 399 and fig. 15; Denys Sutton, "A Bouquet for Sargent," *Apollo* 79 (May 1964), p. 399 and fig. 3; Birmingham City Museum and Art Gallery, England, *Exhibition of Works by John Singer Sargent, R.A.,* 25 September-18 October 1964, mentioned in entry no. 7 (not in exhibition); Wildenstein and Co., New York, *Treasures from the Clark Art Institute,* 2-25 February 1967, no. 48; Richard Ormond, *John Singer Sargent: Paintings, Drawings, Watercolors,* New York and Evanston: Harper & Row, 1970, p. 30; *List of Paintings in the Sterling and Francine Clark Art Institute,* Williamstown, Mass.: Sterling and Francine Clark Art Institute, 1972, no. 575; John H. Brooks, *Highlights: Sterling and Francine Clark Art Institute,* Williamstown, Mass.: Sterling and Francine Clark Art Institute, 1981, p. 88; Rafael Fernandez, *A Scene of Light and Glory: Approaches to Venice,* Sterling and Francine Clark Art Institute, Williamstown, Mass., 10 March-25 April 1982, no. 58.

53 Venetian Water Carriers, 1880 or 1882
Oil on canvas, 25⅜ × 27¾ in. (64.5 × 70.5 cm)
Signed, lower right: *John S. Sargent*
Worcester Art Museum

In response to an inquiry from the then owner of this and another painting, Sargent wrote in a letter of February 1896,
The pictures you refer to were both painted in Venice some fifteen years ago. One is the interior of a bead manufactory or glass work shop of some sort [cat. no. 57]. *I gave them to their late owner* [Friedrich Wilhelm Carl Bechstein of Berlin, Germany] *in exchange for a piano of his make,*[1]
which would date this work to 1880 or 1882. A label on the back indicating Sargent's ownership suggests that it was exhibited before 1886, the date that the trade was accomplished.[2]
The scene is a small courtyard in which two women

are engaged in the daily chore of supplying their plumbingless households with fresh water. The level of interest in this picturesque task, evident in travelers' reports and painters' records, suggests the rarity of this scene elsewhere in urban western Europe. Venice was not only technologically eccentric in her circulation system but also technologically primitive, and as such had a time-capsule quality for visitors. One of the few Sargent paintings to capture whole-body physical labor, this picture reminds us of Degas's contemporary study of laundresses and other women at work. The telling gesture, the frank record of strain, gives the image a very different quality than that perceivable in all but one of Duveneck's figures in his canvas of a very similar subject (cat. no. 15).

The composition is symmetrical and stable, with the well marking the center of both the courtyard and the canvas, a departure from the experiments in radical asymmetry and plunging spatial recession that we see in other early works. And here, more than in other Venetian paintings, we feel the truth of Sargent's remark, "Monet bowled me over," for the slabs of paving stone have been rendered with independent slabs of paint, and the very visible brushstroke is reminiscent of the work of that luminous contemporary.[3]

1. Worcester Art Museum records, per William Macbeth Gallery.
2. Worcester Art Museum records.
3. Letter of 20 March 1911 or 1912, quoted in Charteris, p. 124.

Provenance: Traded by the artist to Friedrich Wilhelm Carl Bechstein, Berlin, Germany, for a piano, ca. 1886; sold at the Hôtel Drouot, Paris, ca. 1895; Frederick Crane, New York; William Macbeth, New York; bought by the Museum, 1911.

Exhibition History and Bibliography: National Academy of Design, New York, 1910; Worcester Art Museum, *Catalogue of Paintings and Drawings*, 1922, p. 202; Museum of Fine Arts, Boston, *Memorial Exhibition of the Works of the Late John Singer Sargent*, 3 November-27 December 1925, no. 17; William Howe Downes, *John S. Sargent: His Life and Work*, Boston: Little, Brown, 1925, p. 145; The Metropolitan Museum of Art, New York, *Memorial Exhibition of the Work of John Singer Sargent*, 4 January-14 February 1926, no. 9; Evan Charteris, *John Sargent*, New York: Scribner's, 1927, p. 282; Worcester Art Museum, *News Bulletin and Calendar* 19 (May 1954), p. 33; Charles Merrill Mount, *John Singer Sargent: A Biography*, New York: Norton, 1955, p. 444; Worcester Art Museum, *News Bulletin and Calendar* 29 (May 1964), n. p.; Donelson F. Hoopes, *The Private World of John Singer Sargent*, Corcoran Gallery of Art, Washington, D.C., 18 April-14 June 1964, no. 17; The Minneapolis Institute of Arts, *Fiftieth Anniversary Exhibition*, 4 November 1965-2 January 1966; Worcester Art Museum, *Art in America, 1830-1950*, 1969; Coe Kerr Gallery, New York, *John Singer Sargent, His Own Work*, 28 May-27 June 1980, no. 12; Carter Ratcliff, *John Singer Sargent*, New York: Abbeville Press, 1982, pl. 103; Susan E. Strickler, "John Singer Sargent and Worcester," *Worcester Art Museum Journal* 6 (1982-1983), pp. 19, 27, fig. 12.

54   Venetian Interior, ca. 1882

Oil on canvas, 27 × 34 in. (68.6 × 86.4 cm)
Signed, lower left: *John S. Sargent*
Museum of Art, Carnegie Institute, Pittsburgh, Pennsylvania. Museum Purchase, 1920
Color plate

Venetian Interior is the largest of three genre paintings that depict women standing and working in the principal upper hallway of an unknown Venetian palace. The close association of this painting with *Venetian Bead Stringers* (cat. no. 55) and *A Venetian Interior* (Sterling and Francine Clark Art Institute) extends to the tone of the works and the models employed, as well as the identity of the room. It is a high-ceilinged space lit at one end by a set of partially blocked windows leading onto an elegant Baroque balcony, visible in the background here. The other end of the long room is lit by the large windows of a stairwell that leads directly into this space (see cat. no. 55). In this painting the central figure suggests by her posture and expression that we have just descended the stairs and entered the hall. The building has not been identified, but it is neither the Palazzo Rezzonico in which Sargent had a studio in 1880 nor the Palazzo Barbaro where Sargent was a guest during most of his stay in Venice in 1882/83. Although it is clearly a domestic space, it has the appearance in these three paintings – given the number of women present and the tasks in which they are engaged – of a workshop.

Beyond the irony of the juxtaposed impressive historic structure and its modest use, there is a slightly unsavory languor discernible in these paintings. The backlit apertures (in this case the balcony vignette) draw our eyes away from the figures in the dimly lit interior in a deliberate reversal of painterly expectations. A piercingly bright and abrupt spear of sunlight, prominent in both this and the Clark Art Institute picture, is rendered in thick, disruptive impasto on the smoothly brushed marble floor, rivaling the foreground figures for our attention. For such arbitrary and anti-hierarchical visual objectivity, Sargent gained a reputation among his contemporaries as "one of the least conventional of painters."[1]

In a letter of 27 September 1880, Sargent indicated that he intended to stay in Venice until completing a painting for the Salon.[2] We know that he had several works in progress at the time, and in the absence of any Venetian paintings – beyond two watercolors – submitted to the Salon, there is room for speculation on which painting he had in mind. *Venetian Interior*, because of its relatively large size, is not an improbable candidate.

1. Cortissoz, p. 518.
2. Ormond, p. 29.

Provenance: Henry Lerolle, Paris

Exhibition History and Bibliography: Carnegie Institute, Pittsburgh, *Nineteenth Annual International Exhibition*, 29 April-30 June 1920, no. 297; Grand Central Art Galleries, New York, *Retrospective Exhibition of Important Works of John Singer Sargent*, 23 February-22 March 1924, no. 44; Museum of Fine Arts, Boston, *Memorial Exhibition of the Works of the Late John Singer Sargent*, 3 November-27 December 1925, no. 23; William Howe Downes, *John S. Sargent: His Life and Work*, Boston: Little, Brown, 1925, p. 132; Fine Arts Gallery, San Diego, Opening exhibition, 1926; California Palace of the Legion of Honor, San Francisco, *First Exhibition of Selected Paintings by American Artists*, 15 November 1926-30 January 1927, no. 163; Evan Charteris, *John Sargent*, New York: Scribner's, 1927, p. 283; Art Gallery of Toronto, *Loan Exhibition of Great Paintings in Aid of Allied Merchant Seamen*, 4 February-12 March 1944; Columbus Gallery of Fine Arts, 4 March-9 April 1952; Munson-Williams-Proctor Institute, Utica, *Expatriates: Whistler, Cassatt, Sargent*, 4-25 January 1953, no. 29; Charles Merrill Mount, *John Singer Sargent: A Biography*, New York: Norton, 1955, p. 444; Grand Rapids Art Gallery, *Sargent, Whistler, and Cassatt Print Show*, 15 September-15 October 1955; John L. Sweeney, ed., *The Painter's Eye: Notes and Essays on the Pictorial Arts by Henry James*, Cambridge: Harvard University Press, 1956, p. 213; Carnegie Institute, Pittsburgh, *American Classics of the Nineteenth Century*, Summer 1957, no. 109; Westmoreland County Museum of Art, Greensburg, Pa., 1961; Charles Merrill Mount, "Carolus-Duran and the Development of Sargent," *Art Quarterly* 26, no. 4 (Winter 1963), p. 400, fig. 10; Fred A. Myers, "Venetian Interior: John Singer Sargent (1856-1925)," *Carnegie Magazine* (September 1966), p. 249; Carnegie Institute, Pittsburgh, *Catalogue of Painting Collection*, 1973, p. 153; Theodore E. Stebbins, Jr., Carol Troyen, and Trevor J. Fairbrother, *A New World: Masterpieces of American Painting, 1760-1910*, Museum of Fine Arts, Boston, 7 September-13 November 1983, no. 90.

55   Venetian Bead Stringers, 1880-1882

Oil on canvas, 26⅜ × 30¾ in. (67 × 78.1 cm)
Signed, upper right: *John S. Sargent*
Albright-Knox Art Gallery, Buffalo, New York. Friends of the Albright Art Gallery Fund, 1916

As in the two other paintings depicting groups of women in the upper hall of a dark Venetian palazzo, *Venetian Interior* (cat. no. 54) and *A Venetian Interior* (Sterling and Francine Clark Art Institute), the dominant tones in *Venetian Bead Stringers* are gray, white, and black. And, as in the other works, the only true opaque black is found in the figures: their shawls, shoes, and hair. Unlike Whistler's gray-based "harmonies," Sargent's compositions exploit the juxtapositions of color areas, the abrupt intrusion of one color area on another, seen here where the molten sunlight outside the stairwell irrupts into the darkness of the hall.

It is characteristic of Sargent's visual wit and dexterity that he achieves one effect by two different means: the white of the left and center windows is rendered in thick impasto, while that of the slatted windows on the right is

55

bare canvas. Reminiscent of Thomas Eakins – another artist who found Velasquez a compelling mentor – Sargent here introduces one startlingly chromatic hue into a basically white-black-gray palette. But where Eakins's note of color is fully saturated, indeed, almost alarming in its intensity (see *Frances Eakins*, The Nelson-Atkins Museum of Art, Kansas City, Missouri, and *Elisabeth Crowell at the Piano*, Addison Gallery of American Art, Phillips Academy, Andover, Massachusetts), Sargent's is, as here in the fan with its delicate fillets of mauve, violet, and vermilion, more muted, more subtly sensuous.

Our view of this hall is basically the same as that in the Clark Art Institute painting, but we have moved closer to the center of the space – away from the balcony visible in *Venetian Interior* (cat. no. 54). In all three pictures we see the long wall, against which sits a leather-upholstered settee. And yet – giving the lie to those who would claim that Sargent "belongs to the class of observers, rather than to that of the composers" – the wall is subtly different each time.[1] In the Clark Art Institute picture, which has the most complex arrangement of figures, more than a dozen dimly-perceived paintings in gilt frames are scattered over the wall in a pattern apparently as random and as complicated as that in which the figures dispose themselves on the floor. In *Venetian Interior* five vague squares suggest prints or pictures on the wall behind a somewhat less complicated figural group. *Venetian Bead Stringers* is even more straightforward with only three women, and the wall is bare, save one lone oval in the far corner.

The tone of languid boredom that invests the other pictures in this set is also evident here. The middle figure stares off into space, and the standing onlooker watches with indifferent interest as one woman unhurriedly threads glass beads onto strings with long wire 'needles. The unseen beads are kept in a soft bag which, in turn, is contained in the shallow wooden trough she holds on her lap. The activity was a universal cottage industry in late-nineteenth-century Venice, one small but very visible aspect of the revival of the glass industry which, like the lace industry, had all but vanished before the Arts and Crafts movement (and English capital) spread to Italy.[2] But unlike lacemaking or the fabrication of intricate glass vessels, the activity we see here was unskilled and essentially tedious.

These three women seem to be simultaneously individuals and types: the fair, sturdy brunette; the delicate red-head with a transparent complexion; and the swarthy, black-haired woman, lost in dreams. Variations on these types are evident in the other paintings in this set and in a related work, one of the few Sargent dated, *Italian Woman with Fan* (1882 and 1883, Cincinnati Art Museum).

Although the precise dating of *Venetian Bead Stringers* is not possible at this point, we know that it was given to the painter James Carroll Beckwith as a wedding present in 1887.[3] When asked about the picture thirty years later, Sargent wrote: "The picture 'Venetian Bead Stringers' was painted by me in Venice in, I should think 1880 to 1890," a remark that suggests, among other things, that the genre scenes more probably represent intermittent work throughout the decade than – as some have speculated – the work of 1880 and 1882 alone.

1. Cox, pp. 256-257.

2. James Jackson Jarves, *Italian Rambles: Studies of Life and Manners in New and Old Italy* (New York: Putnam's, 1883), p. 249.

3. Charlotte Kotik and Steven A. Nash, *Albright-Knox Art Gallery: Painting and Sculpture from Antiquity to 1942* (New York: Rizzoli, 1979), p. 309.

4. Albright-Knox Museum records.

Provenance: Presented by the artist to James Carroll Beckwith, New York, 1887; purchased from Beckwith, 1916

Exhibition History and Bibliography: Henry James, "John S. Sargent," *Harper's Monthly Magazine* 75 (October 1887), p. 689, reprinted in *Picture and Text*, 1893, pp. 108-109; National Academy of Design, New York, 1888, no. 219; Copley Hall, Boston, *Exhibition of Paintings and Sketches by J. S. Sargent*, 1899, no. 37; Buffalo, *Pan American Exposition*, 1901, no. 29; C. H. Caffin, "The Picture Exhibition of the Pan-American Exposition," *International Studio* 14 (September 1901), pp. xxi, xxii; Royal Cortissoz, "John S. Sargent," *Scribner's Magazine* 34 (November 1903), p. 520; idem, *Art and Common Sense*, New York: Scribner's, 1913, p. 225; Albright Art Gallery, Buffalo, *8th Annual Exhibition of Selected Paintings by American Artists*, 1913, no. 102; *Buffalo Fine Arts Academy Notes* (July 1913), pp. 94-95; Detroit Institute of Arts, *2nd Annual Exhibition of Selected Paintings by American Artists*, 1916, no. 81; *Blue Book of the Buffalo Fine Arts Academy*, 1917, p. 34; *Buffalo Fine Arts Academy Notes* (October-December 1917), pp. 142-143; Dallas Museum of Fine Arts, *3rd Annual Exhibition of American Art from the Day of the Colonists to Now*, 1922, no. 78; Grand Central Art Galleries, New York, *Retrospective Exhibition of Important Works of John Singer Sargent*, 23 February-22 March 1924, no. 52; Museum of Fine Arts, Boston, *Memorial Exhibition of the Works of the Late John Singer Sargent*, 3 November-27 December 1925, no. 24; William Howe Downes, *John S. Sargent: His Life and Work*, Boston: Little, Brown, 1925, pp. 93, 144-145; A. D. Patterson, "Sargent: A Memory," *Canadian Magazine* 65 (March 1926), p. 31; Art Gallery of Toronto, *Inaugural Exhibition*, 1926, no. 71; Evan Charteris, *John Sargent*, New York: Scribner's, 1927, p. 283; Royal Academy of Art, Stockholm, *Exhibition of American Art*, 1930, no. 86; M. H. de Young Memorial Museum, San Francisco, *Exhibition of American Painting*, 1935, no. 200; *The Index of Twentieth Century Artists* 2 (March 1935), no. 6, p. 85; Andrew C. Ritchie, ed., *Catalogue of the Paintings and Sculpture in the Permanent Collection*, Buffalo: Albright Art Gallery, 1949, pp. 38-39, 187, no. 16; Roberson Memorial Center, Binghamton, N.Y., *Treasure House – New York State*, 1954-1955; Charles Merrill Mount, *John Singer Sargent: A Biography*, New York: Norton, 1955, p. 444; Chautauqua Art Association, *Fifteen American Painters from the Albright Collection*, 1961; Charles Merrill Mount, "Carolus-Duran and the Development of Sargent," *Art Quarterly* 26, no. 4 (Winter 1963), fig. 13; Donelson F. Hoopes, *The Private World of John Singer Sargent*, Corcoran Gallery of Art, Washington, D.C., 18 April-14 June 1964, no. 21; Nelson Lansdale, "John Singer Sargent: His Private World," *American Artist* 28 (November 1964), p. 59; "The Private World of John Singer Sargent," *Munson-Williams-Proctor Institute Bulletin* (December 1964), n. p.; Richard Ormond, *John Singer Sargent: Paintings, Drawings, Watercolors*, New York and Evanston: Harper & Row, 1970, pp. 29, 69, 238 and pl. 21; Allen Staley, ed., *From Realism to Symbolism: Whistler and His World*, Wildenstein and Co., New York, 4 March-3 April 1972, no. 129; Adeline R. Tintner, "Sargent in the Fiction of Henry James," *Apollo* 102 (August 1975), p. 128; Steven A. Nash, et al., *Albright-Knox Art Gallery: Painting and Sculpture from Antiquity to 1942*, New York: Rizzoli, 1979, pp. 308-309; James Lomax and Richard Ormond, *John Singer Sargent and the Edwardian Age*, Leeds Art Galleries, 5 April-10 June 1979, no. 9; Carter Ratcliff, *John Singer Sargent*, New York: Abbeville Press, 1982, pl. 84.

56 The Bead Stringers of Venice

Oil on canvas laid on board, 22⅛ × 32¼ in.
(56.2 × 81.9 cm)
Signed and inscribed, bottom center: *To my friend Lawless / John S. Sargent*
The National Gallery of Ireland

This unfinished work is, in many ways, one of the most interesting, as well as the most puzzling, of Sargent's interior "subject pictures." We are told that the painting was executed in the company of Valentine Lawless, later Lord Cloncurry, to whom it is inscribed.[1] He apparently requested the work and had the upper right section, which the artist had cut out, roughly repaired with cardboard.[2] Beyond this disfigurement, the picture is hauntingly beautiful.

Primary among the work's eccentricities is the fact that the most prominent figures turn their backs to us as they continue their patient labor. A distant group of figures and a bright swath of sunlight draw our eye back into the gaunt room. To find a precedent for this composition one need look no further than Sargent's own copy of a segment of Velasquez's *The Spinners: The Fable of Arachne*, executed early in 1880 (Sir Alfred Beit Collection, Dublin). There the foreground figure is turned from us as she attends to her handwork. Sunlight spotlights the figures, a tapestry-tableau, in the rear. That Sargent shared Velasquez's more general interest in women at work (whether allegorized, as in *The Spinners*, or vernacular, as in *The Servant Girl with the Supper at Emmaus*, also in the Beit Collection), as well as specific compositional arrangements, is evident in this series of works.

Sargent's two foreground figures face a third, partially obliterated by his cutting of the canvas. The characteristic lap trough and her low hand gesture indicate that she, too, is a stringer of beads. She takes her ease while she works, tipping her chair back against the wall, as does the female figure in another Sargent work of the period, *The Sulphur Match* (private collection). Intent on their beads, the women do not speak; the silence is palpable, and characteristically Venetian. As one nineteenth-century visitor to Venice put it,

The very nature of the employments, in Venice, conduces to its Sybaritic quiet. The whole population, wander where you will through its narrow lanes, is employed in fabricating pretty trifles for Europe and America. Shops after shops – streets after streets – devoted solely to the production of millions of curious trinkets. I really thought, today, after rambling for hours around, that there was hardly an article of merchandise in the city, that weighed twenty pounds, or an artisan, who wielded an instrument bigger than a darning-needle.[3]

Among those "pretty trifles" were glass beads, small agents of commerce that found their way to Plains Indians' moccasins and to the deepest Congo, as well as to the urban centers of Europe and America.

Sargent's bead stringers concentrate on their task, dutifully exercising their modest and tedious skill in the shadows of a monumental city. They are unlike Whistler's bead stringers (see cat. nos. 96 and 111), whose decorative contours give scale and an element of habitation to architectural apertures, or Blum's lacemakers (cat. no. 7), who exude a sense of lively coquetry. Sargent's women constitute a community of labor, cohorts who seem to personify the stoicism and silence of their city.

1. *Venice Rediscovered*, exh. cat. (London: Wildenstein, 1972), p. 56.

2. *Catalogue of Oil Pictures in the General Collection* (Dublin: National Gallery of Ireland, 1932), pp. 113-114.

3. Anon., *Sketches of a Summer Tour* (New York: William J. Read, 1866), p. 182.

Provenance: Given by the artist to Valentine Lawless, Lord Cloncurry, by whom bequeathed, 1929

56

Exhibition History and Bibliography: National Gallery of Ireland, Dublin, *Catalogue of Oil Pictures in the General Collection*, 1932, pp. 113-114; Charles Merrill Mount, "Carolus-Duran and the Development of Sargent," *Art Quarterly* 26, no. 4 (Winter 1963), pp. 400, 405, fig. 17; National Gallery of Ireland, Dublin, *Centenary Exhibition 1864-1964*, 1964, no. 180; Wildenstein and Co., London, *Venice Rediscovered*, 8 November-15 December 1972, no. 34; National Gallery of Ireland, *Illustrated Summary Catalogue of Paintings*, 1981, p. 147.

57   Venetian Glass Workers, 1880 or 1882
Oil on canvas, 22¼ × 33¾ in. (56.5 × 85.7 cm)
Signed, lower left: *John S. Sargent*
The Art Institute of Chicago. Mr. and Mrs. Martin A. Ryerson Collection

Among Sargent's Venetian genre scenes, *Venetian Glass Workers* is unusual in the very free handling of the paint, the density of the room's darkness, and the inclusion of male figures in an interior scene. It also suggests a more concentrated labor effort than is apparent in the other images.

   It is impossible to judge the type of space in which the three women and two men work but, from the bars on the window, it appears to be a lower floor. When Sargent was asked about this picture and another in 1896, he responded that this was "the interior of a bead manufactory or glass workshop of some sort."[1] Sheaves of glass rods – or, more precisely, glass tubes, for these are to be

drawn rather than wound beads – are being sorted, and cut into bead-sized pieces.[2] Once tumbled with abrasives, the beads are round, smooth, and ready to be passed on to the bead stringers who will make up rough or ornamented strands for sale.

   One of Venice's few exportable commodities in the nineteenth century, glass manufactures of all kinds were of great interest to visitors. In a cryptic journal entry, Herman Melville recorded his expedition of 3 April 1857 "to glass bead manufactury. Drawing the rods like twine – making, cutting, rounding, polishing, coloring a secret."[3] And William Dean Howells, American consul in Venice a decade later, comments in *Venetian Life* that "Murano [the island on which most of the glass furnaces were concentrated] beads are exported to all quarters in vast quantities, and the process of making them is one of the things that strangers feel they must see when visiting Venice."[4] The simple alchemy of altering sand, even expensively imported sand, to create lustrous, delicate glasswares is a very fitting field for Venetian preeminence, for it is analogous to the culture of Venice itself.[5] But the making of glass beads is a very different enterprise, one which John Ruskin inveighs against, in a famous passage in "The Nature of Gothic," as the very epitome of the debasement of human intellect, aesthetic expression, and humane labor:
Glass beads are utterly unnecessary, and there is no design or thought employed in their manufacture. They are formed by

first drawing out the glass into rods; these rods are chopped up into fragments the size of beads by the human hand, and the fragments are then rounded in the furnace. The men who chop up the rods sit at their work all day, their hands vibrating with a perpetual and exquisitely timed palsy, and the beads dropping beneath their vibration like hail. Neither they, nor the men who draw out the rods, and fuse the fragments, have the smallest occasion for the use of any single human faculty; and every young lady, therefore, who buys glass beads is engaged in the slave-trade, and in a much more cruel one than that which we have so long been endeavoring to put down.[6]

The alienating nature of the labor involved in the chopping of the glass tubes is suggested in Sargent's hunched figures and tenebrous interior.

In this painting Sargent portrays the glass tubes with rough, summary strokes of white, pale blue, and buff pigment. Lustrous against the dark browns of the rest of the work, these stiff bundles on which the figures bend their energy seem precious and vibrant. Yet Sargent's subject is not simply the semi-abstract rendering in paint of these gleaming tubes of glass; he is also intent on capturing the gesture and pose of those skilled in the handling of the material. He fixes the character of the labor involved as surely as he fixes the optical qualities of these extraordinary filaments.

1. Letter addressed to Charles H. Pepper, 28 February 1896, courtesy Macbeth Gallery, The Art Institute of Chicago files; see also letter from Charles Pepper to Mr. Macbeth of 10 January 1912, Macbeth Gallery Papers, Roll NMc 10, frame 480, AAA.

2. W. G. N. van der Sleen, *A Handbook on Beads* (York, Pa.: Liberty Corp. Books, n.d.), pp. 22-43.

3. Herman Melville, *Journal of a Visit to Europe and the Levant, October 11, 1856-May 6, 1857*, Howard C. Horsford, ed. (Princeton, N.J.: Princeton University Press, 1955), p. 228.

4. William Dean Howells, *Venetian Life* (London: N. Trübner & Co., 1866), p. 181; the tradition continued into the twentieth century (see Elise Lathrop, *Sunny Days in Italy* [New York: James Pott & Co., 1907], p. 302), and indeed to the present.

5. Shirley Guiton, *A World by Itself: Tradition and Change in the Venetian Lagoon* (London: Hamish Hamilton, 1977), p. 83.

6. John Ruskin, *The Stones of Venice*, 3 vols., originally published 1852 (New York: John W. Lovell, n.d.), vol. 2, pp. 166-167.

Provenance: Traded by the artist to Friedrich Wilhelm Carl Bechstein, Berlin, Germany, for a piano, ca. 1886; sold at the Hôtel Drouot, Paris, ca. 1895; Charles Hovey Pepper, Paris (?), 1896; Macbeth Gallery, New York, 1911; Mr. and Mrs. Martin A. Ryerson, Chicago, 1912; bequeathed to The Art Institute by Mr. Ryerson, 1932

Exhibition History and Bibliography: Museum of Fine Arts, Boston, *Memorial Exhibition of the Works of the Late John Singer Sargent*, 3 November-27 December 1925, no. 14; William Howe Downes, *John S. Sargent: His Life and Work*, Boston: Little, Brown, 1925, opp. p. 88; Evan Charteris, *John Sargent*, New York: Scribner's, 1927, p. 282; The Art Institute of Chicago, *A Century of Progress: Exhibition of Paintings and Sculpture*, 1 June-1 November 1933, no. 480; idem, *A Century of Progress: Exhibition of Paintings and Sculpture*, 1 June-1 November 1934, no. 411; New Alexander Gymnasium, Lawrence College, Appleton, Wis., *Loan Exhibition of Oil Paintings at Lawrence College*, 22 September-4 October 1937, no. 6; San Francisco, *Golden Gate International Exposition: Historical American Paintings*, 18 February-29 October 1939, no. 20; Milwaukee Art Institute, *Nineteenth Century American Masters*, 20 February-28 March 1948, no. 36; Charles Merrill Mount, *John Singer Sargent: A Biography*, New York: Norton, 1955, p. 445; Donelson F. Hoopes, *The Private World of John Singer Sargent*, Corcoran Gallery of Art, Washington, D.C., 18 April-14 June 1964, no. 15; Richard Ormond, *John Singer Sargent: Paintings, Drawings, Watercolors*, New York and Evanston: Harper & Row, 1970, p. 30; Michael Quick, *American Expatriate Painters of the Late Nineteenth Century*, Dayton Art Institute, 4 December 1976-16 January 1977, no. 43; Musée Toulouse-Lautrec, Albi, France, *Trésors Impressionistes du Musée de Chicago*, 27 June-31 August 1980, no. 55.

58 Venetian Women in the Palazzo Rezzonico, ca. 1880

Oil on canvas, 17¾ × 25 in. (45.1 × 63.5 cm)
Signed, lower right: *SARGENT*
Peter G. Terian
Color plate

A few years after the fact, Henry James recalled the paintings by Sargent exhibited at the Grosvenor Gallery in London in May of 1882, two of which had been executed in Venice in 1880:

There stands out in particular, as a pure gem, a small picture exhibited at the Grosvenor, representing a small group of Venetian girls of the lower class, sitting in gossip together one summer's day in the big, dim hall of a shabby old palazzo. The shutters let in a chink of light; the scagliola pavement gleams faintly in it; the whole place is bathed in a kind of transparent shade; the tone of the picture is dark and cool. The girls are vaguely engaged in some very humble household work; they are counting turnips or stringing onions, and these small vegetables, enchantingly painted, look as valuable as magnified pearls.[1]

It is probable that *Venetian Women in the Palazzo Rezzonico* is the painting to which James alludes. Less well-known than the paintings of the bead stringers, this and several other Venetian works with onion stringers as subjects clearly constitute a second important set of interiors. Two others, *Stringing Onions* (cat. no. 59) and *Venetian Onion Seller* (private collection), also include prominent strings of "magnified pearls." When looking at the onions in this picture or at the *Octopi on Deck of Fishing Smack* (1875, private collection), one wonders at Sargent's restraint in not doing more still-life pictures.[2] These passages are marvels of just that transformation of the valueless into the priceless that is the essence of still life.

In several ways this painting is reminiscent of the *Venetian Bead Stringers* (cat. no. 55), in which a major standing figure turns obliquely away from the viewer and toward a group of seated women, with a series of apertures beyond. The setting is different, however; in this case it is probable that the Rezzonico, in which Sargent rented a studio, is the site, the balcony in the background overlooking the first bend in the Grand Canal.

At the same time that Sargent was renting space in the palace, the poet Robert Browning was renting a suite of rooms – he eventually bought the building in 1888. In October of 1880, perhaps the very month that Sargent painted this work, the poet wrote to a friend of witnessing daybreak from his room in the Rezzonico:

Every morning at six I see the sun rise; far more wonderfully, to my mind, than his famous setting which everybody glorifies. My bedroom window commands a perfect view; the still, gray lagune, the few sea-gulls flying, the islet of San Giorgio in deep shadow and the clouds in a long purple rock behind which a sort of spirit of rose burns up till presently all the rims are on fire with gold, and last of all the orb sends before it a long column of its own essence apparently; so my day begins.[3]

But this is the poet's Venice, a Venice that had no allure for Sargent. His subject pictures dwell on small matters invested with meaning or beauty only by the artist's rendering of them. His women take their ease here, reclining

57

58

on the bare floor or leaning against the walls as Sargent's *Daughters of Edward Darley Boit* (Museum of Fine Arts, Boston) sit and lean without regard for proprieties. Back-lit by the wide arching windows, these women are reduced in part to silhouette while a "transparent shade" suffuses the enormous, empty space. James continues his discussion of this work with his admiration for the rightness of the figures:

The figures are extraordinarily natural and vivid; wonderfully light and fine is the touch by which the painter evokes all the small familiar Venetian realities . . . and keeps the whole thing free from that element of humbug which has ever attended most attempts to reproduce the Italian picturesque.[4]
And indeed one can judge from a quick survey of contemporary works that Sargent knew much of the "humbug" picturesque and sought consciously to avoid it.

This work and *A Venetian Interior* (Sterling and Francine Clark Art Institute) are signed eccentrically with "SARGENT" in printed capitals rather than script letters. This cousinship may place the pair as products of a single season and as the two exhibited in London in the spring of 1882.

1. James, p. 689.
2. David Sellin, *Americans in Brittany and Normandy, 1860-1910,* (Phoenix: The Phoenix Art Museum, 1982), p. 136, no. 13.
3. Whiting, p. 407.
4. James, p. 689.

Provenance: David Nisinson Fine Art, New York, New York

59

59   Stringing Onions, ca. 1882
Oil on canvas, 17 × 13 in. (43.2 × 33 cm)
Signed and inscribed, upper left:
To my friend Miss R____son [Robinson?] *John S. Sargent*
Private collection
Color plate

Stringing Onions picks up the subject of *Venetian Women in the Palazzo Rezzonico* (cat. no. 58) but places the figures in a more vernacular, less spatially complex setting reminiscent of that in a third, larger work, *Venetian Onion Seller* (private collection).[1] In this smaller, gem-like study, globular onions hang from the shutter, spill across the sunlit window ledge, and scatter about the floor. The standing woman attentively weaves her strand of onions while a girl, seated on a low stool against the far wall, cradles a particularly large example in her hands. The subject is a modest one, yet it affords Sargent the opportunity to study the action of bright sunlight intruding into a shaded interior inhabited only by handsome women and their even handsomer onions.

Of these genre pictures as a whole, Sargent's contemporary Royal Cortissoz wrote that he felt they were "casual . . . if not exactly unstudied, . . . chiefly admirable for the spontaneity and almost artless vivacity with which they record impressions of things seen."[2] The writer's judgment seems as apt today. Certainly the figures' poses are "casual," the one leaning against the wall, the other concentrating on the bright, round onions that weigh down the skirt in her small lap. Sargent in-

jects the element of spontaneity here, as elsewhere in his work, with fluid visible brushwork, most notably in the gathered, pale pink apron of the upright figure and in the slashing, impasto white on her blouse.

This work, like so many other Sargent paintings, is inscribed (in this case probably to Mary Robinson), suggesting its donative function. It is interesting to speculate on Sargent's intentions in creating and (apparently) giving these works; were they in fact 'private' works, painted in a different spirit from that of the commissioned and speculative paintings? Evidence suggests otherwise. Not only are 'gift' pictures indistinguishable from the other genre pictures in manner, subject, and approach, they are inconsistently so marked. Similarly, these friendly inscriptions seem often to record a trade of the artwork for goods or services. Of the genre pictures, four bear donative inscriptions: this painting, the unfinished *The Bead Stringers of Venice* (cat. no. 56), *Venetian Interior* (Sterling and Francine Clark Art Institute), and *Venetian Onion Seller* (private collection). This last work is inscribed "A Monsieur Lemercier/Souvenir Amicale," yet, as Lemercier was Sargent's landlord in Paris, it is fair to assume this his "friendly token" was also partial settlement for studio rent.[3] *The Bead Stringers of Venice* was evidently a discarded work specifically requested by the recipient. On the other hand, other "subject pictures" that we know to have been gifts or barter items bear no donative inscription: *Venetian Bead Stringers* (cat. no. 55) was given as a wedding present to fellow painter, J. Carroll Beckwith, yet it is uninscribed; similarly, neither *A Street in Venice* (cat. no. 52), evidently a gift to J. Nic-

60

olopoulo, the Greek Minister to France, nor the pair,
Venetian Water Carriers (cat. no. 53) and *Venetian Glass
Workers* (cat. no. 57), paintings given in exchange for a
piano, bear notations.[4] One is tempted to conclude from
such evidence that Sargent's gift and barter "subject pictures" only became such at the point of exchange, and
that they received bestowal inscriptions inconsistently
on the whim of the artist or at the request of the recipient. A complete study of Sargent's donative inscriptions
in this context would yield useful insights into his patronage networks and his basic career decisions.

1. Illustrated in *Maestri Americani della Collezione Thyssen-Bornemisza*
(Lugano and Milan: Electa International, 1983), pp. 91, 178.
2. Cortissoz, p. 520.
3. Mount chronicles similar instances of portrait "commissions" for
Sargent's restaurateur and landlord's family during these lean years
("New Discoveries," p. 313); letter from K. Hirago to Mr. Dlogosz of
8 April 1951, courtesy Thyssen-Bornemisza Collection, FO + 95, Frick
Art Reference Library.
4. Kotik and Nash, p. 309; Sterling and Francine Clark Art Institute
records; letter from John S. Sargent to Charles H. Pepper, courtesy Macbeth Gallery, Worcester Museum and Art Institute of Chicago records.

Provenance: Harold W. Parsons; Newhouse Galleries, New York; Mrs.
Elizabeth R. Fisher, Los Angeles; Mrs. G. B. Oxnam, Scarsdale, N.Y.; by
descent to an anonymous owner; sale, Christie, Manson & Woods, New
York, 3 June 1983

Exhibition History and Bibliography: *Art News* 28 (15 March 1930).

60   An Interior in Venice, 1899
Oil on canvas, 25½ × 31¾ in. (64.8 × 80.7 cm)
Signed, lower left: *John S. Sargent 1899*
Royal Academy of Arts, London

An Interior in Venice, painted two decades after Sargent

began to chronicle Venetian interiors (see cat. nos.
54-59), is very different in subject, composition, and tone
from the earlier paintings. While they recall the conventions of genre painting, this evokes the British
conversation piece, even to the tea equipage. Although
most of the genre works from the decade of the eighties
are set in palaces, the figures inhabit the broad hallways,
bare spaces furnished scantily or roughly; they are Venetians, and they are, however languidly, working. Here we
observe Anglo-American expatriate gentry ensconced in
the rococo dignity of "the [Palazzo] Barbaro with its exquisite salon, by far the most beautiful in Europe."[1]
A Gothic palace on the Grand Canal embellished by
Tiepolo, this setting – carefully recorded a few years later
by Walter Gay (*Palazzo Barbaro*, Museum of Fine Arts,
Boston) – gives us a glimpse of a very different aspect of
fin de siècle Venice.

In the lower right of *An Interior in Venice*, Daniel Curtis,
a Bostonian whose family was distantly related to
Sargent's own, leafs through a folio volume; his wife,
British by birth and the subject of a small portrait head by
Sargent two decades earlier (1882, Spencer Museum of
Art, Lawrence, Kansas), observes the viewer. In the middle distance on the left their son Ralph, an artist, a friend,
and a contemporary of Sargent's, sits nonchalantly on a
large gilt table among the objets d'art. His wife, Lisa,
heiress to the Colt firearm fortune, attends to the tea
things.[2] Around them stucco putti, exquisite glass
chandeliers, and comfortable antique furniture are
discernible in the darkness. Expatriate from the 1860s,
the family had occupied a portion of the Palazzo Barbaro
from 1878, purchasing it in 1885.[3] The Curtises were hos-
pitable to a wide circle of Americans notable in the arts:

61

Sargent made extended visits, and Isabella Stewart Gardner, the prodigious Boston collector, regularly rented the establishment.[4] Henry James came often and immortalized the building as the "great gilded shell" in which Milly Theale's odd courtship and necessary betrayal take place in *The Wings of the Dove* (1902). For Sargent it was clearly more than a convenient, handsome hostelry; we sense more than courtesy in his note of May 1898 to his hostess: "The Barbaro is a sort of Fontaine de Jouvence, for it sends one back twenty years, besides making the present seem remarkably all right."[5]

Yet in spite of the memory-filled, elegant, and comfortable atmosphere of the palace, Sargent has made of it a very uncomfortable picture. The raking light from the windows on the right flatters neither of the older people; the one is illuminated primarily on the back of his head, the other boldly reduced to a demi-visage by the glare. But more significantly, these two figures are sliced horizontally, as though accidentally, by the bottom edge of the canvas. None of the genre pictures from the 1880s exhibits this arbitrary truncation of their human subjects, a phenomenon we observe, however, in two other later figurative Venetian works: *Campo Behind the Scuolo di San Rocco, Venice* (private collection) and *Venetian Interior* (Philadelphia Museum of Art). All three appear to relate to Sargent's early twentieth-century experiments in slicing architectural forms.[6]

According to Sargent's early biographer, Evan Charteris, Mrs. Curtis, for whom the work was intended, disliked the picture.[7] When it was exhibited in London in 1900, however, the critics were enthusiastic, responding perhaps to the aptness of the composition to its period as well as to its painterly qualities.[8] One dissident was Sargent's friend and rival, Whistler, who objected here, as always, to Sargent's abrupt and apparently arbitrary use of tone and light, so unlike Whistler's own:

Sargent is a good fellow, I like him extremely – but – really. . . . A smudge for a nose, a great brown shadow anywhere, anything at all that happened to be on his palette, even to pure white squeezed out of his tube. It is preposterous. And the little picture [An Interior in Venice] – smudge everywhere. Think of the finish, the delicacy, the elegance, the repose of a little Terborgh or Metsu – these were masters who could paint chandeliers and the rest, and what a difference![9]

Half portrait, half 'situation' piece, this hybrid aims less at Whistlerian or Metsuian delicacy than at an image congruent with a sense of modernity. As one perceptive critic put it, the subject is a "great rococo room of a Venetian palace occupied by ordinary modern people."[10] In its own way, this image is the counterpart of the other earlier Interiors in which the architectural shell of the past provides the context for an incongruent human present. Declined by Mrs. Curtis, *An Interior in Venice* was selected by Sargent to be his Diploma picture for the Royal Academy.

1. F. Hopkinson Smith, *Gondola Days* (Boston: Houghton Mifflin, 1902), p. 157.
2. Ormond, p. 251; Tharp, p. 201.
3. Leon Edel, *Henry James: The Middle Years: 1882-1895* (New York: Avon Books, 1962), pp. 227-228.
4. Tharp, pp. 146-147, 160-161, 182, 185, 200.
5. Quoted in Ormond, p. 251.
6. Illustrated in Lee Hall, "American Individualism," *Arts Magazine* 42, no. 7 (May 1968), p. 49.
7. Charteris, p. 163.
8. Quoted in William Howe Downes, *John S. Sargent: His Life and Work* (Boston: Little, Brown, 1925), pp. 189-190.
9. Elisabeth Robins Pennell and Joseph Pennell, *The Whistler Journal* (Philadelphia: J. B. Lippincott Co., 1921), p. 39.
10. Quoted in Downes, p. 190.

Provenance: Diploma Work, 1897

Exhibition History and Bibliography: Royal Academy of Arts, London, Diploma Catalogue, no. 102; Royal Academy of Arts, London, 1900, no. 729; Royal Cortissoz, "John S. Sargent," *Scribner's Magazine* 34

(November 1903), p. 527; Elisabeth Robins Pennell and Joseph Pennell, *The Whistler Journal*, Philadelphia: J. B. Lippincott Co., 1921, p. 39; Nathaniel Pousette-Dart, *John Singer Sargent*, New York: Frederick A. Stokes, 1924; Hamilton Minchin, "Some Early Recollections of Sargent," *Contemporary Review* 127 (June 1925), p. 743; William Howe Downes, *John S. Sargent: His Life and Work*, Boston: Little, Brown, 1925, pp. 30, 55, 189-190; Royal Academy of Arts, London, *Winter Exhibition of the Works of the Late John Singer Sargent*, 1926, no. 14, p. 101; Evan Charteris, *John Sargent*, New York: Scribner's, 1927, pp. 57, 163, 285; Charles Merrill Mount, *John Singer Sargent: A Biography*, New York: Norton, 1955, p. 448; Russell-Cotes Art Gallery, Bournemouth, *Diploma Works from the Royal Academy*, 1957, no. 840; Donelson F. Hoopes, *The Private World of John Singer Sargent*, Corcoran Gallery of Art, Washington, D.C., 18 April-14 June 1964, no. 63; Nelson Lansdale, "John Singer Sargent: His Private World," *American Artist* 28 (November 1964), p. 81; Royal Academy of Arts, London, Winter Exhibition, 1968, no. 414; Jeremy Maas, *Victorian Painters*, London: Barrie and Jenkins, 1969, p. 222; Richard Ormond, "The Diploma Paintings, from 1840 Onwards," *Apollo* 89 (January 1969), pp. 60-61; Richard Ormond, *John Singer Sargent: Paintings, Drawings, Watercolors*, New York and Evanston: Harper & Row, 1970, pp. 63, 70, 251, and pl. 90; Columbus Gallery of Fine Arts, *British Art, 1890-1928*, 5 February-7 March 1971, no. 91; Wildenstein and Co., London, *Venice Rediscovered*, 8 November-15 December 1972, no. 37; South London Art Gallery, *Edwardian Artists*, 1973, no. 90; Wildenstein and Co., London, *American Artists in Europe, 1800-1900*, 1976-1977, no. 62; Royal Scottish Academy, Edinburgh, *150th Anniversary Exhibition*, 1976; Grey Art Gallery and Study Center, New York University, *Walter Gay: A Retrospective*, 16 September-1 November 1980; Great Linford Art Centre, *Royal Academy Retrospective*, 1982; International Exhibitions Foundation, Washington, D.C., *Paintings from the Royal Academy: Two Centuries of British Art*, 1982, no. 41.

62

61 A Note (Libreria, Venice), ca. 1902-1908
Watercolor on paper, 13⅜ × 19¾ in. (34 × 50.2 cm) (sight)
The Fine Arts Museums of San Francisco, Achenbach Foundation for Graphic Arts. Gift of George Hopper Fitch

The use of serial images that we find in Sargent's Venetian work of the last two decades of the nineteenth century is continued, with a difference, in the early twentieth. Instead of his bead stringers or his onion stringers, we find two dramatic architectural series: the Libreria and the Salute, executed primarily in watercolor.

This image, *A Note*, appears to have always been so named, and aptly so. Not without a trace of wit, its nomination makes no allusion to a "Nocturne" or even a "Harmony," Whistler's preferred terms – just to a single, vibrant note. It presents itself modestly then, and as something both whole and simultaneously a fragment of a larger composition. The image depicted is a glimpse of the statue of St. Theodore on his crocodile and the upper section of the narrow Bacino façade of Jacopo Sansovino's Libreria, a building described in the Baedecker guide at this period as "perhaps the most magnificent secular edifice in Italy."[1]

Sargent views the Libreria from a standing position on the narrow docks used by the gondoliers, for this section of the Molo is a gondola cab-stand. If we can trust his topographical accuracy (a fragment of San Marco 'should' be visible just left of the column of St. Theodore but is omitted), the watercolor was painted between 1902, when the Campanile fell, and about 1908, when it was sufficiently rebuilt to appear above the balustrade in the background. The fact that *A Note* predates 1909 is evident in its inclusion in the watershed purchase that year by The Brooklyn Museum of eighty-three Sargent watercolors.

A Note is unusual in Sargent's oeuvre in two respects. First, the composition is selected to suppress our sense of deep complex space, focusing on a two-dimensional pattern of repetitive façade parallel to the picture plane. Second, because Sargent's subject is a white marble building, he has – and we suspect that this was the primary artistic problem he perceived here – described the building entirely in negative terms. The structure has been carefully ruled and marked in graphite, but the pigment is applied almost entirely to describe the voids and intervals between architectural features or the shadows they cast. The building itself is described primarily with white paper.

Beneath the molding that appears at the bottom edge of the image, Sargent had begun to paint a course of triglyphs and metopes that separates this story from the one below. They are in deep shade and are rendered in gray jarring tonally with the rest of the image, a fact that Sargent quickly perceived, as he drew a line at the base of the visible molding and noted "to be cut off." Fortunately, the sheet was not cut, and we have this modest (and unique) evidence of Sargent composing his 'sliced' views with a knife.

1. Karl Baedecker, *Northern Italy* (Leipzig: Karl Baedecker, Publisher, 1913), p. 359.

Provenance: Sold by the artist to The Brooklyn Museum, 1909; sold by The Brooklyn Museum to Knoedler's, New York, 1926; bought by George Hopper Fitch from Knoedler's, 1956; given by George Hopper Fitch to the Achenbach Foundation for Graphic Arts, 1976

Exhibition History and Bibliography: M. Knoedler and Co., New York, *Sargent Watercolors*, February 1909; Brooklyn Institute of Arts and Sciences; The Cleveland Museum of Art, *Fourth Exhibition of Watercolors and Pastels*, 16 February–14 March 1927; The Fine Arts Museums of San Francisco, Achenbach Foundation for Graphic Arts, *Recent Acquisitions, 1976–1977*, 27 August–23 October 1977.

62 The Library in Venice
Watercolor and pencil with white gouache on paper,
22⅜ × 17¾ in. (56.8 × 45.1 cm)
National Gallery of Art. Ailsa Mellon Bruce Collection, 1970

"As you know," Sargent wrote to a friend in 1920, "enormous views and huge skys do not tempt me."[1] What clearly did tempt him were small views radically perceived and artfully depicted. This second view of the Libreria shows an even smaller section of the elegant building than *A Note* (cat. no. 61); it is seen from a slightly oblique angle against a clear patch of blue sky. The artist's interest focuses on the round-headed aperture flanked by two lower rectangular sections, a window known elsewhere as a 'Venetian' window. Sargent's fascination with the sixteenth-century building leads him in this instance to explore its ornament with more descriptive and suggestive detail than we find in most of his architectural watercolors. Very close in subject to *A Note*, it is, nevertheless, a much more three-dimensional, plastic rendering of the marble structure. The slightly oblique angle, the inclusion of the lower, deeply shadowed cove and frieze, and the more explicit rendering of the architectural features give depth and substance where *A Note* focuses on overall two-dimensional pattern.

A Note and *The Library in Venice* also exhibit different aspects of Sargent's versatile technique. Although the crisp, ruled underdrawing is virtually identical in manner in the two works, the handling of the watercolor medium differs. The former is more dependent on washes and wetter, quicker strokes than is the latter, which includes several passages where a dry, thin brush articulates detail over a more generalized wash. The columns here are rendered in white paper as in the other image, but in this instance the short balustrade is described in opaque gouache layered over the dark wash of the aperture.

Because his forms are so crisp, his formatting so ahistorical, and his rendering so analytical, Sargent's contemporaries spoke of his work as "unemotional" and "passionless."[2] And recent critics have suggested that Sargent's watercolors were "painted in one session with no afterthoughts," yet the subtle shift in composition and level of detail between these two images suggest the pressure of important, even passionate, afterthoughts.[3] It is, in fact, a characteristic instance of Sargent's reinterpreting and rethinking an architectural subject. Sargent is known to have returned to the same subject on different trips to the city, so it is difficult to determine whether the observable differences represent immediate revision or another expedition altogether.

1. Quoted in Ormond, p. 69.
2. "Studio Talk," *The International Studio* 40, no. 160 (June 1910), p. 307; Catherine Beach Ely, "Sargent as a Watercolorist," *Art in America* 11, no. 2 (February 1923), p. 98.
3. *American Artists in Europe 1800–1900*, exh. cat. (Liverpool: Walker Art Gallery, 1976–1977), p. 25.

Provenance: Sale, Christie, Manson, & Woods, London, 24 July 1925, no. 11, contents of the artist's residence and studio

Exhibition History and Bibliography: The Cleveland Museum of Art, *10th Annual Exhibition of Watercolors and Pastels*, 10 January–12 February 1933.

63 The Piazzetta, Venice, ca. 1904
Watercolor on paper, 13½ × 21⅛ in. (34.3 × 53.6 cm)
Signed, lower left: *John S. Sargent*
The Trustees of The Tate Gallery

A very different painting from *A Note* (cat. no. 61), *The Piazzetta, Venice* portrays the lower section of the same building from almost the same prospect. However, instead of standing, Sargent is seated in a moored gondola. Although many artists mimicked the gondola prospect, Sargent was the one artist who consistently used it, announcing the fact through the inclusion of his prow or stern in this and other images (see cat. nos. 64, 72, 81).

The painting is eccentrically named, for the Piazzetta, that strip of open space between the Libreria and the Doge's Palace, is directly ahead of us but scarcely visible from this low prospect. A jumbled cluster of figures suggests, in the sketchiest way, the busy site. Sargent includes the bottom of the column of St. Theodore, but he has displaced the buildings at the far end of the Piazzetta, eliminating the clock tower, interjecting instead the misplaced, single column bearing the lion of St. Mark against a clear blue sky. Below this void and across most of the picture surface he has rendered the dusky, soaring forms of gondolas.

Washed in gray-purple, the vacant boats read as black hulls against the bright, bare-paper marble of the building. Blacker than the gondolas are the voids of the archways with their sheltering protection from the sun. The work includes a wide variety of watercolor techniques, notably the introduction of resist in the capitals of the pilasters. In the water, broad washes are overlaid by abrupt calligraphic strokes. Particularly characteristic of Sargent is the treatment of the crooked mooring posts. Their color shifts not as the result of a local color change or reflected color, but in response to the color they are silhouetted against, for instance, in the middle example, shading from violet against the white building to light brown against the deep purple boat.

Quite startling in its composition, *The Piazzetta, Venice* is, nevertheless, an image more readily grasped than *A Note* (cat. no. 61) or *The Library in Venice* (cat. no. 62). Here the horizon line is located at mid-page, and the vanishing point is 'visible' within the painting. We have a 'footing', eccentric as it is, rather than the more abstract aerial prospect of these two more radical companion works.

63

Provenance: Presented by Lord Duveen, 1919

Exhibition History and Bibliography: Possibly exhibited at Carfax Galleries, April 1905; Royal Watercolour Society, Summer 1914, no. 38; W. T. Whitley, *The Art Collections of the Nation (Studio Special Number)*, 1920, p. 107; Birmingham City Museum and Art Gallery, England, *Exhibition of Works by John Singer Sargent, R.A., 1856-1925*, 25 September-18 October 1964, no. 80; Mary Chamot, Dennis Farr, and Martin Butlin, *Tate Gallery Catalogues: The Modern British Paintings, Drawings and Sculpture*, 2 vols., London: Oldbourne Press for the Tate Gallery, 1964, vol. 2, no. 3408.

64 **Bridge of Sighs,** ca. 1902 or 1904
Watercolor on paper, heightened with gouache,
10 × 14 in. (25.3 × 35.5 cm)
The Brooklyn Museum. Special Subscription

Lord Byron begins the fourth canto of *Childe Harold's Pilgrimage* with the lines "I stood in Venice, on the Bridge of Sighs; /A palace and a prison on each hand," aptly summing up the paradox of Venice's historic reputation – a city of luxurious palaces and oppressive social institutions. For Byron, as for later Anglo-American generations who followed in his wake, the city represented both supreme human achievement and reprehensible clandestine authority asserting the good of the state over the possibility of individual identity and achievement. For him as for others, architecture stood in for, or re-enacted, historic human reality. Writers tended to dwell on the darker side of the historic record, using such specific structures as "Desdemona's House" or the Bridge of Sighs to prompt their imaginations. American painters, on the other hand, avoided the Byronic posture, neither rendering historical tableaux nor portraying grimly suggestive structures. In spite of its prominent position, dramatically visible from the Ponte della Paglia, the Bridge of Sighs was almost never painted by Americans.

Sargent is the exception; he paints the scene from

water level, lifting the sunstruck arch of the enclosed, faintly humanoid bridge high on the sheet. He has chosen a horizontal format and uses it to give us a long look at the dark mass of the sixteenth-century prison. Against the wet washes that describe the building's somber walls he interjects a pair of parasoled women, swiftly rowed toward the Ponte della Paglia and the Bacino by white-clad, yellow-sashed gondoliers. This group is rendered in body color, standing out dramatically from the deep violet prison walls. With this one swift stroke, the introduction of a figurative group into an architectural watercolor (an unusual move for Sargent), he modifies the ominous presence and reputation of the bridge. For their own part, we can be confident that the ladies have experienced the prescribed shiver: "You look up, shuddering as you trace the outlines of the fatal Bridge of Sighs. For a moment all is dark. Then you glide into a sea of opal, of amethyst and sapphire."[1]

1. F. Hopkinson Smith, *Gondola Days* (Boston: Houghton Mifflin, 1897), p. 5.

Provenance: Sold by the artist to The Brooklyn Museum, 1909

Exhibition History and Bibliography: Carfax Gallery, London 1908; M. Knoedler and Co., New York, exhibition and sale of Sargent watercolors, February 1909, no. 13; Carnegie Institute, Pittsburgh, *Winslow Homer and John Singer Sargent: An Exhibition of Water Colors*, 1-27 November 1917, no. 25; Copley Society, Boston, *Paintings in Water Color by Winslow Homer, John S. Sargent, Dodge MacKnight*, 5-22 March 1921, no. 61; William Howe Downes, *John Singer Sargent: His Life and Work*, Boston: Little, Brown, 1925, p. 266; Berkshire Museum, Pittsfield, Mass., *Watercolors by J. S. Sargent*, February 1944, no. 11; Donelson F. Hoopes, *Sargent Watercolors*, New York: Watson-Guptill, 1970, p. 54, pl. 55; Sarah Faunce, *Homer and Sargent: Watercolors, Prints, and Drawings*, The Brooklyn Museum, 12 July-27 August 1972, no. 58; Davis and Long Co., New York, *Masterpieces of American Painting from the Brooklyn Museum*, 30 April-29 May 1976, no. 32; The Brooklyn Museum, *American Watercolors and Pastels from the Museum Collection*, 3 July-19 September 1976; Union League Club, New York, *American Watercolor Treasures: A Tribute to the Brooklyn Museum*, 1-30 November 1977; Carter Ratcliff, *John Singer Sargent*, New York: Abbeville Press, 1982, pl. 331.

64

65

65 The Salute, Venice

Watercolor over pencil on paper, 20 × 14 in.
(50.8 × 35.6 cm)
Inscribed with gray ink on reverse, upper left:
147/35/The Salute/Venice/by J. S. Sargent; annotated in
pencil: *ES* or *S3*, and in red chalk: *W/16*
Yale University Art Gallery. Christian A. Zabriskie Fund
Color plate

In an act of gratitude for relief from a devastating plague,
the people of Venice commissioned Baldassare Longhena
in 1631 to build a church, Santa Maria della Salute, on
the most prominent site in the city. The exuberantly Baroque, octagonal building was finished fifty years later,
its dramatic domes buttressed by rolling volutes, its skyline punctuated by attendant towers; almost immediately it became a favorite subject for painters. Sargent,
who in his Venetian architectural studies was drawn
to Renaissance and Baroque monuments, returned repeatedly to the Salute and to the neighboring Dogana
(Custom House). His studies differ from those of his predecessors and contemporaries in their cryptically sliced
and partial compositions. "No one," the French artist,
Edgar Degas, had observed, "has ever done monuments
or houses from below, from beneath, up close, as one
sees them going by on the streets."[1] It was a challenge
Sargent enthusiastically, if unwittingly, picked up.

One of seven views of the Salute and the Dogana included here, *The Salute, Venice* takes a view of the church
from beneath in a manner we have come to identify as
distinctly Sargentesque.[2] In *A Note* (cat. no. 61), *The Library in Venice* (cat. no. 62), and *Venice: La Dogana* (cat.
no. 69), we look up at a small but telling fragment of
marble structure which fills the visual field. But, in fact,
the matter is more complex, for in both the Libreria
paintings and this, Sargent is far enough away from the
structure to easily, comfortably, view it whole; yet he
zeros in on a fragment, willfully ignoring the architect's
overall composition and artificially divorcing the part
from the whole. The strategy is not unlike that which
Georgia O'Keeffe was to employ when she greatly enlarged botanical fragments to the point at which they
took on abstract qualities. Part of the decontextualizing

process for both artists is the elimination of a horizon
line or a vanishing point from the visual field, a loss that
we experience subtly, find disorienting, and identify as
characteristically modern.

As in the very different genre works of the 1880s,
Sargent in *The Salute, Venice* has narrowly restricted his
palette. But here, rather than the somber tones of the
oils, transparent blue and brown provide his basic vocabulary. Combined and separately they describe with wash
and stroke the brilliant light and elaborate detail on this
white building. Like an enormous oculus, the thermal
window in the center arrests our attention with its
brown-blue density; the angels, volutes, and staccato
dentils hover suggestively above this cyclopean presence. Two facets of the octagonal building are visible
here, progressing obliquely on separate trajectories; the
whole composition takes on a life of its own, vibrantly
independent of the historic, associational, and visual
facts of the church as a whole.

1. Theodore Reff, ed., *The Notebooks of Edgar Degas: A Catalogue of the
Thirty-eight Notebooks in the Bibliothèque Nationale and Other Collections*,
2 vols. (Oxford: Clarendon Press, 1976), vol. 1, pp. 134-135.
2. Fronia E. Wissman, "Sargent's Watercolor Views of Santa Maria
della Salute," *Yale University Art Gallery Bulletin* 37, no. 2 (Summer
1979), p. 16.

Provenance: Reine Pitman, London; Gertrude Stein Gallery, New York

Exhibition History and Bibliography: Gerald W. R. Ward, ed., *The Eye of*

the Beholder: Fakes, Replicas and Alterations in American Art, Yale University Art Gallery, New Haven, 14 May-10 July 1977, no. 73; Theodore E. Stebbins, Jr., "Collecting American Art for Yale, 1968-1976: A Curatorial Report," Yale University Art Gallery Bulletin 36 (Spring 1977), p. 13; Fronia E. Wissman, "Sargent's Watercolor Views of Santa Maria della Salute," Yale University Art Gallery Bulletin 37 (Summer 1979), pp. 15-19.

1. Quoted in Ratcliff, p. 221.

2. Catalogue of Paintings and Drawings in Water Color (Boston: Museum of Fine Arts, 1949), p. 157.

3. "J.G.," Museum of Fine Arts [Boston] Bulletin 10, no. 57 (June 1912), p. 19.

Provenance: Purchased, Charles Henry Hayden Fund, 1912

Exhibition History and Bibliography: New English Art Club, London, 1907; "The Water-Colors of Edward D. Boit and John S. Sargent," Museum of Fine Arts [Boston] Bulletin 10, no. 57 (June 1912), pp. 18-20; Hôtel de la Chambre Syndicale, Paris, Exposition d'Art Américain, 1923, no. 22; Museum of Fine Arts, Boston, Memorial Exhibition of the Works of the Late John Singer Sargent, 3 November-27 December 1925, no. 61; William Howe Downes, John S. Sargent: His Life and Work, Boston: Little, Brown, 1925, p. 272; Tate Gallery, London, American Painting from the 18th Century to the Present Day, 1946, no. 186; Catalogue of Paintings and Drawings in Water Color, Boston: Museum of Fine Arts, 1949, p. 157; Dartmouth College Art Gallery and Library, Hanover, N.H., Exhibition of Sargent Watercolors, 1950; Society of the Four Arts, Palm Beach, Fla., February 1971.

66 Venice: The Salute, before 1907
Watercolor on paper, 16 × 21 in. (40.7 × 53.3 cm)
Museum of Fine Arts, Boston. The Hayden Collection

In a few cases, Sargent executed watercolors and oil paintings of very similar subjects; the near identity of this work with Santa Maria della Salute (cat. no. 67) provides us with such an instance. In both images, the viewer looks up from the steps beneath the church toward the lower section of the entranceway and the neighboring pavilion of this great octagonal Baroque church. But Sargent shifts his palette, the time of day, and his point of view, as well as the scale and medium in these two paintings, and we can conclude that the watercolor is an independent work, a second interpretation, rather than a study for the oil.

With deft washes of blue and buff-brown, Sargent describes the hard morning light striking the approach steps and giant orders of the church. The underdrawing is crisp and ruled in places but freehand and generalized in others. Over this guide Sargent has applied suggestive, rather than descriptive, strokes of watercolor, depicting particular forms at a precise and fleeting moment. As he once commented, "I can't paint vedutas [views]. I can paint objects."[1] This allegiance to 'objectness' has, for critics, cloaked the interpretive element involved. Sargent is often seen primarily as a depicter of light on form, spontaneously recording facts in a spirit of visual neutrality. Yet his eccentric formatting and insistent return-with-a-difference to the same subject presents us with an artistic sensibility by no means neutral to the object of its attention. The Salute was for Sargent more than a convenient light-struck building on which he could practice the difficulties of describing whiteness on a white sheet; it was a subject close to the hearts of his great predecessors Canaletto, Guardi, and Turner. His will to establish his own interpretation, one congruent with his own era, is evident.

It has often been asserted that Sargent's architectural watercolors – because many bear bestowal inscriptions – were private works, exercises to clear his mind and soul of the social and artistic pressures on him as the premier portraitist of his day, exercises undervalued by the artist. Yet the genre works bear proportionately as many donative inscriptions, and in both cases Sargent seems to have been eager to exhibit his work. Public presentations of his watercolors, which began shortly after he recommenced serious work in the medium, include the Carfax Gallery exhibitions in 1903 and 1905, as well as the New English Art Club exhibition of 1907, in which this work was listed.[2] By 1909, museums were vying for the purchase of whole exhibitions, but the Museum of Fine Arts in Boston had to wait until 1912 before acquiring this and forty-five other watercolors, almost sight-unseen.[3]

67 Santa Maria della Salute, 1904 or 1908
Oil on canvas, 25¼ × 36⅜ in. (64.1 × 92.4 cm)
The Syndics of the Fitzwilliam Museum, Cambridge

The close similarity between this work, Venice: The Salute (cat. no. 66), and a third work at the Johannesburg Art Gallery suggests not so much stages in the development of an idea as Sargent's experimentation with serial images.[1] He exhibits in this concentration on the Salute his cousinship with the French Impressionists, especially Claude Monet, whose Haystacks, Poplars, and Rouen Cathedral series establish the norm for this close scrutiny of a single subject under slightly varying conditions.

The Fitzwilliam painting differs from the Boston watercolor (cat. no. 66) in its size, composition, and palette. It is twice the size of the watercolor; the visual field is shifted sufficiently to the left to encompass the perimeter of the building, and the coloration moves from contrasting blue and buff in the watercolor to a more monochromatic cream and brown with piquant touches of gray-green in the oil painting. But the most significant change occurs in the handling of the sculptural elements. In Sargent's Venetian architectural watercolors, figurative sculpture is handled summarily rather than descriptively (see cat. nos. 61, 62, 65, 69), and Boston's Venice: The Salute is no exception. In the Fitzwilliam painting, on the other hand, the sculptural program within the visual field is carefully inventoried and described. Five figures occupy niches on the visible façade; they are depicted in shades of brown, their attributes, gestures, and drapery highlighted with opaque white in a manner reminiscent of the early seventeenth-century figure studies of Annibale Carracci. This witty appropriation of an Old Master manner within a very clipped and twentieth-century composition is unusual in Sargent's work and singularly successful.

There is both internal and documentary evidence to suggest that Sargent worked from photographs in this and other works.[2] As in the case of Prendergast, it is logical that Sargent used photographs as points of departure and as memory aids for his paintings. The exact role played by photographic images in the work of late nineteenth-century American artists, even in such well-documented cases as that of Thomas Eakins, remains an insufficiently explored field. The significant issue here, however, is not so much whether photographs were employed, but what use Sargent made of them. Most professional architectural photographers active in Italy during this period relied on traditional painterly conventions in arranging their compositions: buildings are whole, horizon lines are low, and the central feature is artfully bracketed by secondary elements.[3] Because of the eccentric formatting of this and related images, one suspects that the professional photograph of this view of the Salute, allegedly in Sargent's studio and which art historian R. H. Wilenski relates to this work, either was taken under the artist's direction or was a fragment of a larger photograph he reformatted to suit his own uses.[4]

1. J. W. Goodison, *Fitzwilliam Museum, Cambridge, Catalogue of Paintings, Vol. 3, British School* (Cambridge: Cambridge University Press, 1977), pp. 215-216.

2. Van Deren Coke, *The Painter and the Photograph from Delacroix to Warhol* (Albuquerque, N.M.: University of New Mexico Press, 1972), p. 204.

3. Wendy M. Watson, *Images of Italy: Photography in the Nineteenth Century* (South Hadley, Mass.: Mount Holyoke College Art Museum, 1980).

4. Coke, p. 204.

Provenance: Sold by the executors of the artist's estate; Christie, Manson & Woods, 24 July 1925, no. 102; bought Martin; Harold, 1st Viscount Rothermere, 1926; given by him to the Museum in that year

Exhibition History and Bibliography: Royal Academy of Arts, London, *Works by the Late John S. Sargent, R.A.*, 1926, no. 22; Evan Charteris, *John Sargent*, New York: Scribner's, 1927, p. 289; Wildenstein and Co., London, *Venice Rediscovered*, 8 November-15 December 1972, no. 39; J. W. Goodison, *Fitzwilliam Museum, Cambridge, Catalogue of Paintings, Vol. 3, British School*, Cambridge: Cambridge University Press, 1977, pp. 215-216; Nottingham University Art Gallery, England, *Queen of Marble and Mud, The Anglo-American Vision of Venice: 1880-1910*, 20 February-20 March 1978, no. 30.

68 Venice, ca. 1903-1912
Watercolor on paper, 9⅞ × 14 in. (25.2 × 35.5 cm)
Signed and inscribed in pencil, lower right: *To my friend Rolshoven/John S. Sargent*
Worcester Art Museum. Gift of Mr. and Mrs. Stuart Riley, Jr.

The steps ascending from the Grand Canal to the wide pavement that sets off Santa Maria della Salute occupy the foreground of *Venice*. Gondolas and fishing boats cluster on the left, while a large, single-funnel steamer occupies the distant horizon. A band of bare white paper between the blue wash of the sky and the blue wash of the Bacino represents the buildings along the Riva, its structures only faintly suggested by a few pale rectangles. On the right, a corner of the Dogana (Custom House) is visible, topped by its golden ball. The weathervane figure of Fortuna that stands atop the globe-orb is abruptly eliminated by the edge of the sheet.

Much less precisely drawn and much more wetly painted than other views of the front of the Salute (cat. nos. 65, 66), this watercolor exhibits an interestingly selective focus. While much of the view has the hazy and generalized look of watercolor washes applied to wet paper, the ball of Fortuna is enlarged and sharply focused as though Sargent wished to mimic the effect of a visitor to the Salute catching a surprised glimpse of the ball from this unusual viewpoint.

It is characteristic of Sargent that our eye level is extremely low, the view apparently random, and the image a composite of seemingly disparate elements. Prendergast's *Rainy Day, Venice* (cat. no. 43) gives us an image of the same steps from a point of view equally eccentric, but very different. Prendergast preferred a high prospect on his subject but he devised strategies to avoid the panoramic view usually associated with that height, often by directing his gaze precipitously down at a slice of the human and architectural action below. Sargent, on the other hand, kept his eye level low, a tendency that helps give his compositions their accidental, deliberately baffling character.

68

This watercolor is inscribed – one of the few in this group so marked – "to my friend Rolshoven," apparently a gift to Sargent's friend and fellow artist, Julius Rolshoven. An enthusiast, like Sargent, for watercolors and for post-Gothic Venice (he made several watercolor studies after Venetian Tiepolos), Rolshoven was an apt recipient for this painting of the Salute steps, the Dogana, and the golden orb of Fortuna.[1] In their admiration for this period of Venetian architecture and design, both artists depart radically from the Ruskinian perspective. While the Salute in John Ruskin's eyes was not totally devoid of proportion, he regarded the Dogana as "a barbarous building of the time of the Grotesque Renaissance, rendered interesting only by its position."[2]

1. *Inventory of American Painting.* Rolshoven at this time was living in Italy near Rome (Quick, p. 126).
2. Arnold Whittick, ed., *Ruskin's Venice* (New York: The Whitney Library of Design, 1976), p. 44.

Provenance: Grand Central Art Galleries, New York; Dr. Loring H. Dodd, Worcester

Exhibition History and Bibliography: Worcester Art Museum, *Annual Report*, 1975, p. 15.

69

69   Venice: La Dogana, ca. 1911
Watercolor on paper, 19¾ × 14 in. (50.2 × 35.5 cm)
Museum of Fine Arts, Boston. The Hayden Collection

Sargent's *Venice: La Dogana* is among the most theatrical of his views of Venice. As in *A Note* (cat. no. 61), *The Library in Venice* (cat. no. 62), and *The Salute, Venice* (cat. no. 65), this watercolor depicts a fragment of one of the city's best-known monuments from below. The view here is a small section of the tower on the Custom House. It occupies the preeminent position opposite the Piazza San Marco at the mouth of the Grand Canal and next to the church of Santa Maria della Salute. A favorite subject with artists, the Dogana and the Salute appear in numerous other works, including the dramatic *Santa Maria della Salute – Sunset* by William S. Haseltine (cat. no. 18). But where Haseltine is careful to explain the relationships of the buildings to one another and to ourselves, Sargent explains nothing except the particular circumstances of the sky, the statue, and the little tower.

Bernardo Falcone's seventeenth-century statue includes two muscular, bronze giants supporting an enormous gilt orb on which stands the allegorical figure of Fortuna. This bronze maiden holds a shield which catches the wind and swivels her from side to side. Her function is twofold: to mark the entrance to the city for arriving vessels, and to indicate – in this most maritime of cities – the direction of the wind for embarking sailors. Sargent's watercolor captures her at a moment of auspicious weather conditions. Silhouetted against an energetic, blue sky which is punctuated by billowing clouds rendered in body color, the statue and tower gesture boldly in the strong sunlight. Pointing up the self-dramatizing element in Venetian design, Sargent gives us here a glimpse of boldly operatic allegory, and simultaneously he suggests a single, caught moment in the observer's experience.

Sargent's perspective underdrawing in *Venice: La Dogana* is careful but not as precise as in some images. The building is rendered in the buff wash and blue shadows familiar from *Venice: The Salute* (cat. no. 66) and other watercolors. Fortuna's bronze is rendered in bright orange, contrasting vividly with the deep blue of the sky. *Venice: La Dogana* is a very different image in technique, point of view, and composition from *Venice* (cat. no. 68) although it portrays the same subject. In the latter painting, however, the gilt ball is an unexplained visual episode; here its enthusiastic but decontextualized description is the primary object of the artist's effort.

Provenance: Purchased, Charles Henry Hayden Fund, 1912

Exhibition History and Bibliography: "The Water-Colors of Edward D. Boit and John S. Sargent," *Museum of Fine Arts* [Boston] *Bulletin* 10, no. 57 (June 1912), pp. 18-20; Museum of Fine Arts, Boston, *Memorial Exhibition of the Works of the Late John Singer Sargent*, 3 November-27 December 1925, no. 51; William Howe Downes, *John S. Sargent: His Life and Work*, Boston: Little, Brown, 1925, p. 272; The Metropolitan Museum of Art, New York, *Memorial Exhibition of the Work of John Singer Sargent*, 4 January-14 February 1926, no. 27; *Catalogue of Paintings and Drawings in Water Color*, Boston: Museum of Fine Arts, 1949, p. 157; Dartmouth College Art Gallery and Library, Hanover, N.H., *Exhibition of Sargent Watercolors*, 1950.

70 Santa Maria della Salute, Venice
Watercolor on paper, 18 × 12 in. (45.8 × 30.5 cm)
Victoria and Albert Museum

The church of Santa Maria della Salute is one of the most recognizable landmarks in Venice. A very frontal building, it faces north across the Grand Canal. It was often painted from the area near the Piazzetta to the east, from the range of hotel-palaces directly across the canal, or from the area of the Accademia Bridge to the west. F. Hopkinson Smith in his *Over a Balcony, View of the Grand Canal, Venice* (cat. no. 82) captures the effect of this western prospect, the domes soaring above the line of palaces along the wide waterway of Venice's principal thoroughfare. None of Sargent's interpretations of the Salute set it into its context in this manner, but few are as radically 'accidental' in their composition as the views from the south, such as *Rigging* (cat. no. 71) and this painting.

In *Santa Maria della Salute* Sargent has placed himself and the observer in a gondola on the Giudecca Canal among the large sailing vessels moored in the deep water behind the Salute. We are dwarfed equally by the looming, brown-black forms of the hulls and the pink-blue presence of the church. Sargent often sought the effect of spontaneity in his painting, but few works seem as rapidly executed as this. His pencil underdrawing is entirely freehand and very generalized, his washes are very wet, and his brush is broad throughout, obliterating all detail. Most dramatically, he has scratched pigment away to describe hawsers and stays with fluid gestural strokes. The technique of this watercolor is worlds apart from that of such tightly detailed images as *The Library in Venice* (cat. no. 62), demonstrating Sargent's wide range and extraordinary versatility. It is significant to note that most of Sargent's wetter, more 'spontaneous' watercolors were executed in a rocking boat, while the tighter, more carefully worked views were made from a land-based, seated position. And few water sites in Venice could be rockier than the Giudecca Canal, a major shipping channel. Sargent once remarked that painting a watercolor was a matter of "making the best of an emergency" as he strove to capture the effect of light, color, and form which struck him as an apt subject.[1] The "emergency" of this situation – the odd conjunction of three vertical elements: the practical construction of the rigging, the natural growth of the cypress trees, and the aesthetic construction of the towers and domes of the Salute – is most aptly captured on a vertical sheet in this abbreviated, calligraphic style.

1. Charteris, p. 95.

Provenance: Presented by Mrs. Ormond and Miss Emily Sargent, sisters of the artist, 1925

Exhibition History and Bibliography: Wildenstein and Co., London, *Venice Rediscovered*, 8 November-15 December 1972, no. 42; Nottingham University Art Gallery, England, *Queen of Marble and Mud, The Anglo-American Vision of Venice: 1880-1910*, 20 February-20 March 1978, no. 29.

70

71 Rigging, ca. 1905-1908
Watercolor on paper, 11⅛ × 18 in. (28.3 × 45.7 cm)
The Brooklyn Museum. Special Subscription

Describing the moored sailing vessels in the Giudecca Canal behind the Salute in 1906, one observer remarked, *The ships lie close together along the quay, ten deep, their masts etched against the sky. . . . A few voices raise from the boats; the hulls creak gently, as if they were talking together; there is a faint plashing of water.*[1]
The nautical character of Venice in the last era of the tall ships was best seen on the Zattere, the broad quay behind the Salute where the confusion of complicated rigging systems was captured by Sargent in this sketchy watercolor painted from a gondola about 1905. As though dwarfing our merely human point of view, the large ocean-going vessel refuses to fit onto the page: the bowsprit disappears to the left while the bulk of the ship continues beyond the edge of the image on the right to a distant, invisible stern. The violet domes of the Salute merge together behind the rigging to form – it appears – a single dome. This illusion by which the mast and ratlines unknowingly modify the noble architecture suggests the quality of Sargent's visual wit.

1. Arthur Symons, "The Waters of Venice," *Scribner's Magazine* 39, no. 4 (April 1906), p. 386.

71

Provenance: Sold by the artist to The Brooklyn Museum, 1909

Exhibition History and Bibliography: M. Knoedler and Co., New York, Exhibition and Sale of Sargent Watercolors, February 1909, no. 9; Catherine Beach Ely, "Sargent as a Watercolorist," *Art in America* 11 (February 1923), pp. 101-102; Pennsylvania Academy of Fine Arts and Philadelphia Water Color Club, *22nd Annual Philadelphia Water Color Exhibition*, 1924, no. 387; William Howe Downes, *John S. Sargent: His Life and Work*, Boston: Little, Brown, 1925, p. 268; Colorado Springs Fine Arts Center, *Exhibition of Water Colors: Homer, Sargent, and Marin*, 7 April-11 June 1947, no. 29; Frederick A. Sweet, *Sargent, Whistler and Mary Cassatt*, The Art Institute of Chicago, 14 January-25 February 1954, no. 72; The Brooklyn Museum, *Homer and Sargent: Watercolors, Prints, and Drawings*, 12 July-27 August 1972, no. 61.

72 Sketching on the Giudecca, ca. 1904

Watercolor and gouache on paper, 14½ × 21 in.
(36.8 × 53.3 cm)
From the collection of the late Lady Richmond

The word "sketching" in the title refers simultaneously to the activity of Sargent executing this work and also to the activity of the male figure in the nearby gondola. The couple has been identified as Jane and Wilfred de Glehn, both artists; they were frequent traveling companions of Sargent's.[1] She was a portraitist, and he, a painter of landscapes and portraits, was Sargent's assistant on the Boston Library mural project.[2] In Sargent's possession at the time of his death were two works by de Glehn, a drawing entitled *Venice* and a painting of the same title, dated 1909, with a donative inscription to Sargent.[3]

Sargent portrays his friends here, in one of the few Venetian watercolors to include figures, "on the Giudecca." It is clear from the size of the vessels that the de Glehns and Sargent are on the Giudecca Canal, not the sleepy Giudecca Island, picturesque haunt of fishermen and their more modest craft. It is summer: the de Glehns are clothed in white and are armed against the sun with

canopy and hats. Impressively dramatic diagonal mooring lines of the large ship on the left sweep across the picture surface and provide anchorage for the smaller craft. From just such a mooring, dwarfed by the large, dark hulls, Sargent painted *Santa Maria della Salute, Venice* (cat. no. 70) and *Rigging* (cat. no. 71). But here he turns his attention to the immediate surroundings: the stern of his own gondola, the de Glehn's craft, and the moored ship whose bowsprit disappears above the edge of the paper, all jumbled and layered in a trajectory marked by the curving mooring lines, and all almost perpendicular to the picture surface.

Although parts of the watercolor – both foreground and background – are executed with great washes of pigment, the de Glehns and their gondola are described in some detail with carefully articulated, layered strokes. The water is a deep blue-green, vivid against the pinks of the far building and the floorboards of Sargent's little vessel. A telling document of artists at work, *Sketching on the Giudecca* is also an arresting, complex image improbably organized around the sweeping line of a homely rope.

1. Lomax and Ormond, p. 96.
2. *American Artists in Europe 1800-1900*, p. 25; *Venice Rediscovered* (London: Wildenstein, 1972), p. 57.
3. Typescript of "Catalogue of Pictures and Watercolour Drawings by J. S. Sargent, R.A. and Works by Other Artists, the Property of the late John Singer Sargent, R.A., D.C.L., LL.D., Removed from 31 and 33 Tite Street, Chelsea, S.W. and from the Studio, 12 The Avenue, Fulham Road, S.W.," Christie, Manson & Woods, 24 and 27 July 1925.

Provenance: William G. Rathbone; his daughter, Lady Richmond; thence by family descent

Exhibition History and Bibliography: *Studio* 90 (15 April 1925), p. 82; Tate Gallery, London, 1926, p. 9; David McKibbin, *Sargent's Boston*, Museum of Fine Arts, Boston, 3 January-7 February 1956, p. 98 (not in exhibition); Birmingham Museum and Art Gallery, England, *Exhibition of Works by John Singer Sargent, R.A.*, 25 September-18 October 1964, no. 60; Richard Ormond, *John Singer Sargent: Paintings, Drawings, Watercolors*, New York and Evanston: Harper & Row, 1970, p. 255 and pl. 106;

72

Wildenstein and Co., London, *Venice Rediscovered*, 8 November-15 December 1972, no. 38; Walker Art Gallery, Liverpool, *American Artists in Europe, 1800-1900*, 14 November 1976-2 January 1977, no. 53; Nottingham University Art Gallery, England, *Queen of Marble and Mud, The Anglo-American Vision of Venice: 1880-1910*, 20 February-20 March 1978, no. 33; James Lomax and Richard Ormond, *John Singer Sargent and the Edwardian Age*, Leeds Art Galleries, 5 April-10 June 1979, no. 83; Coe Kerr Gallery, New York, *John Singer Sargent: His Own Work*, 28 May-27 June 1980, no. 29.

73 Venice, Under the Rialto Bridge, before 1910
Watercolor on paper, 13 × 20½ in. (33 × 52.1 cm)
Museum of Fine Arts, Boston. The Hayden Collection

The most memorable images Sargent made of the sixteenth-century Rialto Bridge are this watercolor and the closely related oil, *The Rialto, Venice* (cat. no. 74). It is a negative image of the bridge, as eccentric in its way as Prendergast's *Market Place, Venice* (cat. no. 47), and each view is typical of the artist's strategy for avoiding the standard, recognizable, lateral view of the well-known structure. Where Prendergast looks down at a fractional and almost unrecognizable section of the bridge, Sargent keeps his point of view low and oblique. From a gondola near the southwestern corner of the bridge, he looks northeast, catching a glimpse of the Fondaco de' Tedeschi, a handsome Renaissance palace once renowned for façades frescoed by Giorgione and Titian. But the principal part of his image records the great arch of the Rialto. As Ruskin recalled, "The shadowy Rialto threw its colossal curve slowly forth . . . that strange curve, so delicate, so adamantine, strong as a mountain cavern, graceful as a bow just bent."[1] For Sargent the "colossal curve" *was* the bridge; the cavernous space below signified the architectural presence above, while also taking on its own curious identity.

The case of *Under the Rialto* and *The Rialto, Venice* (cat. no. 74) appears to be as close an instance as we have of

Sargent's using a Venetian watercolor as a preparatory study for a more finished oil. The composition and color relationships worked out are repeated in the oil, as is the gondola emerging from shadow into the sunlight on the far left. But the fact that Sargent exhibited this work at the Royal Water Colour Society in 1910, before the oil was painted, as well as in 1912, after the oil was executed, suggests that he considered it an autonomous, finished work.[2]

1. John Ruskin, "The Approach to Venice," excerpted from *The Stones of Venice*, *The Crayon* 2, no. 1 (4 July 1855), p. 6.
2. "Exhibited Works by Sargent," typescript in Victoria and Albert Museum Records.

Provenance: Purchased, Charles Henry Hayden Fund, 1912

Exhibition History and Bibliography: Royal Water Colour Society, 1910 and 1912; "The Water-Colors of Edward D. Boit and John S. Sargent," *Museum of Fine Arts* [Boston] *Bulletin* 10, no. 57 (June 1912), pp. 19-20; Hôtel de la Chambre Syndicale, Paris, *Exposition d'Art Américain*, 1923, no. 24; Museum of Fine Arts, Boston, *Memorial Exhibition of the Works of the Late John Singer Sargent*, 3 November-27 December 1925, no. 62; William Howe Downes, *John S. Sargent: His Life and Work*, Boston: Little, Brown, 1925, p. 272; The Metropolitan Museum of Art, New York, *Memorial Exhibition of the Work of John Singer Sargent*, 4 January-14 February 1926, no. 29; Tate Gallery, London, *American Painting from the 18th Century to the Present Day*, 1946, no. 187; *Catalogue of Paintings and Drawings in Water Color*, Boston: Museum of Fine Arts, 1949, pp. 157-158; Dartmouth College Art Gallery and Library, Hanover, N. H., *Exhibition of Sargent Watercolors*, 1950; Donelson F. Hoopes, *The Private World of John Singer Sargent*, Corcoran Gallery of Art, Washington, D.C., 18 April-14 June 1964, no. 120.

74 The Rialto, Venice, ca. 1911
Oil on canvas, 22 × 36 in. (55.9 × 91.5 cm)
Signed, lower left: *John S. Sargent*
Philadelphia Museum of Art. The George W. Elkins
Collection

The Rialto, Venice is closely related to the watercolor
Venice, Under the Rialto Bridge (cat. no. 73), yet there are
significant differences. The painting is nearly double in
size, and a number of important elements have been
added. The emphasis has shifted from the yawning void
of the bridge itself to the busy life that passes beneath its
generous arch. To the single vessel emerging out of the
shadow into the daylight in the watercolor, the artist has
added three gondolas, a skiff, and – in a unique instance
for Sargent – juxtaposed clusters of native Venetians and
visiting elegant ladies. These disparate groups share the
public space and the historic presence of the Rialto; each
pursues its own trajectory, yet, for a moment, both are
caught within the same framework.

The market-bound skiff in the foreground contains a
sleeping youth and two women, reminiscent, in their
posture and treatment, of the genre works Sargent
painted two decades earlier (cat. nos. 52-59). And, as in
those works, Sargent explores here the difficulties of a
dark space into which bright sunlight intrudes from two
different directions, lighting the foreground figures and
backlighting the background figures. The bottom frame
of the canvas bisects the small vessel, abruptly slicing the
near figures in a manner familiar from *An Interior in Venice* of 1899 (cat. no. 60) and related works of that period.

The Rialto, Venice was purchased by the important sec-
ond-generation Philadelphia collector George Elkins
shortly after it was painted, joining significant examples
by Whistler and Homer, as well as a remarkable group of
eighteenth-century English and nineteenth-century
French paintings.[1] Whether Elkins was attracted by its
painterly qualities (such as the bright, sharply contrasting blue and yellow dashes that describe the water), by its

seemingly accidental, truncated, aggressively modern
composition, or by the memory of a scene familiar from
his travels is not known. But the work is notable for its
radical revision of our notion of the Rialto and for its
novel treatment of a picturesque subject.

The little vignette of Venetian fruit boats, which
Sargent focuses on here, was a familiar sight. As one
observer eloquently recorded,
*At evenfall a stream of boats and rafts are seen slowly wending
their way across the Giudecca or along the Riva, bringing the
produce of their gardens from Mazzorbo, from Malamocco and
Palestrina, to the Venetian market. They are among the most
picturesque craft in Venice these market-boats, piled up with
grapes and pomegranates and vegetables, and rowed by
strong-limbed fishermen with bronzed faces or black-eyed
lads in torn blue hose and slouching hats. Sometimes a curly-
headed child lies asleep in the stern, his head resting on a big
cabbage; and I have a vivid remembrance of a brown-faced
maiden . . . who sat throned like a goddess among the fruit-
baskets. The cloud-like masses of her wavy hair were gathered
in loose tresses about her brow . . . and her dark eyes turned
with I know not what dream of yearning . . . while the bark
with its precious freight moved slowly over the green waters. It
was a picture worthy of being painted by the hands of a Millet
or a Costa.*

*These boats are often to be seen on the outskirts of the city
. . . but if you want to study them at your leisure, you must go
to the Rialto at evening . . . as one by one the fruit-laden rafts
come in.*[2]
Sargent's painting captures one small instance of this
daily flow of bounty into Venice; the low western sun in
the background marks the time of day, as the skiff, rowed
by an unseen "black-eyed lad in torn blue hose and
slouching hat" makes its way to the market.

Yoked together in this tableau are the representatives
of three disparate cultures: the bridge which, as surro-
gate for its builders, vividly evokes the Renaissance
builders of Empire, the modern Venetians tied to the
most modest aspects of a preindustrial economy, and the

Anglo-American tourists who come to observe the first
two. One might add a fourth persona here, that of the
artist who, with the analytical eye of an anthropologist,
records the visual facts of the three remarkable and
different cultures before him. There is something
unaccountably uncomfortable in the conjunction of
these two vessels and their occupants. The elegantly
turned-out trio in the far gondola, in their quest for
the historic past and the picturesque present, provide
employment to the Venetians and a market for their
produce, yet they are the least integral to the place.
Pictorially, Sargent suggests this little tension in the
inclusion of the bare-limbed, reclining youth, who basks
among the melons with a kind of social innocence
which, in this context, takes on a wonderful insolence.

1. Fiske Kimball, ''The George W. Elkins Collection,'' *Pennsylvania
Museum Bulletin* 31, no. 168 (November 1935), p. 3.
2. Julia Cartwright, ''The Artist in Venice,'' *The Portfolio* (1884), p. 39.

Provenance: George W. Elkins, Philadelphia

Exhibition History and Bibliography: The Art Institute of Chicago, *13th
Annual Exhibition of American Paintings*, 1917; Pennsylvania Academy of
Fine Arts, Philadelphia, 112th Exhibition, 1917; Philadelphia Museum
of Art, *Catalogue of Paintings in the Elkins Gallery*, 1925, no. 38; William
Howe Downes, *John S. Sargent: His Life and Work*, Boston: Little, Brown,
1925, p. 242; Evan Charteris, *John Sargent*, New York: Scribner's, 1927,
p. 291; ''The George W. Elkins Collection,'' *Pennsylvania Museum Bul-
letin* 31 (November 1935), p. 19; Charles Merril Mount, *John Singer
Sargent: A Biography*, New York: Norton, 1955, p. 450; Donelson F.
Hoopes, *The Private World of John Singer Sargent*, Corcoran Gallery of
Art, Washington, D.C., 18 April-14 June 1964, no. 84.

75 Doorway of a Venetian Palace, ca. 1906-1910
Watercolor and pencil on paper, 23 × 18 in.
(58.4 × 45.7 cm)
Signed and inscribed, lower left: *To my friend Mrs.
Hunter/John S. Sargent*
Westmoreland Museum of Art, Greensburg,
Pennsylvania

Sargent's interest in painting the white marble Renais-

sance and Baroque buildings of Venice extended beyond
the Libreria on the Piazzetta (cat. nos. 61-63) and the
church of Santa Maria della Salute (cat. nos. 65-67) to
include several less well-known structures. In this case
he has elected to describe the lower portion of the Palazzo Balbi on the Grand Canal in bright, early morning
light. Sargent stalked other buildings in this stretch of the
canal at the turn halfway between the Salute and the
Rialto; his *Gondoliers' Siesta* (private collection), for instance, includes a glimpse of the Palazzo Contarini delle
Figure, which faces the Palazzo Balbi across the broad
waterway.

The principal steps of the palace, its wide band of molding, and the deep recesses of doorways and windows are rendered in a broad spectrum of colors ranging from deep violets and blues through bright yellows and browns. As though vying to outdo the brilliant chromatics of the façade, the canal reflects in deep, opaque color the muted orange of the mooring posts and the dense blue of the sky. The colorless, white building and the transparent water take on such a vivid life of their own that the faint areas in which local colors are recorded – the distant rooftops and wooden mooring posts – become negligible in the operatic gesture, hue, and vibrating contrast of mere reflections.

Sargent inscribed this work "To my friend Mrs. Hunter," a close friend whose seventeenth-century home, Hill Hall near Epping Forest, was one of the great pre-war sanctuaries for international musical, literary, and artistic talent. Her guests included William Butler Yeats, Henry James, Auguste Rodin, Bernard Berenson, and the Daniel Curtises (see cat. no. 60).[1] Edith Wharton was also in her circle, and when the cataclysm of the First World War and private reversals altered Mrs. Hunter's fortunes, it was the charitable Mrs. Wharton who came to her assistance.[2] In the pre-war years, she was close to Sargent, and this token of their friendship is particularly apt, for she was an enthusiast for things Italian.

1. R. W. B. Lewis, *Edith Wharton: A Biography* (New York: Harper & Row, 1975), p. 347; Leon Edel, ed., *Henry James: Letters* (Cambridge, Mass.: The Belknap Press of Harvard University Press, 1984), vol. 4, p. 722.
2. Lewis, pp. 508-509.

Provenance: Mrs. Charles Hunter, London; Mrs. Francis F. Garvan, Roslyn, New York; sold Sotheby Parke-Bernet, 10 December 1970, no. 47; bought John J. McDonough, Youngstown, Ohio; sold Sotheby Parke-Bernet, Dr. John J. McDonough Collection, 1978, no. 29; bought The Westmoreland County Museum of Art

Exhibition History and Bibliography: Royal Academy of Arts, London, *Winter Exhibition of the Works of the Late John Singer Sargent*, 1926, p. 107; E. John Bullard, *A Panorama of American Painting: The John J. McDonough Collection*, New Orleans Museum of Art, 18 April-8 June 1975, no. 50; The Westmoreland County Museum of Art, Greensburg, Pa., *Catalogue of the Permanent Collection*, 1978, p. 123, pl. 13; Coe Kerr Gallery, New York, *Americans in Venice, 1879-1913*, 19 October-16 November 1983, no. 37.

76 Venetian Doorway

Watercolor and pencil on paper, 21½ × 14⅝ in.
(54.6 × 37.1 cm)
The Metropolitan Museum of Art. Gift of Mrs. Francis Ormond, 1950
Color plate

Faced with the rather grand and very Gothic façade of the Palazzo Giustiniani Faccanon on the narrow Rio de la Fava, Sargent selected for his subject a single rope column at the edge of the building and a dusky passageway skirting its side. A convenient portal with a large stoop opposite might have suggested itself as a steady location from which to paint the scene. But even more important, the abrupt contrasts of bright sunshine and deep shadow, between flat surface pattern and layered three-dimensional pattern, and the asymmetrical nature of the doorway would have appealed to him, as these problems are recurrent issues in his work.

Restricting his palette to a rich green-blue and shades of buff-brown, he has eloquently described languid water, damp wall, iron grillwork, and, most poignantly, the twisting masonry rope. It is a vacant scene, rich in the suggestion of human presence, but void of present activity. James Jackson Jarves, the notable collector of medieval paintings, described in 1883 the visual and emotive qualities of these familiar Venetian scenes:

I wish to speak of Venice of a hot summer's early eve, when the lengthening shadows cross its network of green waters, and, climbing fast up its marble façades, give quaint gloom and suggestive mystery to the many picturesque portals with their medieval sculptures and inviting coolness, sometimes leading the eye to inviting patches of brilliant green in verdant courtyards, but oftener into passages and halls dark and grim with the stains of many humid centuries in deep-tinted picturesque decay.[1]

Clearly it is the quality of "suggestive mystery," readable in the stones, that appeals to him and, we can surmise, to Sargent as well. The absence of present habitation permits the viewer to read the factors of time and the unknown into this ancient architectural assemblage. The small cluster of steps, passageway, wall, and window are then read interrogatively and imaginatively; the viewer is drawn beyond observation into speculative musing on the passage of those "humid centuries."

1. James Jackson Jarves, *Italian Rambles: Studies of Life and Manners in New and Old Italy* (New York: Putnam's, 1883), p. 213.

76

Provenance: Gift of Mrs. Francis Ormond, 1950

Exhibition History and Bibliography: The Metropolitan Museum of Art, New York, *200 Years of Watercolor Painting in America: An Exhibition Commemorating the Centennial of the American Watercolor Society*, 8 December 1966-29 January 1967, no. 117; Larry Curry, *Eight American Masters of Watercolor*, Los Angeles County Museum of Art, 23 April-16 June 1968, no. 15; Donelson F. Hoopes, *Sargent Watercolors*, New York: Watson-Guptill, 1970, pp. 30, 31, pl. 5; The Metropolitan Museum of Art, New York, *John Singer Sargent: A Selection of Drawings and Watercolors from the Metropolitan Museum of Art*, 1 December 1971-15 February 1972, no. 24; Carter Ratcliff, *John Singer Sargent*, New York: Abbeville Press, 1982, pl. 266.

77   Venice

Watercolor on paper, 9⅞ × 13¾ in. (25 × 35 cm)
Inscribed in ink on reverse, upper left: *31/Venice/by J. S. Sargent*
The Metropolitan Museum of Art. Gift of Mrs. Francis Ormond, 1950

Sargent's handling of the watercolor medium is full of variety, and on occasion he used a very wet, 'spontaneous' technique. Many of these more loosely drawn and painted works were apparently executed in a gondola, and we can conjecture that this looser handling of the medium was at least in part a response to the technical difficulties of the waterborne situation. But there is a second reason *Venice* may display more fluid, 'rapid' brushwork, and that is the sought-for effect of a scene glimpsed at dusk. The indistinctness of forms and the ambiguity of architectural planes in *Venice* mimic the visual effect of moving through the city at twilight. As one visitor recorded,
You see in flashes: an alley with people moving against the light, the shape of a door or balcony, seen dimly and in a wholly new aspect . . . the water lapping against the green stone of a wall which your elbow all but touches.[1]
Sargent's subject here is not the description of architectural fact as in so many of his Venetian watercolors (such as cat. nos. 61-66) or of architectural space (as in cat. no. 78), rather it is the record of a situation. A single light

illuminates a small landing near the corner of two palaces while a still canal reflects the walls and dusky apertures above. Undramatic and suggestive, this watercolor remarks on the eccentric and haunting visual quality of Venetian experience off the Grand Canal as one passes by in the fading light of evening.

1. Symons, p. 387.

Provenance: Gift of Mrs. Francis Ormond, 1950

78   Venice

Watercolor on paper, 9⅞ × 14 in. (25 × 35.5 cm)
Inscribed in ink, on reverse, upper left: *109 Venice/by J. S. Sargent*
The Metropolitan Museum of Art. Gift of Mrs. Francis Ormond, 1950

Although most of Sargent's later paintings and watercolors of Venice are unpeopled studies of architectural facts, in few is humanity as feelingly absent as in *Venice*. We are confronted with a rectangular space, a box. A patchwork of wooden doorways, iron-grilled windows, and other deep-set apertures lines the walls which retreat to an oppressively blank, but brightly-lit wall parallel to the picture plane. The artist's interest here is not focused on the masonry facts of the little *calle* but on the claustrophobic quality of the space itself. It is a Venetian social fact that, usually, canal and water-access buildings are aristocratic, the *campi* (squares) are religious and mercantile, while the paved streets and enclosed areas are working-class neighborhoods. And one can quickly feel here how the airless, vistaless, pedestrian zones at the centers of the islands provided less desirable habitation. Sargent appeals to our sense of empathy with architectural space and form here, confronting us with the baffling character of Venetian streets through which one wanders – it was often remarked – as in a maze.
Venice is one of several intensely felt and brilliantly executed *calle* views, none of which appear to be studies for the genre street scenes, for the latter are associated

77

with the decade of the 1880s (see cat. nos. 52, 53) and these watercolors were probably painted in the early twentieth century. Moreover, the sites differ considerably. They share, however, some tonal and technical elements, which we recognize as Sargentesque: the image presents itself to us as a conundrum, as an interrogative or incomplete puzzle, and the darkly lit or shaded area in the foreground is thrown into relief by intense light in the background (cat. nos. 54-58, 73-74). But in few instances has Sargent as eloquently caught the distilled and faintly disturbing otherness of Venetian space as in this portrait of a 'dead end.'

Provenance: Gift of Mrs. Francis Ormond, 1950

Exhibition History and Bibliography: The Metropolitan Museum of Art, New York, *John Singer Sargent: A Selection of Drawings and Watercolors from the Metropolitan Museum of Art,* 1 December 1971-15 February 1972, no. 22.

79   Campo S. Agnese, Venice
Oil on canvas, 18 × 25½ in. (45.7 × 64.8 cm)
Collection of the Wellesley College Museum
Color plate

Less well-known than the genre works or the architectural watercolors is a small group of architectural oils Sargent produced in the 1880s and 1890s. Three are particularly memorable: *Venise par Temps Gris* (ca. 1882, private collection), a Whistlerian study of the Riva from the roof garden of the Hotel Sandwirt, *The Pavement* (ca. 1896, private collection), a chiaroscuro rendition of the interior of San Marco, and *Campo S. Agnese, Venice,* an extraordinary record of a deserted campo behind the Accademia. All three cloak meditative solitude and a faint disquiet in painterly brilliance.

Campo S. Agnese is particularly evocative of a sense of the past, a robust past juxtaposed to the diminishment of the present. Against the backdrop of a red-pink stucco Gothic palazzo, a broad gray-green pavement sets off a jewel-like Baroque wellhead, its massive volutes and carved garlands sparkling in the sun. In the 1880s, when this painting was probably executed, there were about 2,000 public wells in Venice providing fresh ground water to most of the population.[1] In his memoirs, Maitland Armstrong describes the tone of these little spaces, so aptly punctuated by their exuberant wells:
Our favorite haunts were the old courtyards, surrounded by gray palace walls, with their wonderful marble wells, the sculptured curbs furrowed inside by the ropes and chains of countless years and bearing on their sides the coats of arms of the former knightly owner. The wrought-iron gratings which covered them, works of art in themselves, used to be kept locked, as the water-supply was limited in those days.[2]
The wellheads were often, as in this case, carved of white Istrian stone, and much care was lavished on their design. Sargent's well, more crisply rendered than the other elements in the image, is self-consciously Baroque, its naturalistic architectural ornament is starkly contrasted with a small flock of irreverent Venetian hens. Rendered, as is the rest of the work, in summary, 'spontaneous' strokes, these small fowl, nevertheless, have presence, even individuality. A fifth hen has been painted out of the foreground with a single stroke. The whole composition is freely painted and seemingly rapidly executed in a spectrum of subtle color variations. Yet despite Sargent's lavish brush and the bright sunshine, the place is an empty one; it vibrates with the emptiness of completion, not of potential, and in that fact Sargent locates a subtle melancholy note which we do not often feel in the more constricted watercolor studies.

1. Museum records indicate that the work was executed in 1884 and given to Gervase Ker in Venice in 1890; Cartwright, p. 42.

2. Maitland Armstrong, *Day Before Yesterday: Reminiscences of a Varied Life* (New York: Scribner's, 1920), p. 242.

Provenance: Given by the artist to Gervase Ker, Venice, 1890; purchased by Whitney Morss, 1936; given to the Museum by Strafford Morss, 1969

80   Venetian Canal, ca. 1904

Watercolor on paper, 15½ × 20⅞ in. (39.4 × 53 cm)
Signed, upper right: *John S. Sargent*
The Metropolitan Museum of Art. Purchase, Joseph
Pulitzer Bequest, 1915

Venetian Canal provides us with a rare instance of
Sargent's employing a 'classic' composition, one with
which we are familiar from the work of numerous contemporary artists. In the center of the image, a narrow
canal reflects two vertical ranges of buildings; a bridge
arches over the waterway, parallel to the picture plane,
connecting the two lateral points of closure. In the background, a tower overlooks the scene and provides a point
of orientation and focus. *A Canal in Venice* by G. W. Stevens (cat. no. 85) and *Rio di San Barnaba, Venice* by
Sargent's friend Edward D. Boit (cat. no. 8) provide other
instances of, and variations on, this familiar pictorial arrangement. Sargent's interpretation places the observer
low on the water, and he introduces a horizontal format,
rather than the more customary vertical, emphasizing expanse rather than closure. The scene is suffused with a
golden glow; bright sunlit areas contrast sharply with
violet shadows on the buildings and deep green reflections in the water.

Because of Sargent's adoption of a familiar pictorial
arrangement and because of the general non-problemati-
cal nature of the image, it seems likely that this is among

the earliest of his Venetian watercolors, dating from before 1905. With very few exceptions, Sargent did not
again bend his formidable talents on a Venetian architectural subject of even this broad a scope.

Sargent's mother was an amateur watercolorist, and he
had gained facility in the medium with her tutelage before he began his formal art training. His return to
watercolor as a mature artist reflects not only his appreciation of the pictorial quality of transparent color and
the portability of the medium in the itinerant phases of
his life, but it also signaled a broader professional legit-
imization of a technique formerly the province of ladies,
amateurs, and British topographical draftsmen.

Provenance: Purchased in 1915

Exhibition History and Bibliography: Pennsylvania Academy of Fine
Arts and Philadelphia Water Color Club, *Second Annual Philadelphia
Water Color Exhibition*, 3-29 April 1905, no. 128; Catherine Beach Ely,
"Sargent as a Watercolorist," *Art in America* 11 (February 1923), p. 98;
Exposition d'Art Américain, Paris, 18 May-25 June 1923, no. 36; William
Howe Downes, *John S. Sargent: His Life and Work*, Boston: Little, Brown,
1925, p. 278; Albert Ten Eyck Gardner, *History of Water Color Painting in
America*, New York: Reinhold, 1966, pl. 73; Larry Curry, *Eight American
Masters of Watercolor*, Los Angeles County Museum of Art, 23 April-16
June 1968, no. 16; The Metropolitan Museum of Art, New York, *John
Singer Sargent: A Selection of Drawings and Watercolors from the Metro-
politan Museum of Art*, 1 December 1971-15 February 1972, no. 17.

79

80

81 Rio di Santa Maria Formosa, Venice

Watercolor, pen and ink, wash and gouache over pencil
on paper, 13⅞ × 19⅜ in. (35.2 × 49.2 cm)
Signed in brown ink, upper right: *John S. Sargent*
Museum of Art, Rhode Island School of Design. Gift of
Mrs. Murray S. Danforth

Very similar in its subject to *Venetian Canal* (cat. no. 80),
Rio di Santa Maria Formosa, Venice is, even so, a radically
different sort of picture, one more congruent with the
partial views of monumental and vernacular spaces for
which Sargent is better known (see cat. nos. 61-63,
65-68, 73-78). Both this image and *Venetian Canal* are
views of a narrow, placid canal lined with buildings and
moored boats, but in this view Sargent has lifted his horizon line, truncated the buildings, and introduced two
over-sized and partial elements into the immediate foreground, elements he and other artists would have
avoided or overlooked in such views as *Venetian Canal*.
The two major elements whose almost disturbing proximity obstructs the rest of the scene are the stern of
Sargent's gondola intruding directly into the picture
plane and, perpendicular to the boat, the arching presence of the underside of a small bridge which joins the
Calle del Paradiso to the Calle del Dose. Linking the
bridge and the boat is the slashing, diagonal, in-
completely explained presence of an unmanned oar.

By reformatting his image and by including these
abrupt and partial forms, Sargent adds considerable visual complexity to his scene and a note of ambiguity and
immediacy that is not present in *Venetian Canal*. Slicing
and arbitrarily terminating his bridge, gondola, and

buildings, he emphasizes the abstract conjunction of
curves and the linear play of these graceful curves –
associated with the water section of the image – against
the rectilinearity of the buildings. In this move toward
abstract pattern and visual immediacy, *Rio di Santa Maria
Formosa* is the vernacular equivalent of Sargent's watercolor exploration of Venice's great Baroque monuments.
His strategy here, as there, is to take that which is familiar
and insist that we see it anew.

Francis Hopkinson Smith
1838-1915

A successful New York-based marine engineer and writer
as well as self-taught watercolorist, Smith traveled widely, observing and enjoying the picturesque. In the last
two decades of the nineteenth century and the first decade of the twentieth, he made nineteen trips to Europe
and spent almost every summer in Venice.[1] Throughout
his career his watercolors retained the quality noted in
an early review: "Mr. Smith's paintings are all of a summer-like character."[2] A cheerful, "summer-like," almost
self-indulgent tone invests his travel writings about Venice as well as his pictures. In the Preface to his very
popular *Gondola Days*, Smith notes,

*I have made no attempt in these pages to review the splendors
of the past, or to probe the many vital questions which concern
the present, of this wondrous City of the Sea. . . .*

*I have contented myself rather with the Venice that you see
in the sunlight of a summer's day — the Venice that bewilders
with her glory when you land at her water gate; that delights
with her color when you idle along the Riva; that intoxicates
with her music as you lie in your gondola adrift on the bosom
of some breathless lagoon — the Venice of mould-stained palace, quaint caffè and arching bridge; of fragrant incense, cool,
dim-lighted church, and noiseless priest; of strong-armed men
and graceful women — the Venice of light and life, of sea and
sky and melody.*[3]

The act of painting itself, for Smith, seems to have had
much of the tone of a summer's picnic. Describing the
preparation for a painting expedition, Smith records his
gondolier's report: "Everything is ready, he says: the
sketch trap, extra canvas, fresh siphon of seltzer, ice,
fiasco of Chianti, Gorgonzola, all but the rolls which he

will get at the baker's on our way over to the Giudecca, where I am to work on the sketch begun yesterday."[4] But "Hop," as he was known, was not as indolent as this might suggest; he was industrious at his craft. One source records that on one trip to Venice he produced a picture a day for fifty-three days.[5]

Although Smith spoke very little Italian, he (like many of his patrons and much of the American public) had a deep affection for the picturesque aspects of Italian life and felt they provided appropriate foils within the context of "this selfish, materialistic, money-getting age."[6] For the 1893 World's Columbian Exhibition in Chicago, Smith arranged for boats, built in exact replication of Venetian gondolas and manned by Italian gondoliers, to grace the lagoon.[7] Although to modern eyes the Chicago Fair seems overwhelmingly Roman and imperial in nature, contemporaries saw a Venetian cityscape on the shores of Lake Michigan in the Exposition's

beauty, its harmonious grouping, its splendid landscape and architectural effects. This is best comprehended as a whole in the approach from the lake. The view then, especially at the coming of evening, when the long rows of classic columns, the pillars, and domes are in relief against a glowing sunset sky, is a vision of beauty that will surprise most and will appeal most to those familiar with man's triumphs of genius elsewhere. The little city of the lagoon, reflected in the water as distinctly as it stands out against the sky, seems like some fairy exhalation on the shore, suggesting . . . the canals and palaces of Venice as seen from the Lido. In its light and airy grace it is like a city of the imagination.[8]

Despite their visual specificity, Smith's books on and views of Venice suggest more this sense of an imaginary cityscape, a vernacular world of "summer-like" charm, than a city of specific historic architectural monuments.

1. Soria, *Dictionary*, pp. 271-272.
2. *Art Journal* (11 March 1876), cited in Clement and Hutton, vol. 2, p. 262.
3. F. Hopkinson Smith, *Gondola Days* (Boston: Hougton, Mifflin, 1897), n. p.
4. Smith, pp. 134-135.
5. *Literary World*, p. 245, cited in *The Dictionary of American Biography*, vol. 9, p. 266.
6. Joseph Pennell, *The Adventures of an Illustrator* (Boston: Little, Brown, 1925), p. 286; Smith, Preface, n. p.
7. Soria, *Dictionary*, p. 272; John J. Flinn, ed., *Official Guide to the World's Columbian Exposition* (Chicago: The Columbian Guide Co., 1893), p. 20; photographs of these gondolas in action are to be found in James W. Shepp and Daniel B. Shepp, *Shepp's World's Fair Photographed* (Chicago: Globe Bible Publishing Co., 1893), n. p.
8. "Editors Study," *Harper's New Monthly Magazine* 86, no. 63 (February 1893), p. 477.

82 Over a Balcony, View of the Grand Canal, Venice, before 1894
Watercolor on paper adhered to fabric fastened on wooden stretchers, 31⅝ × 20⅞ in. (80.3 × 53 cm)
Signed, lower right: *F. Hopkinson Smith*
Walters Art Gallery

In his travel book describing the pleasures of Venice, *Gondola Days*, published in 1897, Smith describes his arrival at the Grand Hotel Britannia, a noble palazzo on the Grand Canal:
You pass out, cross a garden, cool and fresh in the darkening shadows, and enter a small room opening on a staircase. You walk up and through the cozy apartments, push back a folding glass door, and step out upon a balcony of marble.

How still it all is! Only the plash of the water about the bows of the gondolas, and the little waves snapping at the water steps. . . .

You look about you, — the stillness filling your soul, the soft air embracing you, — out over the blossoms of the oleanders, across the shimmering water, beyond the beautiful dome of the Salute, glowing like a huge pearl in the clear evening light.[1]
A few years earlier he had painted a balcony view of the Salute invested with the same pleasurable qualities of stillness and fragrant blossoms, *Over a Balcony, View of the Grand Canal, Venice*. Poised high above a placid, summer-struck Grand Canal, Smith looks east toward the distant dome of San Biagio on the horizon. Punctuating the skyline on the right, the buoyant Salute domes, like "huge pearls," lift themselves above a cluster of tile-roofed palazzi. The unfinished eighteenth-century Palazzo Venier (which now houses the Peggy Guggenheim Collection), with its oleandered balcony hanging over the canal and its eccentric, truncated columns, is clearly visible to the immediate right of our own perch in the fifteenth-century Palazzo Contarini del Zaffo with its lion-corbeled ledges. Like most of Smith's interpretations of Venice, this scene is redolent with the peaceful and picturesque qualities for which he prized the city.

Smith uses here, as in many of his other compositions, a tinted paper, allowing it to become variously 'wall' and 'water.' In his treatment of value and hue he is — as one contemporary remarked — "a little old-fashioned." The reviewer goes on to remark that
in his work there is always a deliberate selection of a darkest dark and a lightest light, . . . a carrying off of . . . emphatic touches by echoing subordinates, which repeat themselves in fainter and fainter reverberations till the scheme fades out of the painting. In color, too, the same expedient is used, the red note or the blue note being never isolated impertinently in the picture, but persuaded away in minor keys of suggestive colors till it is lost in a margin or dissolved in a variation.[2]
And *Over a Balcony* is no exception. Smith plays here particularly on the subtle variations in the blues of water, sky, and shadow, and the reds of roof and flower pot against the warm texture of his buff paper.

Smith was active in arts organizations (he was treasurer of the American Watercolor Society, 1873-1878), and he aggressively promoted his watercolors. They were acquired by such distinguished collectors as John Jacob Astor, Charles F. Havermeyer, Isabella Stewart Gardner, and, in the case of this work, William Thompson Walters.[3] Purchased directly from the artist in 1894, *Over the Balcony* was the last work by an American to enter W. T. Walters's collection.[4]

1. Smith, *Gondola Days*, pp. 6-7.
2. Edward Strahan, "F. Hopkinson Smith's Water Color Drawings," *The Art Amateur* 8, no. 3 (February 1883), p. 63
3. Kathleen A. Foster, "The Watercolor Scandal of 1882: An American Salon des Refusés," *Archives of American Art Journal* 19, no. 2 (1979), pp. 19-25 passim; Clement and Hutton, vol. 2, p. 261.
4. William R. Johnston, "American Paintings in the Walters Art Gallery," *The Magazine Antiques* 106, no. 5 (November 1974), pp. 856-858.

Provenance: Purchased from the artist by W. T. Walters, 1894

Exhibition History and Bibliography: Walters catalogues: 1897, 1899, 1903, no. 272; Gruelle (1895), p. 131; *The Walters Collection*, Baltimore:

83

The Friedenwald Co., 1897, p. 131, no. 272; Edward S. King and Marvin C. Ross, *The Walters Art Gallery Catalogue of the American Works of Art Including French Medals Made for America*, Baltimore: The Trustees of the Walters Art Gallery, 1956, no. 105, p. 27; William R. Johnston, "American Paintings in the Walters Art Gallery," *Antiques* 106 (November 1974), pp. 856-858.

83 Venice: Canal Scene I

Watercolor and gouache on paper, 23¾ × 13 in.
(60.3 × 33 cm)
Signed, lower right: *F. Hopkinson Smith*
Museum of Fine Arts, Boston. Gift of the Estate of Nellie P. Carter

Characteristic of "Hop" Smith's vernacular views of the city, this vignette focuses on a narrow canal, an architecturally interesting cluster of buildings, and a few Venetians going about their chores under a hot summer sky. Pellucid and green, the canal soon loses itself among a jumble of closely packed, stucco-on-brick dwellings.

Adding interest to the scene, and, we surmise, contrib-

uting that element which prompted Smith to set up his easel and umbrella in this spot, is the garden in the middle distance. Not only does the abundant foliage repeat the deep green of the water and interrupt the flat buff-red of the walls, it also adds a note of closure, mystery, and elegance to an otherwise vernacular scene—for gardens in Venice are, *de facto*, aristocratic and closed. As Smith puts it in the chapter entitled "In an Old Garden" in his *Gondola Days*, "almost every Palace hides a garden nestling beneath its balconies, and every high wall hems a wealth of green, studded with broken statues, quaint arbors festooned with purple grapes, and white walls bordered by ancient box."[1] For Smith, a leap of the imagination, catapulted by the fact of a walled garden, takes him, in that essay, quickly into the realm of aristocratic history, intrigue, and tragedy which is as important to him as the visual facts artfully recorded.

Unlike Charles Coleman, whose monumental *Bronze Horses of San Marco, Venice* (cat. no. 12) recalls the public tale of Venice's political history, Smith prefers the realm of romance; his modest *Canal Scene* evokes the private histories of notables long gone while it celebrates the picturesqueness of the vernacular present.

1. Smith, *Gondola Days*, p. 58.

Provenance: Gift of the estate of Nellie P. Carter, 1935

Exhibition History and Bibliography: Museum of Fine Arts, Boston, *Catalogue of Paintings and Drawings in Water Color*, 1949, p. 175, repro. p. 276.

Joseph Lindon Smith
1863-1950

A Boston-based artist, Smith was best known during his lifetime for his documentary paintings – in watercolors and oils – of Egyptian, Mayan, and Far Eastern, as well as European, antiquities and architectural subjects. His penchant for vibrant accuracy is visible in his painterly records of distinguished Venetian buildings.

Smith was in Venice during the summers of 1892, 1894, and 1906, and probably on several other occasions as well.[1] While there, he bought paintings and objets d'art for the Museum of Fine Arts, Boston, and for the collection of Isabella Stewart Gardner, whose Venetian-styled Fenway Court was built and assembled (using many Venetian architectural fragments) not far from the museum between 1899 and 1903.[2]

While in Venice in 1892, he studied the paintings of the Venetian masters and in the fall of that year lectured on Giovanni Bellini, Titian, and Veronese for the Boston Art Students' Association.[3] He was a friend of John Singer Sargent, and they met frequently during their peregrinations in Florence (1886), in London (1901), at Henry James's Lamb House in Rye, and in Boston where they worked on the Boston Public Library mural project together.[4]

Smith was also a dramatist, producing elaborate pageants including "The Festival of the Doge of Venice" at The Art Institute of Chicago.[5] In keeping with this enthusiasm, his Venetian paintings include costume pieces as well as topographically accurate records of architectural monuments.[6]

1. Isabella Stewart Gardner papers, roll 410, frames 121 and 129, AAA.
2. Isabella Stewart Gardner Papers, roll 410, frames 129ff and 276, AAA; Rollin van N. Hadley, *Museums Discovered: The Isabella Stewart Gardner Museum* (New York, 1981), n. p.
3. New York Public Library Papers, Art Division, roll N47, frame 253, AAA.
4. Corinna Lindon Smith, *Interesting People: Eighty Years with the Great and Near-Great* (Norman: University of Oklahoma Press, 1962), pp. 113-122, 125-127.
5. *The National Cylopaedia of American Biography* (New York: James T. White & Co. 1954), vol. 39, p. 32.
6. *Catalogue of Paintings and Drawings in Water Color* (Boston: Museum of Fine Arts, 1949), p. 175.

84

84 Venetian Scene (Palazzo Dario)
Watercolor on paper, 19¼ × 14 in. (48.9 × 35.6 cm)
Signed, lower right: *Joseph Lindon Smith.*
The Metropolitan Museum of Art. Gift of the Estate of Mrs. Edward Robinson, 1952

A portrait of the Palazzo Dario, Pietro Lombardo's late fifteenth-century masterpiece near the mouth of the Grand Canal, Smith's watercolor captures its patinaed facade in the warm afternoon light. Jewel-like, intensely colored roundels in red, blue, and green enrich the façade, adding what John Ruskin characterized as a "careful and noble use of inlaid marbles as a means of color" to an already noble structure.[1] An instructor of architecture at Harvard early in his career, Smith was clearly sensitive not only to the details of the building's façade but also to the structural infirmities which have compressed and canted its lines out of plumb.

Smith has depicted the little palace's facade parallel to the picture plane from across the canal. Setting off his subject with a strip of sky above, rippling water below, and glimpses of adjoining structures, he has concentrated our attention on the isolated dignity of the building as a container for human habitation and history. The palace is an historic event surviving into and experienceable in the present, and Smith treats it as such with respect, recording its accidents and irregularities as a portraitist does the visage of a noble but elderly sitter. It is summer: windows are open to catch chance breezes, and long curtains – almost the only three-dimensional elements in the picture – shield the implied inhabitants from the glaring sun. Smith seems to have executed his pictures entirely on site, unlike many other artists who recorded only sketches and then composed their finished works in the studio.[2]

Although he is best known for the documentary nature of his images, it is interesting to note that Smith uses selective focus here: the flanking vernacular building and Gothic palazzo are differentiated not only in their physical incompleteness but also in the relative abbreviation of their rendition. That Smith could paint more loosely, less literally than was his wont in documentary work, is evident from John Singer Sargent's praise (recorded by Smith's wife, Corinna) for another work's *few strokes of the brush on a narrow bit of cardboard. Several brilliant spots of light, with thin lines of color below, in deep blue sky had produced an impression of a tremendous display of fireworks, with sparks flying, in Venice. He [Sargent] had been so impressed, he said, that he had invited the younger painter to show his studies on Greece and Italy in his London studio that summer.*[3]

130   *J. L. Smith*

1. John Ruskin, *The Stones of Venice* (New York: John W. Lovell, n. d.), vol. 3, p. 20.
2. Isabella Stewart Gardner Papers, roll 410, frame 276, AAA; Smith, *Interesting People*, p. 197.
3. Smith, *Interesting People*, p. 114.

George W. Stevens
1866-1926

Best known as the innovative and charismatic first director of The Toledo Museum, Stevens was also a newspaper reporter, poet, writer, amateur astronomer, and Sunday painter.[1] We know very little about his Venetian works, except that they were executed during summer excursions abroad early in this century. A well-trained amateur, Stevens worked primarily in watercolor and achieved a rare poetry in this medium.

1. Blake-More Godwin, "George W. Stevens," *The Toledo Museum of Art Museum News* 9, no. 1, n. s. (Spring 1966), pp. 5-22.

85 A Canal in Venice, ca. 1902
Watercolor on paper, 18⅞ × 12⅛ in. (48 × 30.8 cm)
Signed, lower right: *Geo. W. Stevens*
Lent by The Toledo Museum of Art. Bequest of Carl B. Spitzer

In its subdued palette and balanced composition, *A Canal in Venice* captures the stillness and quiet for which Venice's byways are well-known. The vertical format emphasizes our sense of enclosure, but the sunlit area beyond the dark foreground draws us back into the distant vista. A single boat, a modest sandolo, prompts our

85

John Henry Twachtman
1853-1902

As a student, Twachtman visited Venice with Frank Duveneck and William M. Chase in 1877. Their stay was of nine months' duration, and the work of all three artists at this time was clearly marked by their training in Munich. Carolyn C. Mase reported that later in his life Twachtman critiqued the Germanic tone of his early Venetian works: *Once I recollect his showing me a brownish-black water colour, reeking with all the colours that Nature does not show. "That," he said with a chuckle, "is sunny Venice, done under the influence of the Munich School."*[1]
Yet at the time they seemed sufficient to him, and in 1879 he exhibited two Venetian views at the Society of American Artists Exhibition and three at the National Academy of Design.[2]

In the fall of 1880, Duveneck invited Twachtman to teach at his school, then located in Florence, and after the close of the session, the two spent some weeks in Venice.[3] Twachtman married the following year and toured northern Europe on his honeymoon, stopping again in Venice.[4] After a brief sojourn in America, the couple returned to Europe in 1884, while Twachtman pursued further study, this time based in Paris. The winter of 1884 and the summer and fall of 1885 were passed in Venice in the congenial company of Frank Duveneck and fellow Cincinnatian Robert Blum.[5] Works of this later Venetian period have the lighter tone of a more French palette. In fact, some of the most successful are pastels, which he exhibited at the Exhibition of Painters in Pastel in 1888.[6] The following year he settled permanently in Greenwich, Connecticut, closing the long European chapter in his development and achievement.

1. Carolyn C. Mase, "John H. Twachtman," *The International Studio* 72, no. 286 (January 1921), p. 73.
2. John Douglass Hale, "The Life and Creative Development of John H. Twachtman," 2 vols., Ph. D. diss., The Ohio State University, 1957, p. 20; *NAD*, p. 952.
3. *John Henry Twachtman: A Retrospective Exhibition*, exh. cat. (Cincinnati: The Cincinnati Art Museum, 1966), p. 4.
4. Allen Tucker, *John H. Twachtman* (New York: Whitney Museum of American Art, 1931), p. 12.
5. Eliot Clark, *John Twachtman* (New York: Privately printed, 1924), p. 25; Tucker, p. 13; Richard J. Boyle, *John Twachtman* (New York: Watson-Guptill Publications, 1979), p. 7.
6. Hale, p. 64.

mental excursion. Stevens has rendered the upper half of the image in smooth, even washes while the water is alive with nervous, fluid line. Recording the archetypical Venetian site where "a bridge crosses a narrow canal between high walls and over dark water," Stevens imbues the scene with a faint note of pathos and melancholoy.[1]

1. Arthur Symons, *Cities of Italy* (New York: Dutton, 1907), p. 100.

Exhibition History and Bibliography: Susan E. Strickler, *The Toledo Museum of Art: American Paintings*, William Hutton, ed., Toledo: The Toledo Museum of Art, 1979, distributed by The Pennsylvania State University Press, p. 103, pl. 108.

86 Canal in Venice, ca. 1884
Pastel on paper, 22½ × 17½ in. (57.2 × 44.5 cm)
Signed, lower left: *J. H. Twachtman*; inscribed on the reverse: *Painted by my father, J. H. Twachtman/Venice '84/J. Alden Twachtman/June 16, 1956/Greenwich, Connecticut*
Private collection

The etching revival, which is responsible for so much excellent late-nineteenth-century work, had its counterpart in the revival of pastels, and Whistler may be credited with identifying both with the city of Venice.[1] The application of pastels, or colored chalks, to paper was an important portrait medium in eighteenth-century France, England, and America, but it was not until the

86

nineteenth century that the potential of the medium for landscape and cityscape was fully explored. In the wake of the exhibition of Whistler's Venetian pastels in London in 1881, numerous artists, including Twachtman, essayed the medium, discovering its versatility in the depiction of atmosphere, space, and structure. Like Whistler, Twachtman in *Canal in Venice* uses a colored paper, giving the whole composition coherence and unity, while suggestively vignetting the image and abbreviating the edges of his scene. The subtle pinks and yellows of the building and the shimmering, reflective blue-yellow-black of the canal are applied with the delicacy and confidence of a mature artist discovering the eloquence of a whole new vocabulary.

The scene depicted is the Rio della Guerra, just north of the Piazza San Marco. The serenity, even vacancy, of this small canal signals our removal from the center of the city and our entry into its more domestic areas. It is probable that Twachtman executed this pastel during his visit to the city in 1884 or 1885 in the company of Robert Blum, whose own work in pastel of 1885 takes on a rather different, more painterly tone. Twachtman's experiments with pastel were important in the modification of his painterly style from that of the early Munich work to the delicately toned later landscapes for which he is best known.

1. Dianne H. Pilgrim, "The Revival of Pastels in Nineteenth-Century America," *American Art Journal* 10 (November 1978), pp. 43-62.

Provenance: Mrs. J. H. Twachtman; estate of Albert E. McVitty, Princeton, New Jersey; sold Parke-Bernet Galleries, New York, 15 December 1949, no. 22; Mr. Ned Pines, New York; Philip Morrison by 1953; Mrs. William H. Bender, Bronxville, New York; sold Sotheby Parke-Bernet, New York, 21 April 1977, no. 69

87

Eugene Vail
1857-1934

Vail, who was born in France (his father was American), was educated in the United States but passed most of his working life in France.[1] He was known during his life-time as a portraitist and a figure painter specializing in scenes of Brittany's fisherfolk, but his Venetian views, the fruit of several trips in the first decade of the twentieth century, were also recognized.[2]

An able, although somewhat obscure artist, Vail is probably best known as Peggy Guggenheim's neuras-thenic father-in-law.[3] A large group of his charcoal drawings of Venetian subjects — many evening or night scenes recalling Whistler — are preserved at the Corcoran Gallery.[4] Both these drawings and the Venetian oils often include partial views of well-known buildings, poetically rendered in crepuscular tones.

1. M. A. Banks, ''Memorial Exhibition of Paintings by Eugene Vail,'' *Bulletin of the Rhode Island School of Design* 26, no. 1 (January 1938), p. 9.

2. ''Worcester: A Touring Retrospective of Eugene L. Vail,'' *The Art News* 37, no. 9 (26 November 1938), p. 17.

3. Peggy Guggenheim, *Out of This Century: Confessions of an Art Addict* (New York: Universe Books, 1979), pp. 26, 29, 54, 55.

4. Linda Crocker Simmons, *American Drawings, Watercolors, Pastels and Collages in the Collection of the Corcoran Gallery of Art* (Washington, D.C.: Corcoran Gallery of Art, 1983), pp. 117-118.

87 Venetian Scene, ca. 1904
Oil on canvas, 21⅜ × 25½ in. (53.8 × 64.8 cm)
Signed, lower right: *Eugène Vail*
Museum of Art, Rhode Island School of Design

Pressing his horizon line high on the canvas allows Vail here, in a manner reminiscent of Maurice Prendergast, to devote a majority of his picture surface to the play of light and reflection on water (see cat. nos. 40, 41, 43, 44, 46, 47). Impressionist broken brushstrokes record the elongated, fractured images of pink wall, gaping door-way, and black boat in the rippling canal. Suggesting the omnipresence of the aquatic medium in which Venice floats, this image is also successful in capturing the tone of her structures in the archaic, random patterning of wall and aperture.

The abruptness with which Vail slices the buildings by the top edge of the canvas, as well as the general han-dling of the medium, are both reminiscent of the work of John S. Sargent in Venice. Boldly composed and fluidly executed, this quiet work captures both a sense of the antiquity of Venice and the modernity of Vail's own era.

Provenance: Laurence Vail, Paris?

Exhibition History and Bibliography: Chicago, n. d. [?]; Pennsylvania Academy of Fine Arts, Philadelphia, 1904, no. 333; Rhode Island School of Design, Providence, *Vail*, 1906, no. 4, as *Reflections, Grand Canal, Venice*; Museum of Art, Rhode Island School of Design, Providence, *Days Gone By*, 1 July-26 September 1971; idem, *Selection VII: American Paintings from the Museum's Collection, c. 1800-1930*, 31 March-8 May 1977, pub-lished in *Bulletin of Rhode Island School of Design Museum Notes* 63 (April 1977), pp. 201-202.

James McNeill Whistler
1834-1903

In September of 1879, James McNeill Whistler left London, the notoriety attendant upon his recent libel suit against John Ruskin, and his well-publicized bankruptcy, bound for Venice.[1] He and his mistress, Maud Franklin, arrived in Paris on September 16. On the 18th, he left for his first and only stay in Venice; she followed a month later.[2] Whistler had, for at least three years, contemplated a trip to the Italian city, but it was a timely commission for twelve etchings from the Fine Art Society (a commercial art gallery on London's New Bond Street) that made the journey possible.[3] The contract was precise; as Whistler had capsulized it in a letter to a friend and patron several months before, "I . . . now rush off to Italy instantly where I am to be in Venice until December. I am to do the long promised set of etchings and have engaged to finish them by the 20th Dec."[4]

When Whistler first arrived in the city, he is reported to have taken a studio in the Palazzo Rezzonico.[5] By the winter, he and Maud Franklin moved to modest rooms near the Church of the Frari.[6] The weather during the autumn and winter of 1879 was exceedingly harsh, and Whistler at first suffered much and accomplished little.[7] When, in January 1880, the director of the Fine Art Society inquired about the twelve prints due the month before, Whistler responded with evasive eloquence:
The "Venice" my dear Mr. Huish will be superb – and you may double your bets all round – only I can't fight against the Gods – with whom I am generally a favorite – and not come to grief – so that now – at this very moment – I am an invalid and a prisoner – because I rashly thought I might hasten matters by standing in the snow with a plate in my hand and an icicle at the end of my nose. – I was ridiculous – the Gods saw it and sent me to my room in disgrace . . . Nevertheless, be comfortable, Huish . . . now I have learned to know a Venice in Venice that the others never seem to have perceived. . . . The etchings themselves are far more delicate in execution, more beautiful in subject and more important in interest than any of the old set [probably referring to views of the Thames and its bridges] – Then I shall bring fifty or sixty if not more pastels totaly new and of a brilliancy very different from the customary watercolor – and [they] will sell – I don't see how they can help it – But then my dear Huish, the revers de la medaille: I am frozen – and have been for months – and you cant hold a needle with numbed fingers, and beautiful work cannot be finished in bodily agony – Also I am starving – or shall be soon – for it must be amazing even to you that I should have made my money last this long – You had better send me fifty pounds at once and trust to a thaw which will put us all right—[8]
As late as April, he was able to lodge comparable complaints with his English correspondents:
I am happy to tell you that my own health is capital and the weather alone in all its uncertainties retards my work. . . . It has been woefully cold here – The bitterest winter I fancy that I ever experienced, and the people of Venice say that nothing of the kind has been known for quite a century. . . . At last the ice and snow have left us – and now the rain is pouring down upon us.[9]
There were difficulties beyond the weather. Like others

before and after, Whistler, when surrounded with the visual glories of Venice, had difficulty settling upon a subject. One American resident of the city later reminisced that Whistler used to say Venice was an impossible place to sit down and sketch in – he always felt "there was something still better round the corner."[10] With the coming of spring, the beauty of the city wove its spell. Whistler wrote to his mother of the Venice that existed especially for artists, and for their work:
Perhaps tomorrow may be fine – And then Venice will be simply glorious, as now and then I have seen it – After the wet, the colors upon the walls and their reflections in the canals are more gorgeous than ever – and with sun shining upon the polished marble mingled with rich toned bricks and plaster, this amazing city of palaces becomes really a fairy land – created one would think especially for the painter. The people with their gay gowns and handkerchiefs – and the many tinted buildings for them to lounge against or pose before, seem to exist especially for one's pictures – and to have no other reason for being![11]
By the beginning of May, Whistler, who, when he worked, set to the task with a vigor that made a strong impression upon his fellow artists, remarked in a letter, after noting how awful the winter weather had been, that "I have worked very hard, and bring back with me a perfect gallery of beautiful pastel drawings – about sixty in all."[12]

During the early summer, circumstances again changed for Whistler. Frank Duveneck and other German-trained Americans (including Otto Bacher, Robert Blum, and John Twachtman) descended upon the city. He met them first crossing the iron bridge over the Grand Canal near the Accademia. Bacher, who wrote of the ensuing months, recorded his initial impression of Whistler:
Short, thin, and wiry, with a head that seemed large and out of proportion to the lithe figure. His large, wide-brimmed, soft, brown hat was tilted far back, and suggested a brown halo. It was a background for his curly black hair and singular white lock, high over his right eye, like a fluffy feather carelessly left where it had lodged. A dark sack-coat almost covered an extremely low turned-down collar, while a narrow black ribbon did service as a tie, the long pennant-like ends of which, flapping about, now and then hit his single eyeglass.[13]
At first tentatively, but with increasing frequency, Whistler met with this new circle, the "Duveneck Boys," until he simply changed quarters to join them in the Casa Jankowitz on the Riva degli Schiavoni. He took an upper story room with two windows that looked out on San Giorgio Maggiore, the Doge's Palace, and Santa Maria della Salute.[14] He took advantage of this view, sketching and etching from the window, a fact recorded in a small drawing by Robert Blum (see Introduction, p. 10).

There he and Maud Franklin stayed until the middle of November 1880, when they journeyed to London, never to return. Whistler had stayed, in all, fourteen months and had a substantial body of work to show for his labor, including fifty etchings, over ninety pastel drawings, and perhaps twelve paintings (of which two were major efforts). And while he never again visited Venice, artists that followed him there seemed, with few exceptions, always to be encountering his spirit. As late as 1909, the Pennells report,

And yet today, when two or three artists gather together of an evening at Florian's . . . it is of Whistler they talk. When the prize student arrives and has sufficiently raved, they say, "Oh, yes, but you will have to do it better than Whistler!" When a new discoverer of the picturesque brags, Whistler's old friends tell him of Whistler's discovery.[15]

And with even fewer exceptions, it was Whistler's vision of Venice that determined how those who followed him, especially etchers and pastellists, were in turn to perceive the city (see, for example, the works of Bacher, Duveneck, MacLaughlan, Marin, and Twachtman: cat. nos. 2, 14, 20-24, 86).

Whistler went to Venice, at least in part, to recoup his shattered finances, and in this he was successful. The Fine Art Society exhibited its twelve commissioned etchings ("The First Venice Set") in December of 1880. Displayed in a small room lined with maroon-colored cloth, their catalogue numbers written in chalk beneath, the twelve – for the most part the larger and more finished of the etchings – elicited mixed reviews from the critics, many of whom found them slight or unfinished.[16] But, gradually, they did sell and Whistler, overseeing all aspects of the printing himself, was to work on the edition of one hundred impressions of each plate throughout the next decade.[17]

On 29 January 1881, the Fine Art Society again presented an exhibition of Whistler's Venetian work, this time showing fifty-three of the pastels. The gallery was decorated according to Whistler's specifications, and was carefully described in the press:

First, a low skirting of yellow-gold, then a high dado of dull yellow-green cloth, then a moulding of green-gold, and then a frieze and ceiling of pale reddish brown. The frames are arranged on the line; but here and there one is placed over another. Most of the frames and mounts are a rich yellow gold, but a dozen out of the fifty three are in green gold, dotted about with a view to decoration, and eminently successful in attaining it.[18]

The exhibition was an unqualified success; Maud Franklin reported to Bacher on both London exhibitions:

He has been frightfully occupied every day & hour since we came home [from Venice] in bringing out the etchings and pastels. The etchings of course were exhibited first & were a great success – I dare say you have seen some accounts of them – most of the papers spoke in the highest possible terms of them and everything was as great a triumph as even Jimmy [Whistler] *could wish – but of course all the other artists were furious.*

As to the pastels, well – they are the *fashion – There has never been such a success known – Whistler has decorated a room for them – an arrangement in brown gold and Benedictine red which is very lovely – out in it they look perfectly fine. All the London world was at the private view – princesses painters beauties actors – everybody – in fact at one moment of the day it was impossible to move – for the room was crammed. . . .*

The best of it is all the pastels are selling – Four hundred pounds worth went the first day now over a thousand pounds worth are sold – the prices ran from 20 to 60 guineas – and nobody grumbles at paying that for them.[19]

Over a year later, in February 1883, Whistler and the Fine Art Society drew together yet a third exhibition, this

time a collection of fifty-one etchings: the vast majority of his Venetian prints augmented by more recent etchings of London.[20] Again, the decoration of the gallery was supervised by Whistler, and the effect was striking:

A gallery unique in its artistic accompaniments, has just been opened at the Fine Arts Club, New Bond Street, in which is exhibited a second series of etchings by Mr. J. McNeill Whistler. The room, lighted from the top, is in itself as remarkable as the etchings themselves. The walls, to a height of about 10 ft., are lined with white felt, finished with a moulding or capping painted yellow, while the skirting is also of the same colour; the floor is carpeted with matting of similar tone, the fireplace is draped in yellow plush; and even the attendants are dressed in a costume in which light yellow is the conspicuous colour. Mr. Whistler, by this "arrangement in white and yellow," as it is called, has enhanced the contrast, or rather produced a harmony of tone between his work and its surroundings. The frames are white, plain, square in section, with two light brown lines as their only relief.[21]

The exhibition was a popular and a critical success; a comparable exhibition was held in New York in October.[22] Yet in spite of the increasing favor that his works gained, the relationship between Whistler and the Fine Art Society dissolved as difficulties over financial arrangements arose with increasing frequency.

It was, therefore, through another London gallery, Dowdeswell & Dowdeswells, that the last major project involving the Venetian works took place. This was the publication in April 1886 of *A Set of Twenty-Six Etchings* – twenty-one of Venetian subjects and five of English – known as "The Second Venice Set." Whistler again undertook to print the edition of thirty himself, a task that, contrary to the First Venice Set, he executed with dispatch; it was completed by mid-July 1887.[23] The set also included a "short résumé of the principles" held by Whistler concerning his etching. The eleven propositions dealt primarily with two subjects: the suitable size of the etching plate (which Whistler felt should be small) and the margin of paper beyond the plate mark, a space often used by his contemporaries to include a *remarque*, a design or drawing printed on the margin (which Whistler felt to be, quite simply, "odious").[24] Consistent with this latter belief, most of Whistler's prints from the Venice sets onward are cut to the plate mark, save for the small tab at the bottom edge which he reserved to carry his graceful signature, the delicate (if sometimes barbed) butterfly.

Whistler's Venetian work – etchings, oils, and pastels – was singularly innovative and singularly successful. The London exhibitions were as novel in their repudiation of Victorian concepts of display as his etchings and pastels were in their technique and handling of materials. At the base of this series of breakthroughs was Whistler's uncanny ability to see in radically new terms subjects that had been viewed but not seen before. As he had written Huish, "Now I have learned to know a Venice in Venice that others never seem to have perceived." An extraordinarily apt pupil of visual experience, he then turned and instructed his generation in knowledge of the Whistler "Venice in Venice." In doing so, he established new norms, new canons of depiction, which we (and his contemporaries) recognize as essentially modern and utterly revolutionary.

M.M.L.
M.S.

1. The libel suit issued from Ruskin's published response to Whistler's *Nocturne in Black and Gold: The Falling Rocket* (1875, Detroit Institute of Art):
For Mr. Whistler's own sake, no less than for the protection of the purchaser, Sir Coutts Lindsey [director of the Grosvenor Gallery] ought not to have admitted works into the gallery in which the ill-educated conceit of the artist so nearly approached the aspect of willful imposture. I have seen, and heard, much of cockney impudence before now; but never expected to hear a coxcomb ask two hundred guineas for flinging a pot of paint in the public's face.
The trial was held 25-26 November 1878 and, amid testimony of wit and irreverence, Whistler established and maintained important (and very modern) arguments on the integrity of the artist's vision and taste as distinct from skill of hand or minuteness of finish. The court sided with Whistler, but gave him, for damages, one farthing rather than his sought-for 1,000 pounds. The costs of this legal suit and the recent expenses of building a grand house and studio led to his declaration of bankruptcy on 8 May 1879. See James McNeill Whistler, *The Gentle Art of Making Enemies* (New York: Dover, 1976), pp. 1-18. Has anyone yet noted that the acronym to this witty book – there could be none more apt – is GAME?
2. Dates and times are recorded in the diary of George A. Lucas, quoted by John A. Mahey, "The Letters of James McNeill Whistler to George A. Lucas," *The Art Bulletin* 49, no. 3 (September 1967), p. 254; quoted in Robert Getscher, "Whistler and Venice," Ph. D. dissertation (Case Western Reserve University, 1970), p. 29.
3. Getscher (pp. 4-10) cites letters and newspaper notices from August and September 1876 that make Whistler's intentions clear, and he presents hints of a possible plan to go to Italy (and presumably Venice) as early as 1863 (p. 4). Circumstances, however, prevented the journey until the autumn of 1879.
4. Mahey, p. 254.
5. E. R. and J. Pennell, *The Life of James McNeill Whistler*, 2 vols. (Philadelphia: Lippincott, 1909), vol. 1, pp. 265-266; the two Pennells present conflicting witness accounts, although they seem to view the Palazzo studio as unlikely.
6. Otto M. Bacher, *With Whistler in Venice* (New York: Century, 1909), p. 14.
7. E. R. and J. Pennell, vol. 1, pp. 263-264. He wrote to his sister-in-law in early November: "Now that it has taken to snowing I begin rather to wish myself back in my own lovely London fogs! – They are lovely those fogs – and I am their painter!" (Getscher, p. 115).
8. Undated letter, Birnie Philip Collection, University of Glasgow, quoted in Getscher, pp. 43, 116.
9. Undated letter (no. 176, Freer Gallery of Art, Washington, D.C.), quoted in Getscher, pp. 117-118.
10. E. R. and J. Pennell, vol. 1, p. 263.
11. Undated letter (no. 176), Freer Gallery, quoted in Getscher, p. 118.
12. Undated letter (University of Glasgow, AM 151/2), quoted in Getscher, p. 119. For Whistler's working habits, see the testimony of Henry Woods, quoted in E. R. and J. Pennell, vol. 1, p. 263, as well as other references, pp. 263-265.
13. Bacher, pp. 6-7.
14. Bacher, p. 14.
15. E. R. and J. Pennell, vol. 1, p. 261. See also Elizabeth Robins Pennell, *Nights* (Philadelphia: Lippincott, 1916), pp. 94-95, "[In Venice] I heard far more of the few little inches of Whistler's etchings and of Whistler's pastels than of the great expanse of Tintoretto's *Paradise* . . . the talk could never keep very long from Whistler."
16. See Getscher, pp. 214-218, for a representative selection.
17. The last two of the set were finally finished posthumously in 1903; see Ruth Fine, *Drawing Near: Whistler Etchings from the Zelman Collection* (Los Angeles: Los Angeles County Museum of Art, 1984), pp. 23-24.
18. E. W. Godwin writing in the *British Architect* (February 1881), quoted in E. R. and J. Pennell, vol. 1, p. 292; Getscher, p. 178.
19. Letter postmarked 25 March 1881 (no. 177, Freer Gallery of Art, Washington, D.C.), quoted in Getscher, p. 180.
20. The catalogue of the exhibition, with brown paper wrapper and torn edges, not only set forth the works exhibited, but included snippets (some woefully out of context) of critical response to the 1880 exhibition, chosen to put the critics in an absurdly bad light. The catalogue is included in Whistler, pp. 92-105.
21. *Building News* (23 February 1883), preserved in Whistler Press Cuttings, Birnie Philip Collection, University of Glasgow, quoted in Getscher, p. 194.
22. At H. Wunderlich & Sons. See Fine, p. 24, and *Arrangement in Yellow and White* (New York: Wunderlich, 1983), n.p.
23. In addition to the sets of thirty, fifteen of the prints had twelve extra impressions made to be sold separately. See Howard Mansfield, *A Descriptive Catalogue of the Etchings and Dry-Points of James Abbott McNeill Whistler* (Chicago: Caxton Club, 1909), pp. xlix-l; Fine, p. 24.
24. The text of the "11 Propositions" is in Whistler, pp. 76-77.

88 The Lagoon, Venice: Nocturne in Blue and Silver, ca. 1879/80

Oil on canvas, 20 × 25¾ in. (50.8 × 65.4 cm)
Signed, lower right: butterfly
Museum of Fine Arts, Boston. Emily L. Ainsley Fund

In *The Lagoon, Venice: Nocturne in Blue and Silver*, Whistler stands near the Piazzetta in front of the Royal Gardens and looks south, with the island church of San Giorgio Maggiore on the right balanced by a tall-masted ship on the left; across the horizon between them stretches the Lido.[1] The viewpoint is shifted from, but clearly relates to, Whistler's etching *Nocturne* (cat. no. 99). In the painting, the dark, wet air of an autumn night places veils before and between the things seen, robbing them of substantiality.[2] Only the points of light in the distance, stretched like beads across the horizon, and their bright reflections in the still water of the lagoon have distinct contours. The rest – the ship, the church, the ghostly gondolas in the foreground – assume an air of immateriality, almost as if they were pockets of mist soon to be dispersed, an illusion. One writer in 1884 described the view with elegant simplicity:

On one of those still moonlight nights which belong of right to Venice . . . you may wander undisturbed along the palace wall and gaze your fill on the shining waters beyond, and on the dark mass of S. Giorgio throwing its shadow between the sky and sea. On such a night, the sight is simply the most exquisite which you can ever hope to enjoy on earth.[3]

It was, in fact, a scene Whistler studied many times in the process of his transcription of it. One of his young colleagues described the procedure:

He gave me many lessons there in Venice – real ones. He would hook his arm in mine, and take me off to look at some Nocturne that he was studying or memorising, and then he would show me how to paint it, in the daytime. He let me – invited me, indeed, to stand at his elbow.[4]

Writing to one of the early owners of this painting, the same correspondent, Harper Pennington, refined the anecdote (with a small lapse in geography):

So, dear Dick [Richard A. Canfield], you have let the Whistlers go! You will miss the great Nocturne – possibly the most peace-bringing of all Jimmy's pictures; certainly his finest night scene. I was with him when he painted it, and many a time he and I would stand for as much as twenty minutes looking at St. Mark's while he memorized the tints and tones.[5]

Because Pennington did not arrive in Venice until the summer of 1880, it would seem, on the basis of this testimony, that Whistler turned to his paints only late in his Venetian stay, after concentrating primarily on etchings and pastel drawings for his first year in the city. One imagines him strolling with his young colleagues after a long evening at one of his favorite cafés – Florian's, perhaps, or the Orientale – and, amid his animated conversation, staring out into the moonlit night, memorizing

88

the colors and the effects of the scene. Then, during the day when he had the clear skeleton of the scene before him, he laid on the nocturnal vestments in his thin, liquid washes of pigment. The result of these long hours of nocturnal study and observation is an evocative, "peace-bringing" glimpse of the lagoon.

Somewhat paradoxically, the serenely titled Nocturnes (or "Moonlights") were among the most controversial and inflammatory of Whistler's works. One, *Nocturne in Black and Gold: The Falling Rocket* (1875, Detroit Institute of Arts), was, in fact, partially responsible for the artist's bankruptcy and Venetian sojourn, having prompted Ruskin's immoderate and often-cited criticism and Whistler's answering libel action. A different critic characterized the Nocturnes as easily replicable, hasty works of seemingly little value:

A "Nocturne" or two by Mr. Whistler – and here we have it in the usual style – a daub of blue and a spot or two of yellow to illustrate ships at sea on a dark night, and a splash and splutter of brightness on a black ground to depict a display of fireworks.[7]

But the Nocturnes are, in fact, highly individual and non-formulaic distillations of a lifetime of seeing and art-making – the artist's response to that magic moment "when the evening mist clothes the riverside with poetry, as with a veil. . . . [And] Nature . . . sings her exquisite song to the artist alone."[8]

M.M.L.
M.S.

1. Bacher, p. 558, records one Nocturne as "a scene from a café near the Royal Gardens. Night after night he watched the gondolas pass, singly and in groups, with lanterns waving in the darkness, without making a show with brush or pen. Then he would return to his rooms and paint the scene."

2. Harper Pennington places the painting of this canvas in September of 1880 (E. R. and J. Pennell, vol. 1, p. 271).

3. Julia Cartwright, "The Artist in Venice," *The Portfolio* (1884), p. 20.

4. Pennington, quoted in E. R. and J. Pennell, vol. 1, pp. 271-272.

5. Pennington, quoted in *American Paintings in the Museum of Fine Arts, Boston*, 2 vols. (Boston: Museum of Fine Arts, 1969), vol. 1, p. 285.

6. E. R. and J. Pennell, vol. 1, p. 269.

7. Whistler, p. 317.

8. Whistler, p. 144.

Provenance: Said to have been stolen from Whistler's studio in Paris by his model, Carmen Rossi; sold by her at the Hôtel Drouot, 25 November 1903, no. 1; bought by Marchant, a London dealer, for R. A. Canfield, Providence, R.I.; sold by him to Knoedler, New York, 1914; sold by them to Mrs. William Henry Bliss, New York; bought by Knoedler, 1922, and later owned by C. N. Bliss and Mrs. Robert Woods Bliss, Dumbarton Oaks, Washington, D.C.; bought by the Museum, 1942

Exhibition History and Bibliography: Copley Society, Boston, *Whistler*, 1904, no. 67; B. Sickert, *Whistler*, London, 1908, p. 90; E. R. and J. Pennell, *The Life of James McNeill Whistler*, 2 vols., Philadelphia: Lippincott, 1909, pp. 271-272; Königliche Akademie der Künste, *Ausstellung Amerikanischer Kunst*, 1910, p. 80; Albright Art Gallery, Buffalo, *Oils, Water Colors, Pastels and Drawings: James McNeill Whistler*, 1911, no. 5, lent by Richard Canfield; Elisabeth Luther Cary, *The Works of James McNeill Whistler*, New York: Moffat, Yard, 1913, p. 167, pl. opp. p. 28; M. Knoedler and Co., New York, *Oils, Water Colors, Pastels and Drawings: James McNeill Whistler*, 1914, no. 4; Théodore Duret, *Whistler*, Frank Rutter, trans., London: Grant Richards, 1917, opp. p. 70; Wadsworth Atheneum, Hartford, *Night Scenes*, 15 February-7 March 1940, no. 137; Carnegie Institute, Pittsburgh, *Survey of American Painting*, 1940, no. 137; M. Knoedler and Co., New York, *Cortissoz – Fifty Years*, 1914, no. 25; Santa Barbara Museum of Art, *Painting Today and Yesterday in the United States*, June-1 September 1941, no. 134; Museum of Modern Art, New York, *Romantic Painting in America*, 1943, no. 208; "1,000 Years of Landscape," *Art News* 44 (14 November 1945), p. 21; Brooklyn Museum, *Landscape*, 8 November 1945-1 January 1946, no. 51; Dayton Art Institute and Columbus Gallery of Fine Arts, *America and Impressionism*, 1951; American Federation of Arts, New York, *American Painting in the Nineteenth Century*, 1953-1954, no. 77; Museum of Fine Arts, Boston, *American Marine Paintings*, 1955, no. 22; Brooks Memorial Union Building, Marquette University, Milwaukee, *American Painting of the Past Seventy-Five Years*, 1956, no. 74; Arts Council of Great Britain, London, *James McNeill Whistler: An Exhibition of Paintings and Other Works, Organized by the Arts Council of Great Britain and the English-Speaking Union of the United States*, 1-24 September 1960, no. 43; Munson-Williams-Proctor Institute, Utica, *19th Century American Painting*, 1960, no. 25; Denys Sutton, *Nocturne: The Art of James McNeill Whistler*, Philadelphia: Lippincott, 1964, p. 94, pl. 39; Spencer Museum of Art, Lawrence, Kansas, *Les Mardis: Stéphane Mallarmé and the Artists of His Circle*, 1966 (?), no. 19; Denys Sutton, *James McNeill Whistler: Paintings, Etchings, Pastels and Watercolours*, London: Phaidon, 1966, pp. 43, 192, pl. 84; Donald Holden, *Whistler Landscapes and Seascapes*, New York: Watson-Guptill, 1969, p. 54, pl. 17; Nationalgalerie, Staatliche Museen, Berlin, *James McNeill Whistler*, 1969, no. 33; Philadelphia Museum of Art, 1971; Wanda M. Corn, *The Color of Mood: American Tonalism, 1880-1910*, M. H. de Young Memorial Museum and the California Palace of the Legion of Honor, San Francisco, 22 January-2 April 1972, no. 47; Museum of Fine Arts, Boston, *Impressionism: French and American*, 1973, no. 135; Roy McMullen, *Victorian Outsider: A Biography of J. A. M. Whistler*, New York: Dutton, 1973, p. 203; Dianne H. Pilgrim, "The Revival of Pastels in Nineteenth-Century America: The Society of Painters in Pastel," *American Art Journal* 10 (November 1978), fig. 22; Howard Risatti, "Music and the Development of Abstraction in America: The Decade Surrounding the Armory Show," *Art Journal* 39 (Fall 1979), p. 9, fig. 2; Andrew McLaren Young, et al., *The Paintings of James McNeill Whistler*, 2 vols., New Haven and London: Yale University Press, 1980, no. 212, pl. 151; National Gallery of Art, Washington, D.C., *Post-Impressionism: Cross-Currents in European and American Painting, 1880-1906*, 25 May-1 September 1980, no. 251.

89   St. Mark's, Venice: Nocturne in Blue and Gold, 1879/80

Oil on canvas, 17½ × 23½ in. (44.5 × 59.7 cm)
The National Museum of Wales

St. Mark's, Venice: Nocturne in Blue and Gold shows four bays of the elaborate façade of St. Mark's, perhaps the central Venetian monument for most Anglo-American travelers, and suggests, to the far left, the clock tower, with a play of gaslights illuminating its arched passageway. Shadowy figures are clustered at the lower left. The scaffolding on the façade of the church may be seen in Whistler's only other view of this urban space, the print *The Piazzetta* (cat. no. 104). No doubt this scaffolding is in place for the 'restoration' of the cathedral and its mosaics that, in 1880, so outraged William Morris and other passionate foreign admirers of San Marco.[1]

When Ruskin portrayed St. Mark's, he called upon all his multiple phrases, his poly-clausal constructions, to suggest a small degree of the basilica's richness:

... a vision out of the earth, and all the great square seems to have opened from it in a kind of awe ... a multitude of pillars and white domes, clustered into a long low pyramid of colored light; a treasure heap, it seems, partly of gold, and partly of opal and mother-of-pearl, hollowed beneath into five great vaulted porches, ceiled with fair mosaic, and beset with sculpture of alabaster, clear as amber and delicate as ivory. ...[2]

And he continues on as long again before ending his sentence. Whistler took a rather different tack. Drawing the cover of night around the structure, creating his effects from memory, he swathed the monument in darkness and mist.[3] Neither gold nor opal gleam forth from across the square; Ruskin's wonder at gorgeous materials and constructs is replaced by the painter's joy of depicting dark shadows looming within a darkened building seen at night – the inverse of a talent for monochromatic virtuosity, which Whistler praised in a strong predecessor: "Canaletto could paint a white building against a white cloud. That was enough to make any man great."[4] And, indeed, it would seem that Whistler himself associated this work with Canaletto, for in 1892, when *Nocturne* was exhibited at Goupil's, Whistler's highly ironic catalogue entry for the painting began with an excerpt from Ruskin condemning Canaletto, whose mannerism he termed "the most degraded that I know of in the whole range of art. ... It gives no one single architectural ornament."[5] Thus joined with the admired Venetian by Ruskin's negative judgments, Whistler could laugh his critics to scorn.

But if Whistler here invokes the work of a famous predecessor, a rarity in his oeuvre, he does so obliquely and non-hierarchically, under cover of darkness and from off-center, lopping off the bay to the far right.[6] The artist's willingness to truncate the facade, and his tendency toward the balanced, rather than the symmetrical, is unexceptional within the context of his entire oeuvre. He does, however, seem to have particularly enjoyed abbreviating the reverence-inspiring basilica. He is reported as saying (although the degree of his seriousness is difficult to assess) that his own decorative scheme for the ceiling of the Peacock Room (Freer Gallery of Art, Washington, D.C.) was "more splendid in effect" than

89

the golden domes of St. Mark's. There is, further, the unpleasant anecdote reported that, when John Wharlton
Bunney, an English painter and ardent disciple of Ruskin, was intently concentrating on his painstakingly
precise description of the façade (*The West Front of St.
Mark's*, 1877-1882, The Guild of St. George, Reading,
England), Whistler crept up behind him and pinned a
note to the back of the unwitting painter: "I am totally
blind."[7] Among his own works, Whistler is reported to
have said that *St. Mark's, Venice: Nocturne in Blue and Gold*
"is the best of my noctur-n-nes."[8] Perhaps part of his affection for the work derived from a nostalgia associated with the
site, for one contemporary reports,

*Very late, on hot sirocco nights, long after the concert crowd
had dispersed, one little knot of men might often be seen in the
deserted Piazza San Marco, sipping refreshment in front of
Florian's. You might be sure that was Whistler, in white duck,
praising France, abusing England, and thoroughly enjoying
Italy.*[9]

M.M.L.
M.S.

1. Letter of 29 November 1880, from Morris (Sanford and Helen
Berger Collection, Carmel, California).
2. John Ruskin, *The Stones of Venice*, 3 vols. (New York: John W.
Lovell, n.d.), vol. 2, p. 70.
3. Bacher, p. 55.
4. Andrew McLaren Young reasonably suggests that the picture has
darkened with time (letter to Rollo Charles, 10 July 1969, department
files, National Museum of Wales); quoted in Bacher, p. 29.
5. Whistler, p. 320.
6. E. R. and J. Pennell report that Whistler said that to reproduce the
masterpiece of the master would be an impertinence (vol. 1, p. 165).
7. E. R. and J. Pennell, vol. 1, p. 270.
8. W. D. Scull to Joseph Pennell, 2 January 1909, speaking of
1886-1887, quoted in Getscher, p. 132.
9. Ralph Curtis, quoted in E. R. and J. Pennell, vol. 1, pp. 273-274.

Provenance: Gallimard, Paris; probably reacquired by Whistler, 1892;
John J. Cowan, Edinburgh, by 1905; Wallis, London; bought by Miss
Gwendoline E. Davies, Llandinam, 1912; bequeathed by her to the
Museum in 1952

Exhibition History and Bibliography: Society of British Artists, London,
1886-1887, no. 331; Goupil Gallery, London, *Nocturnes, Marines and
Chevalet Pieces*, March-April 1892, no. 38; Société Nationale des Beaux-
Arts, Paris, 1892, no. 1071; D. Croal Thomson, "James Abbott McNeill
Whistler: Some Personal Recollections," *Art Journal* 55 (September
1903), pp. 266, 268; Mortimer Menpes, *Whistler As I Knew Him*, New
York: Macmillan, 1904, opp. p. 36; T. R. Way and G. R. Dennis, *The Art of
James McNeill Whistler: An Appreciation*, London: George Bell, 1904, p.
94; Mrs. Arthur Bell, *James McNeill Whistler*, London: George Bell, 1904,
p. 29; New Gallery, London, *The International Society of Sculptors, Painters
and Gravers: Memorial Exhibition of the Works of the Late James McNeill
Whistler*, 22 February-15 April 1905, no. 2; Otto Bacher, *With Whistler in
Venice*, New York: Century, 1908, p. 55; E. R. and J. Pennell, *The Life of
James McNeill Whistler*, 2 vols., Philadelphia: Lippincott, 1909, vol. 1, pp.
265, 272, 287; Howard Mansfield, *A Descriptive Catalogue of the Etchings
and Drypoints of James Abbott McNeill Whistler*, Chicago: Caxton Club,
1909, p. xxix; B. Sickert, *Whistler*, 1908, no. 89; T. Martin Wood, *Whistler*,
London: T. C. and E. C. Jack, n. d., pl. 2; National Museum of Wales,
Cardiff, 1913; Elisabeth Luther Cary, *The Works of James McNeill Whistler*,
New York: Moffat, Yard, 1913, no. 366, p. 211; W. Graham Robertson,
"Whistler, Sargent and Others: A Chapter of Memories," *Harper's Magazine* 163 (October 1931), p. 557; National Museum of Wales, Cardiff,
Catalogue of Oil-Paintings, 1955, no. 816; Denys Sutton, *Nocturne: The Art
of James McNeill Whistler*, Philadelphia: Lippincott, 1964, pp. 93, 94;
Andrew McLaren Young, et al., *The Paintings of James McNeill Whistler*,
2 vols., New Haven and London: Yale University Press, 1980, no. 213,
pl. 135.

90

90 **Clouds and Sky, Venice,** 1879/80
Pastel on gray, textured, wove paper, 5 × 8½ in.
(12.7 × 21.6 cm)
The St. Louis Art Museum. Gift of J. Lionberger Davis

Seen from afar, perhaps from the Lido or from one of the
islands at which the steamers briefly stop in their peregrinations of the Lagoon, Venice stretches in a thin line
across the low horizon. Bracketing the city from above
are great, luminous clouds in an azure sky, and from
below, a calm sea lightly flecked with turquoise. The
domes and campanili of the city, given weight by Whistler's heavy application of dark gray pastels, are but
distant eccentricities in the horizontal line of the city.
They are identifiable not by their form, but by their location – it is recognizably Venice, that is, only for one
already familiar with the city. But, of course, here the city
is only an interrupting agent dividing the two major subjects of the drawing – the sea and the sky:
The aspects of Venice are as various, as manifold, as the hues
held in solution upon her waters beneath a sirocco sky. There
is a perpetual miracle of change; one day is not like another,
one hour varies from the next; there is no stable outline such
as one finds among the mountains, no permanent vista, as in
a view across a plain. The two great constituents of the Vene-
tian landscape, the sea and the sky, are precisely the two
features in nature which undergo most incessant change . . .
the bold and buttressed piles of those cloud-mountains will
never be built again.[1]
Whistler has evoked the "two great constituents" of the
scene by elegant but economic means. Upon a gray paper

that provides his middle tones, the artist lightly streaks a
vibrant blue-green; the friable color just catches across
the textured paper and describes 'lagoon.' Three dark
gray dots at the center and a long band of dark chalk
above them create the city with three gondolas before it.
The clouds also build upon the tone of the paper, as
Whistler applies both lighter and darker grays to model
their extravagant swellings before setting their forms by
placing patches of brilliant light blues amid them. When
earlier artists (such as John Constable) sought to capture
the effects of cloud and sky, there was an element of
meteorologic investigation present, emphasized by the
non-pictorial data recorded in the margins of the images:
site, date, time of day, and weather. Whistler eschews this
web of facts, capturing instead an undefined moment of
great beauty, an end in itself.

The sheet betrays traces of another drawing in the
sky – a doorway, perhaps, if the drawing is turned to a
vertical orientation. Whistler's Venetian pastels often reveal earlier projects that were largely rubbed off in order
to reutilize the sheets, possibly a sign of Whistler's forced
economy while in Venice.[2] *Clouds and Sky, Venice* was
once in the collection of Thomas Way, Whistler's friend
and printer; Way's son, Thomas Way, Jr., served as the
artist's assistant and companion during the period in
1881 when Whistler exhibited fifty-three of his pastels.
The thumbnail sketches made by the younger Way and
included in his *Memories* of the artist provide the best
record of Whistler's innovative pastel exhibition of 1881.
M.M.L.
M.S.

91

1. Uncited source, quoted in Lilian Whiting, *Italy: The Magic Land* (Boston: Little, Brown, 1910), pp. 392-393.

2. See, for example, David Park Curry, *James McNeill Whistler at the Freer Gallery of Art* (Washington, D.C.: Freer Gallery, 1984), pp. 259-267.

Provenance: Thomas Way; J. Lionberger Davis, St. Louis

Exhibition History and Bibliography: Macbeth Gallery, New York, *Whistler Loan Exhibition*, 14 April-10 May 1947, no. 43; Frederick A. Sweet, *Sargent, Whistler and Mary Cassatt*, The Art Institute of Chicago, 14 January-25 February 1954, no. 111; Arts Council of Great Britain, London, *James McNeill Whistler: An Exhibition of Paintings and Other Works, Organized by the Arts Council of Great Britain and the English-Speaking Union of the United States*, 1-24 September 1960, no. 85; Frederick A. Sweet, *James McNeill Whistler*, The Art Institute of Chicago, 13 January-25 February 1968, no. 54; The Saint Louis Art Musueum, *On View*, 6 October-17 November 1974; The University of Michigan Museum of Art, Ann Arbor, *James McNeill Whistler: The Later Years*, 27 August-8 October 1978.

91   The Riva, Sunset: Red and Gold, 1879/80
Pastel on brown paper, sight 5½ × 10½ in. (14 × 26.7 cm)
Signed, lower right: butterfly
Yale University Art Gallery. Mary Gertrude Abbey Fund

Looking down the Giudecca Canal, with the Redentore on the left and the Salute on the right, Whistler created, in *The Riva, Sunset: Red and Gold*, a shiveringly brilliant winter sunset. The pastel was probably executed during the harsh winter of 1879/80, when Whistler impressed his colleagues with his "remarkable energy – and actual suffering – when doing those beautiful pastels during the coldest winter for thirty years, and mostly toward evening, when the cold was bitterest."[1] He has here apparently followed the method that Bacher was later to witness and record:

In beginning a pastel he drew his subject crisply and carefully in outline with black crayon upon one of those sheets of tinted paper which fitted the general color of the motive. A few touches with sky-tinted pastels, corresponding to nature, produced a remarkable effect, with touches of reds, grays, and yellows for the buildings here and there.[2]

Applying in this instance rather more than a "few touches" of pastel, Whistler has filled in his line drawing of the architectural elements across the middle of the brown sheet with a cool slate-blue and then woven on either side of this a web of orange, yellow, and pale blue. The application of these colors in the sky is broad and atmospheric. When treating their reflections in the lagoon, however, Whistler instead used a pattern of short horizontal strokes applied with a relatively fine point, thus conjuring up the movement of the water with the pastel representing the top of the wave, catching light, and the untouched paper signalling the waves' troughs.

Among those exhibited in the 1881 exhibition at the Fine Art Society, *The Riva, Sunset: Red and Gold* was one of five (out of fifty-three) carrying the highest price of 60 guineas, an indication, perhaps, of Whistler's high estimation of this pastel among the set.[3] Several critics at the time valued the work equally highly:

The Riva, Sunset: Red and Gold is one of the most successful examples of a power to reject everything that is superfluous, to select everything that is entirely necessary. . . . A few touches of the pastel in various colours, and somehow, the sky is aglow and the water dancing. The thing has been wrought as it were by pure magic.[4]

M.M.L.
M.S.

92

1. Betsy Fryberger, *Whistler: Themes and Variations*, exh. cat. (Stanford, Ca.: Stanford University Museum of Art, 1978), p 40; Henry Woods, quoted in E. R. and J. Pennell, vol. 1, p. 263.

2. Bacher, pp. 75-76.

3. Getscher, p. 181. The pastels ranged in price from 20 to 60 guineas.

4. Frederick Wedmore, quoted in Getscher, p. 222.

Provenance: Thomas Agnew & Sons, Ltd., London

Exhibition History and Bibliography: Fine Art Society, London, *Venice Pastels*, 1881, no. 6; T. R. Way and G. R. Dennis, *The Art of James McNeill Whistler: An Appreciation*, London: George Bell, 1904, p. 93; Society of the Four Arts, Palm Beach, Fla., *Master Drawings from the Collection of Yale University*, 1 February-3 March 1974; Gerald W. R. Ward, ed., *The Eye of the Beholder: Fakes, Replicas and Alterations in American Art*, New Haven: Yale University Art Gallery, 14 May-10 July 1977, no. 130; Betsy Fryberger, *Whistler: Themes and Variations*, Stanford University Museum of Art, 2 May-18 June 1978, no. 33; The University of Michigan Museum of Art, Ann Arbor, *James McNeill Whistler: The Later Years*, 27 August-8 October 1978.

92 Church of San Giorgio, Venice, 1879/80

Pastel on brown paper, 7¾ × 11⅝ in. (19.7 × 29.6 cm)
Signed, lower right: butterfly
Corcoran Gallery of Art, Washington, D.C. Bequest of James Parmelee

Gleaming like an orient pearl in the soft Venetian light, the semi-spherical dome of San Giorgio Maggiore is the exquisite point of focus in Whistler's view of the island church. Below and beside it the artist employs light dustings of pink and rose pastel on the brown paper to evoke the warm and weathered brickwork that forms the bulk of Palladio's masterpiece. A softer pink echoes these hues in the clouds to the left of the campanile and in the church's reflection in the lagoon. The artist creates the sea by horizontal streaks of three shades of blue, their intensity of hue and the pressure of application becoming ever greater with distance, the pigment denser, leaving less paper uncovered as the horizon is approached. Whistler describes the sky in a very different fashion, laying it on with the flat edge of the pastel stick, and leaving wide bands of colors mottled only by the surface of the paper and force of the hand. Amid this glowing scene of blue and rose, the artist introduces intense green, in the trees to the left, and white, in the wall behind the trees and on the stark little lighthouse stretching from sea to sky at the tip of the island, to enrich and intensify the power of his vision. Whistler applies each of these colors without stumping or any blending on the sheet, yet, due in part to the uncovered portions of the brown paper, the whole is a unified, harmonious unit – a lustrous gem.

While at work on this pastel, Whistler probably stood along the Riva degli Schiavoni. A year later, in the spring of 1881, Whistler's compatriot Henry James stayed at No. 4161 Riva degli Schiavoni, in what he called "dirty apartments with a lovely view."[1] He later described that view on a day that must have much resembled Whistler's in light and atmosphere, so close are their two evocations of the scene:

Straight across, before my windows, rose the great pink mass of San Giorgio Maggiore, which, for an ugly Palladian church, has a success beyond all reason. It is a success of position, of colour, of the immense detached Campanile, tipped with a tall gold angel. I know not whether it is because San Giorgio is so grandly conspicuous, and because it has a great deal of worn, faded-looking brickwork; but for many persons the whole place has a kind of suffusion of rosiness.[2]

M.M.L.
M.S.

1. Leon Edel, *Henry James: The Conquest of London, 1870-1881* (New York: Avon, 1978), p. 438.
2. Henry James, *Portraits of Places* (Boston: James R. Osgood, 1885), p. 15.

Provenance: Bequeathed to the Corcoran by James Parmelee, 1941

Exhibition History and Bibliography: Macbeth Gallery, New York, *Whistler Loan Exhibition*, 14 April-10 May 1947, no. 35; Lyman Allyn Museum, New London, Conn., *James McNeill Whistler, 1834-1903*, 1 May-13 June 1959, no. 46; Arts Council of Great Britain, London, *James McNeill Whistler: An Exhibition of Paintings and Other Works, Organized by the Arts Council of Great Britain and the English-Speaking Union of the United States*, 1-24 September 1960, no. 84; Nationalgalerie, Staatliche Museen, Berlin, *James McNeill Whistler*, 3-24 November 1969, no. 83; Corcoran Gallery of Art, Washington, D.C., *American Pastels from the Corcoran Collection*, 18 January-19 March 1978; idem, *Sargent's Contemporaries*, 4 June-28 August 1983; Linda Crocker Simmons, et al., *American Drawings, Watercolors, Pastels and Collages in the Collection of the Corcoran Gallery of Art*, Washington, D.C.: Corcoran Gallery of Art, 1983, no. 462; David Park Curry, *James McNeill Whistler at the Freer Gallery*, Washington, D.C.: Freer Gallery of Art, 1984, p. 260.

93 A Canal in Venice (Tobacco Warehouse), 1879/80
Pastel on buff paper, 11⅞ × 8⅛ in. (30.2 × 20.6 cm)
Signed, lower left: butterfly
Hirshhorn Museum and Sculpture Garden, Smithsonian Institution

The dominant object in this oblique view down a wide canal is the large building to the right, a palazzo perhaps, now come to a different, less elegant use. Whistler has drawn the building with considerable attention to detail, marking not only the window and shutters on either side of the central archway, but details as small as the tiles of the roof, the laundry drying on lines along the façade, and the dentil course just under the roof. On the canal, a lone gondolier propels his craft back toward a small bridge in the distance, while figures in bright colors walk along the quay.

Within his carefully drawn scene the artist has applied his color with great deliberation. Light strokes with the broad edge of his white pastel fill the unbounded sky

with clouds, while small patches of blue gently define their edges. The buildings are likewise lightly dusted with local colors, except where hard strokes of either white or gray are necessary to define form, such as between the first and second floors of the enormous archway, where, if there were no horizontal accents of white, the façade of the palace might read as flat and unbroken. A brilliant coral color touches the occasional pedestrian – the color recurs, with lessened intensity, across the middle of the pastel on wall, shutter, or reflection, as well as picking out the form of Whistler's butterfly signature at the bottom left, thus tying this otherwise empty corner of the sheet to the rest of the composition. Bacher wrote in retrospect of Whistler's expeditions:

He would load his gondola, which was virtually his studio, with materials, and the old gondolier would take him to his various sketching points. It is noticeable in Venice that many subjects were pastel motives, and Whistler was very clever in deciding which these were. He generally selected bits of strange architecture, windows . . . canal views with boats . . . always little artistic views that would not be complete in any other medium. He always carried two boxes of pastels, an older one for instant use, filled with little bits of strange, broken colors of which he was very fond, and a newer box with

93

which he did his principal work. He had quantities of vari-colored papers, browns, reds, grays, uniform in size.[1]
Yet possessing "quantities" of paper did not provoke Whistler to waste. *A Canal in Venice* is a fine example (there are many among the Venetian pastels, including *Clouds and Sky, Venice*, cat. no. 90) of his practice of taking a sheet with previous work and, orienting it differently, beginning another, unrelated drawing on top of it. The artist might take steps to efface a part, perhaps, of the earlier drawing, but certainly not always; in this instance, a faint scene of architecture hovers, upside down, beneath *A Canal in Venice*, and an upside-down inscription inexplicably floats in the sky. Unconcerned with traditional notions of finish, Whistler left such marks faintly visible. This work was included in the group of pastels he chose to exhibit at the Fine Art Society in 1881.[2] There, it was perhaps among those that prompted one critic to write,

As to the few bits of architecture he has drawn, he has given us – with what remains of the marble forms and details, which a knowledge of architecture would have tempted the eye to complete and restore and spoil – that most difficult of effects to render, its gradual decay. Of Venice as it is, in the de-throned, neglected, sad passing away of it, Whistler tells us with the hand of a master, who has sympathised with the noble city's sufferings and loss.[3]

    M.M.L.
    M.S.
    1. Bacher, pp. 74-75.
    2. See T. R. Way, *Memories of James McNeill Whistler, the Artist* (London: John Lane, The Bodley Head, 1912), opp. p. 52.
    3. E. W. Godwin (architect of Whistler's White House) in the *British Architect* (25 February 1881), quoted in Stanley Weintraub, *Whistler: A Biography* (New York: Weybright and Talley, 1974), p. 261.

Provenance: Kennedy and Company, New York, 1914; collection of Henry Harper Benedict; sold Sotheby's, London, 21 November 1962, no. 11; bought by Joseph H. Hirshhorn

Exhibition History and Bibliography: Fine Art Society, London, *Venice Pastels*, 1881, no. 5; T. R. Way, *Memories of James McNeill Whistler, the Artist*, London: John Lane, The Bodley Head, 1912, opp. p. 52; "Whistlers at Kennedy's," *American Art News* (14 November 1914), p. 6; Burlacher Brothers, New York, *Painters of the Beautiful: Lord Leighton, Whistler, Albert Moore and Conder*, 3-28 March 1964, no. 21; Thomas Agnew & Sons, Ltd., London, *Whistler, The Graphic Work: Amsterdam, Liverpool, London, Venice*, 6-30 July 1976, no. 89; Betsy Fryberger, *Whistler: Themes and Variations*, Stanford University Museum of Art, 2 May-18 June 1978, no. 34; The University of Michigan Museum of Art, Ann Arbor, *James McNeill Whistler: The Later Years*, 27 August-8 October 1978.

94   Canal, San Canciano, Venice, 1879/80
Pastel on brown paper, 11¼ × 6½ in. (28.3 × 16.5 cm)
Signed, lower right: butterfly; inscribed, at right margin:
Ponte Raspi = /0 Sansoni-San Cassiano
Westmoreland Museum of Art, Greensburg, Pennsylvania. William A. Coulter Fund

In *Canal, San Canciano, Venice*, Whistler has placed a web of black lines on his brown paper and, using primarily five hues of pastel (white, brick-red, light blue, turquoise, and deep green), created a vision complete with forms, textures – almost sounds and smells. The artist's uncanny ability to turn to these small byways of the magnificent city and, with discerning eye and skillful hand, recreate them with the most economical of means, was

94

noted as soon as the works were shown:
Certain of the simpler subjects are in their own way perfectly successful. . . . their colour is of gem-like purity; they are, at the same time, sparkling and harmonious, faithful indications of the places and effects they seek to chronicle, and to the eye sensitive to such matters, for their own sake most enjoyable arrangements of light and of hue. In speaking of them, it is impossible to avoid prominent recognition of what seem their merely technical triumphs. The historical and poetic associations have little charm for Mr. Whistler, and no place in his art. In the character of humanity he has not time to be interested, preoccupied as he is by its colours and contours. But nearly all that he has intended to do in these pastels he has done beautifully.[1]

At least part of what is being praised here, and a characteristic especially evident in *Canal, San Canciano*, is Whistler's ability to vary the manner of drawing a stick of color across the paper so as to evoke different substances – in the case of the white, first cloud, then stucco, then marble, then reflection. Only in the building at the center has he stumped (or blended) some of the color to aid this modeling. For the rest, all is laid on freshly and cleanly, with no opportunity for reworking for adjustments in intensity. All depends on the pressure upon and the angle of the pastel, guided always by the artist's preconceived notion of the finished work:

In his best work here, Mr. Whistler has been quite unerring; there is a unity in it from beginning to end; the conception was clearly formed, and it has been executed deftly and with uniformity of excellence. Nor would it be doing quite justice to these fascinating pastels to speak of them as the record of rapid impressions. Venetian nature and Venetian art have really been looked at very closely, as well as with an artist's eye, before so many of their essential characteristics came to be recorded in this swift but penetrating way.[2]

M.M.L.
M.S.

1. *The Standard*, quoted in Getscher, pp. 220-221.
2. Frederick Wedmore, *The Academy*, quoted in Getscher, p. 222.

Provenance: Ross Winans, Baltimore; Albert Roullier Galleries, Chicago; Mrs. Diego Suarez, New York; M. Knoedler and Co., New York, 1963

Exhibition History and Bibliography: Fine Art Society, London, *Venice Pastels*, 1881, no. 20; Kennedy and Company, New York, *Pastels, Etchings and Lithographs by Whistler*, November 1914, no. 4; Carroll Carstairs Gallery, New York, *Whistler Pastels and Water Colours*, 12 January-5 February 1938, no. 1; Musée du Jeu de Paume, Paris, *Trois Siècles d'Art aux Etats-Unis*, May-July 1938, no. 182; Lyman Allyn Museum, New London, Conn., *J. McNeill Whistler*, 1 May-13 June 1949, no. 50; University of Pittsburgh, Henry Clay Frick Fine Arts Department, 1963 and 1966; Butler Institute of American Art, Youngstown, Ohio, 1964; William H. Gerdts, *American Impressionism*, Seattle: Henry Art Gallery, University of Washington, 1980, p. 32; Coe Kerr Gallery, New York, *Americans in Venice, 1879-1913*, 19 October-16 November 1983, no. 8.

95 Calle San Trovaso, 1879/80
Pastel on brown paper, 10⅞ × 5 in. (27.7 × 12.7 cm)
Signed, lower right: butterfly
Collection of James Biddle

Called now after the Calle San Trovaso, a street near the Accademia, this drawing might well be the one exhibited at the Fine Art Society exhibition in 1881 under the title *A Red Note* (no. 43). A narrow view from between two buildings, the work shows at its center a cluster of white domestic buildings, laundry hanging before them. The artist lightly suggests a wellhead standing where the four alleys intersect, and touches in figures of women and children scattered around it with the scantest of details. The chief color accent of the work is the red brick of the foremost tenement, exposed beneath its crumbling sheath of white stucco. A sense of gentle, picturesque decay pervades the scene.

Characteristic of many of Whistler's Venetian pastels, and particularly evident here, is the expanse of dark brown paper left virtually bare but which, through the artist's power of implication, reads as positive form. To the right, for example, it is the absence of sky and the slightest touch of one light line that creates a building flanking the viewer. To the left, a few black lines mold the brown mass of the paper into a specific, visitable building. This pastel exemplifies in particular Whistler's "Secret of Drawing," a vignettist's approach of first drawing the object of primary attention and working from there outward — a process stoppable at any moment so that "the picture must necessarily be a perfect thing from start to finish."[1] It was, in fact, the very modesty of the pastels that drew praise from his critics when they were first exhibited in 1881: "These 'pastels' of Mr. Whistler's are his perfect works — suggestive little pictures which, if he tried to make them more than this, would have been deformed into elaborate failures."[2]

M.M.L.
M.S.

95

1. Bacher, p. 215.
2. *The Times*, quoted in Getscher, p. 220.

Provenance: G. Henry Harper Benedict; sold Sotheby's, 21 November 1962; Agnew; acquired 1963

Exhibition History and Bibliography: Fine Art Society, London, *Venice Pastels*, 1881, no. 43.

96 Bead Stringers, Venice, 1879/80

Pastel on brown paper, 11¾ × 7¼ in. (29.8 × 18.4 cm)
Signed, right center: butterfly
The Metropolitan Museum of Art. Harris Brisbane Dick
Fund, 1917

96

*As we float through these narrow canals between tall houses
which shut out the light even at noonday, we catch glimpses of
Rembrandt-like interiors, and of workers in gold, silver, and
bronze, lace-makers, and stringers of beads, pursuing their
craft, each figure against a background where there is certain
to be some beautiful detail – a wreath of flowers with a child's
face . . . a carven portal, arched casement, or Gothic gateway
– which is sure to touch our quickened aesthetic sense.*[1]
Whistler, far more sensitive than most, was so touched
often during his stay in Venice. The simple configuration
of two windows over two doors, each one of radically
different shape and character, must have delighted the
artist. The flamboyant swag of pink laundry hanging
from the left-hand window is aptly juxtaposed to the
neatly symmetrical ironwork of the ovoid beside the
door: a paradigm of Venice's peculiarly vivid past splendor and present poverty coexisting. Bacher reports that
Whistler would often linger in such working-class sections of the city, intrigued by a picturesque bit of
architecture or a group of bead stringers or needle-
workers.[2]

In this instance, the artist has organized his vision on a
central line marked by the mooring post at the center of
the image. Buildings and figures are lightly suggested by
schematic black lines on brown paper. Forms are given
substance by light touches of color that distinguish masonry from exposed brick, open from closed shutters.
Actual weight, however, comes when Whistler presses
down hard on his color stick, lending intensity to white
door and window surrounds, to pink banner, or to the
black void of an open door or window. When the pastels
were first exhibited in 1881, critics of the day immediately recognized Whistler's virtuosity in the medium:
*One of the great secrets of their charm is the perfect frankness
with which they are drawn. We never feel that the hands have
stopped or hesitated for a moment. Problems of color and
light, the most difficult which the artist has to solve, are
grasped with a certainty seldom realized in such variety . . .
the power which Mr. Whistler possesses of getting at, and
presenting to us, the very essence and kernel of his subjects.
This is the power men call genius.*[3]

M.M.L.
M.S.

1. Ellen Olney Kirk, "In a Gondola," *Lippincotts' Monthly Magazine* 50
(November 1892), pp. 646-647.
2. Bacher, pp. 185-186.
3. *The Art Journal*, quoted in Dianne H. Pilgrim, "The Revival of Pastels
in Nineteenth-Century America: The Society of Painters in Pastel,"
American Art Journal 10 (November 1978), pp. 46-47.

Provenance: Purchased 1917

Exhibition History and Bibliography: Fine Art Society, London, *Venice
Pastels*, 1881, no. 26; Ecole des Beaux-Arts, Paris, *Oeuvres de James
McNeill Whistler*, 1905, no. 149; Elisabeth Luther Cary, *The Works of James
McNeill Whistler: A Study, with a Tentative List of the Artist's Works*, New
York: Moffat, Yard, 1907, no. 274; T. R. Way, *Memories of James McNeill
Whistler, the Artist*, London: John Lane, The Bodley Head, 1912, opp. p.
52; The Museum of Modern Art, New York, *American Painting and Sculp-
ture, 1862-1932*, 31 October 1932-31 January 1933, no. 116; Allen Staley,

ed., *From Realism to Symbolism: Whistler and His World*, New York, Co-
lumbia University Press, 1971, no. 32; The Metropolitan Museum of Art,
New York, *Drawings, Watercolors, Prints and Paintings by James Abbott
McNeill Whistler*, 19 September-26 December 1972; Dianne H. Pilgrim,
"The Revival of Pastels in Nineteenth-Century America: The Society of
Painters in Pastel," *American Art Journal* 10 (November 1978), p. 46.

97 The Doorway, Venice, 1879/80

Pastel on gray-brown paper, 11¾ × 7⅞ in.
(29.8 × 19.8 cm)
Signed, right center: butterfly
The St. Louis Art Museum. Gift of J. Lionberger Davis
Color plate

In *The Doorway*, Whistler looks out from an interior
courtyard, where two women lean over an octagonal
well, through a passageway to a brilliant blue canal beyond. The asymmetrical gray and red near wall fills the
bulk of the image; the shutters of the windows, the water
and the costumes of the two women provide bright notes
of complementary colors. Of his pastels, this is among the
simplest and most modern in composition: the near
frontality of the building and the unbroken climb of its
red wall to the very top of the paper simultaneously assert the flatness of the sheet, while implying a question-
ing of borders and edges.

E. R. and J. Pennell, in describing Whistler on foot,
prowling about Venice in search of a fascinating motif,
seem to make specific reference to *The Doorway*:
*When he once found what he wanted, he made his sketch in
black chalk, and then just hinted, but beautifully, the colour
of the old walls, the green shutters, the brilliant spots of the
women's dresses; the colour put in as in a mosaic or stained
glass, mostly a flat tint, the pastel between the black lines. He
always remembered the limitations of the medium and never
attempted to paint with his stick of colour, using greatest pressure to obtain greater brilliancy and less for his more delicate
tones, but keeping his colour pure and fresh.*[1]
Part of what the Pennells consider the limitation of the
pastel is precisely the quality of effervescent, glowing
color that the artist captures in *The Doorway*, where the
brown paper glows beneath lightly dusted layers of pigment. In its delicacy and small size, *The Doorway*, like
many of Whistler's pastels, evokes "a bloom, an airiness,
a tenderness, a decorative grace."[2]

The delicacy in this case is heightened by a distancing
device often used in Whistler's Venetian works: the view
through a doorway. The doors not only frame the various
views or figures, but establish spaces within spaces that
reveal glimpses of removed and unexplored worlds,
while maintaining the privacy of those portrayed.
M.M.L.
M.S.

1. E. R. and J. Pennell, vol. 1, p. 278.
2. M. G. van Rennsselaer, "American Painters in Pastel," *Century Magazine* 29 (December 1884), p. 209.

Provenance: Richard A. Canfield, Providence, R.I., until 1914;
M. Knoedler and Co., New York, 1914; sold Parke Bernet Galleries,
New York, 19 May 1948, no. 62; J. Lionberger Davis, Saint Louis

Exhibition History and Bibliography: Fine Art Society, London, *Venice
Pastels*, 1881, no. 11; Ecole des Beaux-Arts, Paris, *Paintings in Oil and
Pastel by James A. McNeill Whistler*, 15 March-31 May 1910, no. 19; Al-
bright Art Gallery, Buffalo, *Oils, Water Colors, Pastels and Drawings by
James McNeill Whistler, Lent by Mr. Richard Canfield*, 1911, no. 32; T. R.
Way, *Memories of James McNeill Whistler, the Artist*, London: John Lane,
The Bodley Head, 1912, opp. p. 53; Elisabeth Luther Cary, *The Works of
James McNeill Whistler*, New York: Moffat, Yard, 1913, p. 200; M. Knoed-
ler, New York, *Oils, Water Colors, Pastels & Drawings: James McNeill*

97

Whistler, 1914, no. 4; Théodore Duret, *Whistler*, trans. Frank Rutter, Lon-
don: Grant Richards, 1917, opp. p. 82; Frederick A. Sweet, *Sargent,
Whistler and Mary Cassatt*, The Art Institute of Chicago, 14 January-25
February 1954, no. 114; idem, *James McNeill Whistler*, The Art Institute of
Chicago, 13 January-25 February 1968, no. 55.

98   Little Venice, 1880
From the First Venice Set
Etching (brown ink on laid paper)
K. 183, only state, trimmed to plate mark, 7⅜ × 10½ in.
(18.6 × 26.7 cm)
Signed in plate, at left: butterfly; signed on tab: butterfly
and *imp*
The Cleveland Museum of Art. Gift of Mr. and Mrs. Ralph
King

From a site near the Lido across the lagoon, Whistler, in
Little Venice, puts the entire city before the viewer. From
the Public Gardens at the left, to the Salute at the right
(the image is reversed due to the printmaking process)
the southern side of the city stretches in one thin line
across the middle of the plate. Gondolas and other craft
hover on the still water, emphasizing this vision of the
site's splendors suspended between sky and sea. The perceptive critic Théodore Duret, in March of 1881, articulated the magical way in which Whistler evokes the richness of the panorama through an elegant economy:
*Un petit nombre de traits horizontaux figurent de l'eau et
servent à rejeter dans un immense lointain le rivage, la ville et
ses monuments, simplement marqués, au milieu du papier,
par quelques lignes dentelées. Jamais on ne s'est essayé à tant
rendre avec si peu de travail apparent et des moyens si sim-
ples. Mais comme cette eau-forte reproduit l'impression qu'on
se rappelle avoir soi-même éprouvée à l'aspect de Venise!
Comme c'est bien là une ville à fleur d'eau qui, de loin, semble
une apparition prête à rentrer sous la mer!*
(A few horizontal lines mark the water and serve to con-
struct in the far distance, the Riva, the city, and its
monuments, simply denoted in the middle of the sheet by
a few jagged lines. Never has anyone attempted to portray so much with so little apparent effort and with such
simple means. But how this etching reproduces the impression that one remembers having felt oneself on
seeing this view of Venice! It is truly, there, a city at water
level which, from afar, seems an apparition ready to return beneath the sea.)[1]

Although catalogued as the first print in the First Venice Set, the series of twelve etchings commissioned by the
Fine Art Society and exhibited in December of 1880, this
was in fact probably among the last plates that Whistler
made in Venice.[2] Not until after his return to London in
November of 1880 did Whistler actually etch the plate, a
process that the printer T. R. Way observed and recorded
with obvious admiration for the artist's exacting technique:
He brought back [to London] *the plate of the ''Little Venice,'' only drawn with the needle. He had done it from one of
the islands, to which there are excursions by steam boat, allowing an hour or two on shore before returning. The plate I
saw him bite in, holding it in one hand and moving the acid
about with a feather, and without any stopping out. The first
impression of it printed was quite satisfactory, and he did not
need to rebite or reduce any part of it, which . . . showed not
only wonderful skill in biting, but an amazing memory as
well.[3]*
Thus, while *Little Venice* serves as an introduction and
overview to the vision that Whistler brought back to his
London patrons, it should also be seen as the clear summary, the elegant final distillation, of his fourteen-month
stay in the city which so many would recognize in his
''apparition ready to return beneath the sea.''
M.M.L.
M.S.

99

1. Théodore Duret, "Artistes Anglais: James Whistler," *Gazette des Beaux-Arts* 23, 2e période (1881), p. 369, authors' translation.

2. Getscher, pp. 74-75.

3. T. R. Way, *Memories of James McNeill Whistler: The Artist* (London: John Lane, The Bodley Head, 1912) p. 45.

Exhibition History and Bibliography: Edward G. Kennedy, *The Etched Work of Whistler*, New York: The Grolier Club, 1910, no. 183.

99 Nocturne, 1879/80

From the First Venice Set
Etching and drypoint (brown ink on modern laid paper)
K. 184, iv/v, trimmed to plate mark, 8 × 11⅝ in.
(20.3 × 29.5 cm)
Signed on tab: butterfly and *imp*
The Fine Arts Museums of San Francisco, Achenbach Foundation for Graphic Arts. William H. Noble Bequest Fund

One of the earliest of his Venetian prints, *Nocturne* is among the most evocative and poetic etchings in Whistler's entire oeuvre.[1] Viewed looking south over the water from the Riva past gondolas and a tall ship, the scene extends between the church and campanile of San Giorgio Maggiore on the right, to the church of Santa Maria della Salute on the left (due to the etching process, the view is reversed). Whistler suggests these masterworks of Palladio and Longhena, the surrounding stretch of architecture and shipping, and their reflections in the quiet waters of the Bacino di San Marco and Giudecca Canal by the merest clustering of vertical lines across the horizon; all detail and materiality have faded with the advent of night. But if the artist has used the etched line only sparingly to depict specific objects, he has, with great verve and freedom, evoked the sensation of mist and palpable darkness with plate tone (ink left upon the surface of the metal plate rather than held in the incised

lines), creating an aurora-encased view. The narrow line of structures and masts appears to cast radiating streaks of light up into the night sky and out across the water. The effect – mysterious, magical – is the printmaking equivalent of Whistler's painted Nocturnes of London and Valparaiso (one of the former, through Ruskin's intemperate criticism and Whistler's resultant libel suit, had initially helped to spark the bankruptcy that led to the artist's Venetian journey). And as did the paintings, the print at first provoked negative response from London critics:

"Nocturne," is different in treatment to the rest of the prints, and can hardly be called, as it stands, an etching; the bones as it were of the picture have been etched, which bones consist of some shipping and distant objects, and then over the whole of the plate ink has apparently been smeared. We have seen a great many representations of Venetian skies, but never saw one before consisting of brown smoke with clots of ink in diagonal lines.[2]

The necessary individuality of each impression, however, resulting from Whistler's "smearing" of ink for each sheet, allowed the artist to create the illusion of moments ranging from a light-tinged dusk or dawn to the very deepest of midnights. Beauty of effect, rather than an adherence to definitions, was the quality Whistler here sought and achieved.

M.M.L.
M.S.

1. Robert H. Getscher and Allen Staley, *The Stamp of Whistler*, exh. cat. (Oberlin, Ohio: Allen Memorial Art Museum, 1977), p. 95, records one impression now in the University of Glasgow as being inscribed "1st state – 1st proof – Venice 1879."

2. *British Architect* (10 December 1880), quoted in Fine, p. 133.

Exhibition History and Bibliography: Edward G. Kennedy, *The Etched Work of Whistler*, New York: The Grolier Club, 1910, no. 184, iv/v.

100 The Little Mast, 1880
From the First Venice Set
Etching (dark brown ink on laid paper)
K. 185, ii/iv, trimmed to plate mark, 10½ × 7¼ in.
(26.7 × 18.4 cm)
Signed on tab: butterfly and *imp*; in plate upper right:
butterfly; inscribed on reverse in Whistler's hand: *selected
proof* and butterfly
The Zelman Collection

The Little Mast (so called to distinguish it from Whistler's
larger version of a comparable subject, *The Mast*, cat. no.
109) shows a midday scene on the Via Garibaldi, near the
Public Gardens.[1] Relatively modest buildings flank the
open space, and a hot sun draws short, sharp-edged
shadows from their balconies and lowered awnings. A
balustrade and bridge (very similar to those appearing in
Duveneck's *The Water Carriers*, cat. no. 15) border the Riva
degli Schiavoni in the middle ground. The wide street is
filled with men, women, and children; the figures, although lightly suggested and undetailed, are characterized by an outline or gesture so vivid that each has
movement and individuality. As in Prendergast's images,
the viewer is elevated and thus enabled to see the scene
and the figures with clarity and precision. Near the balustrade, standing high above the Venetians, a grand,
eagle-betopped mast asserts the city's past link to, and
dominion over, the sea, the source of her wealth and
pride. Removed now from its proud galleon, the mast
stands incongruously on the dry land, seemingly un-
noticed by the city dwellers of this working-class district.

The contrast between the past and present glories of
Venice was often noted by visitors to the city, as when
Mark Twain wrote of it in 1869:
*This Venice, which was a haughty, invincible, magnificent
Republic for nearly fourteen hundred years; whose armies
compelled the world's applause whenever and wherever they
battled; whose navies well nigh held dominion of the seas, and
whose merchant fleets whitened the remotest oceans with their
sails and loaded these piers with the products of every clime, is
fallen a prey to poverty, neglect, and melancholy decay. Six
hundred years ago, Venice was the Autocrat of Commerce; her
mart was the great commercial centre, the distributing house
from whence the enormous trade of the Orient was spread
abroad over the Western world. Today her piers are deserted,
her warehouses are empty, her merchant fleets are vanished,
her armies and her navies are but memories. Her glory is
departed, and with her crumbling grandeur of wharves and
palaces about her she sits among her stagnant lagoons, forlorn
and beggared, forgotten by the world. She that in her palmy
days commanded the commerce of a hemisphere and made the
weal or woe of nations with a beck of her puissant finger is
become the humblest among the peoples of the Earth – a ped-
dler of glass-beads for women, and trifling toys and trinkets
for schoolgirls and children.*[2]
Whistler makes the point with a far lighter touch.

This impression of *The Little Mast*, evenly wiped with
just enough plate tone to suggest warm sunlight, displays
Whistler's ability to suggest aerial perspective within the
limits of a monochromatic image; dark, heavily-etched
lines detail the foreground while the lightly touched
lines that describe schooners and masts at the center of

100

the plate read convincingly as distant barks bobbing at
anchor in the Bacino.
M.M.L.
M.S.

1. According to Joseph Pennell, cited in *Arrangement in White and
Yellow: A Centennial Celebration*, no. 16. The Via Garibaldi is near the
Casa Jankowitz, into which Whistler and Maud had moved in the summer of 1880. The Pennells report that an inexpensive trattoria near the
Via Garibaldi was the site of many dinners and Sunday breakfasts for
the Anglo-American artist community that Whistler, although impoverished, hosted (E. R. and J. Pennell, vol. 1, p. 168).
2. Mark Twain, *The Innocents Abroad or The New Pilgrim's Progress* (New
York: Grosset & Dunlop, 1911), p. 144.

Exhibition History and Bibliography: Edward G. Kennedy, *The Etched
Work of Whistler*, New York: The Grolier Club, 1910, no. 185, ii/iv.

101 The Little Lagoon, 1880

From the First Venice Set
Etching (warm black ink on wove paper)
K. 186, ii/ii, plate 8⅞ × 6 in. (22.6 × 15.2 cm)
Signed in pencil in lower left margin: butterfly and *imp*;
in plate lower right: butterfly
The Zelman Collection

In *The Little Lagoon*, Whistler turns from the monuments
of Venice, the ''stones'' earlier celebrated by John Ruskin, and concentrates instead on a scene of anecdotal
simplicity and great formal beauty. The still waters of the
Lagoon fill almost three-quarters of the sheet; a cloudy
sky above occupies the remainder. At the horizon, wavy
broken lines suggest the distant shoreline of the Lido.
Only at the far left does a building (a section of the monastery connected with San Giorgio Maggiore, unseen
beyond the paper's edge) intrude on this scene of sea and
sky. Instead of focusing on the city, Whistler centers his
composition on a large ketch, its sails lowered, its deck
empty. Nowhere in his Venice work do we find the fun-
neled steamships or the turtlish vaporetti, which by 1880
were familiar sights; Whistler insists on the technologically more archaic vessels for his carefully balanced
images. Around the moored boat, the man-powered craft
of Venice move through the scene, each propelled by a
wiry gondolier twisted into a pose of vigor and action
worthy of the figures of Jacques Callot. These smaller
craft are depicted quickly, sketchily, as if to convey an
idea of both their form and their gliding movement; we
note, for instance, that the gondoliers strain at their task,
but all lack the oar essential to convert this energy into
forward motion. As completely as any in the set, this
image becomes a formal arrangement of light and dark,
the illusion of deep space held precisely in balance by the
surface pattern on the work's flat surface. The striped
pilings and their reflections in the foreground (echoing
the two masts of the boat) and the butterfly monogram
might almost be placed as much in response to an oriental sense of design as to the facts of the scene.

The Zelman Collection impression, printed with a
warm black ink, signed with a large butterfly, and left
with its margins untrimmed, is perhaps one of those
printed in Venice on either Otto Bacher's portable press
or the old wooden press reportedly used for Canaletto's
etchings.[1]

M.M.L.
M.S.

1. E. R. and J. Pennell, vol. 1, pp. 167, 282.

Exhibition History and Bibliography: Edward G. Kennedy, *The Etched
Work of Whistler*, New York: The Grolier Club, 1910, no. 186, ii/ii.

101

102 The Palaces, 1880

From the First Venice Set
Etching and drypoint (warm black ink on antique laid
paper)
K. 187, iii/iii, trimmed to plate mark, 10 × 14¼ in.
(25.4 × 36.2 cm)
Signed on tab: butterfly and *imp*
The Fine Arts Museums of San Francisco, Achenbach
Foundation for Graphic Arts. Gift of Osgood Hooker

The Palaces is the largest of Whistler's plates, appropri-
ately monumental in subject, treatment, and presentation.[1] From the Fondamenta dell'Olio, next to the fishmarket, he looked across the Grand Canal to make a
straightforward, topographically clear image of the large
Palazzo Morosini-Sagredo and the adjoining fifteenth-
century Palazzo Pesaro Rava'.[2] In its asymmetrical mass-
ing and the detail work of its windows, the Palazzo
Morosini-Sagredo is a splendid example of the Venetian
Gothic and was recognized as such by that style's chief
nineteenth-century champion, John Ruskin:
*Sagredo, Palazzo, on the Grand Canal. Much defaced, but full
of interest. Its sea story* [ground floor] *is restored; its first
floor has a most interesting arcade of the early thirteenth
century third order of windows; its upper windows are the*

102

finest fourth and fifth orders of early fourteenth century; the group of fourth orders in the centre being brought into some resemblance to the late Gothic traceries by the subsequent introduction of the quatrefoils above them.[3]

Ruskin, his interest primarily taxonomic, sought to understand the building through the close scrutiny of its details. Whistler, drawn to the same subject as his nemesis, simply calls his image *Palaces,* avoiding its specific topographic, literary, and historic context. Its ''interesting'' ornament and traceries are but suggested; Whistler's portrayal of them is not so much a scientific exploration of this type of molding or that kind of carving as it is simply the recording of daylight falling across the broken surface of masonry walls and sculptural details. Whistler further deflects attention from the architectural facts and enlivens the scene with summarily noted figures and errant curtains at doorways and windows. Gondolas, particularly those lightly sketched in on the right, and others gamboling and bobbing at the Traghetto della Pescheria on the left, punctuate the Grand Canal, its own surface animated by Whistler's delicate tracery of shadow and reflection.

It is significant that Whistler arrests his pictorial field on the right with a glimpse of the side of the Ca' d'Oro, avoiding any hint of its very recognizable façade. Clearly, like Prendergast in his *Venetian Palaces on the Grand Canal* (cat. no. 44) he wants his palaces to be generic and anonymous rather than specific and heroic. Also like Prendergast, he lifts the buildings high on his sheet, a strategy that enables him to use the ever-shifting surface of the water as an eloquent foil to the impressively permanent masonry structures.

The weightiest, most detailed sections of the etching are the slopes of the two palaces' asymmetrical tiled roofs, elements that Whistler exaggerates in his print, forcing them into far greater prominence than they in fact have. These cap the composition and, with their multitude of tiny, overlapping strokes, provide a rich and velvety surface to contrast with Whistler's predominantly light and shimmering line work. In this and other late impressions of the print, the area along the rooftops is further enriched by tonal areas (perhaps an experiment with a sulphur tint) added to the plate itself.[4]

M.M.L.
M.S.

1. And yet this is not a giant sheet by any means. Whistler inveighed against the large plates fashionable at the end of the century in the ''11 Propositions'' that accompanied the Second Venice Set (see Whistler, pp. 76-77). Fellow American F. Hopkinson Smith painted this same view but included a section of the fishmarket (*Old Fish Market, Venice,* Santa Barbara Museum of Art).
2. Pennell's placing of Whistler at the Palazzo Rezzonico for the making of this print is clearly an error (*Life*, p. 165).
3. Ruskin, *Stones,* vol. 3, p. 374.
4. Fine, p. 123.

Exhibition History and Bibliography: Edward G. Kennedy, *The Etched Work of Whistler*, New York: The Grolier Club, 1910, no. 187, iii/iii.

103   **The Doorway,** 1879/80
From the First Venice Set
Etching and drypoint (black ink on antique laid paper)
K. 188, iv/vii, trimmed to plate mark, 11⅝ × 8 in.
(29.5 × 20.3 cm)
Signed on tab: butterfly and *imp*; in plate upper left: butterfly
The Zelman Collection

One of the richest of Whistler's Venetian etchings, *The Doorway* combines his bold use of linear detail in the architectural section with a heavy, atmospheric plate tone in the water. The scene is of an intricately detailed Renaissance doorway located on the Rio della Fava, just east of the Rialto.[1] Whistler viewed the scene from across the narrow canal, near the water terminus of the Calle del Zocco opposite. The sites for Marin's *Della Fava* (cat. no. 24) and Sargent's *Venetian Doorway* (cat. no. 76) are close by. The focus here is on a group of figures seen through a doorway, a subject that runs through Whistler's oeuvre. The palace, gently decaying, is used by a chairmaker or caner; his wares can be seen suspended from the ceiling, glimmering ghost-like across the top of the large space, while the tradesman himself sits at the center of the sheet beneath the distant, grilled window.

In a departure from his practice in many of the Venetian works, objects such as the chairs, the interior figures, and the iron grills are described less by line than by the negative presence of white paper surrounded by deep black areas. In the foreground, two women face the viewer, one posed meditatively with her chin cradled on her upraised hand, the other, younger girl bending somewhat enigmatically out over the water of the canal (other states of the print explain her stance by including a cloth that she rinses in the water). Whistler models the figures and the interior space with close, lightly etched lines that create around them a softened, shadowy light. The exterior doorway, with its floral relief carvings and iron grills, on the contrary, he treats with bold, heavy lines suggesting strong shadows cast by direct sunlight. Across the bottom of the sheet, a beautifully modulated area of plate tone combines with both the ribbed quality of the laid paper and the light etching of the canal's surface to create a powerful illusion of dark, moving water.

Whistler's adaptation of the vignette format, here and in other Venetian prints, unobtrusively focuses the viewer's attention at the center of the image, letting the details of the subject fade at the edges of the sheet. The effect of the symmetrical arrangement of *The Doorway*, with its large central arch and two smaller flanking ones, lends the work a sacred tone, suggesting a triptych. Whistler's monogram-derived signature, the butterfly, finds a place in the architecture to the left of the central arch, added by the artist as if it were simply another carved ornament on the elaborate façade – Whistler here leaving his mark, quite literally, on the Venetian scene.

The impression from the Zelman Collection, one of particularly fine quality, was chosen by Whistler to give to his principal American dealer, Hermann Wunderlich.[2]

M.M.L.
M.S.

1. A photograph of the site is reproduced in Bacher, p. 195.
2. From inscription on reverse of print.

Exhibition History and Bibliography: Edward G. Kennedy, *The Etched Work of Whistler*, New York: The Grolier Club, 1910, no. 188, iv/vii.

103

104 The Piazzetta, 1880
From the First Venice Set
Etching (black ink on laid paper)
K. 189, iii/v, trimmed to plate mark, 10 × 7⅛
(25.4 × 18 cm)
Signed on tab: butterfly and *imp*; in plate on column: butterfly
The Cleveland Museum of Art. Gift of Mr. and Mrs. Ralph King

The Piazzetta, located at the very heart of Venice, is bordered on three sides by the foremost architectural symbols of the city's spiritual, temporal, and intellectual power, and on the fourth, by the Bacino. Whistler's only version of this evocative geographical confluence is, characteristically, oblique. In the distance, closing off the scene, is the elaborately etched clock tower viewed slightly off-center, the subject of memorable works by Charles Coleman (cat. no. 12, cover) and Maurice Prendergast (cat. no. 35, back cover). The façade of San Marco is partially obscured by scaffolding, visible again in Whistler's nocturnal portrait of the church (cat. no. 89). Here the familiar façade, its encrustations and elaborations reduced to thin outlines (even the famous horses are but lightly suggested), is largely hidden by the granite pillar of St. Theodore. This, the column erected in 1180 and dedicated to Venice's first protector, is truncated,

104

illusion is boldly undermined, however, as the column reaches upward and loses not only the parallel hatchings, but its very contour lines; solid and void meet and mingle, and where the illusion of rounded granite ceases and the sky begins is impossible to determine. Equally remarkable is Whistler's uncanny ability, in this most linear of media, to suggest motion in a fashion that directly foreshadows the experiments of the Italian Futurists two decades and more later: the fabled pigeons of St. Mark, omnipresent, but rarely depicted, here fly across the square, their wings a blur, marking the vitality of the living occupants of the city.

M.M.L.
M.S.

1. John Ruskin, in *St. Mark's Rest: The History of Venice* (New York: John Wiley, 1877), pp. 1-2, begins his book with an account of these columns, "the most beautiful columns at present extant and erect in the conveniently visitable world," and, granting them pride of place, hangs his discussion of Venice's history upon their importance and beauty.

Exhibition History and Bibliography: Edward G. Kennedy, *The Etched Work of Whistler*, New York: The Grolier Club, no. 189, iii/v.

105 Traghetto, No. 2, 1880

From the First Venice Set
Etching and drypoint (black ink on antique laid paper)
K. 191, iv/vi, sheet 10½ × 13⅜ in. (26.7 × 33.9 cm); plate 9¼ × 12 in. (23.5 × 30.5 cm)
Signed in plate, center left: butterfly
The Fine Arts Museums of San Francisco, Achenbach Foundation for Graphic Arts. Gift of Dr. Ludwig A. Emge

In *Traghetto, No. 2*, Whistler again depicts a darkened interior space separating two lit exterior zones. In the distance, gondolas glide along the sunstruck canal, and one man (perhaps a gondolier of the traghetto, or ferry) basks in the heat, his broad-brimmed hat shielding his face and casting a shadow across his body. In the foreground, also in the light, a young girl holds a child not substantially smaller than herself, and, to the right, a group of mustachioed men in large, dark hats sits casually around a table set with glasses and a carafe. At the center of the foreground, young trees, the light playing upon their falling leaves, divide the image. Spreading across the breadth of the scene and plunging diagonally into deep space is a broad, high-ceilinged passageway. It is here that the artist has concentrated his principal effort, clustering hundreds of short parallel lines to differentiate the darkened rafters from their yet darker shadows, and modeling the stone moldings that line the side walls of the cavernous space. This large archway finds a smaller echo towards the back, where a detached gondola felze mimics the same arched shape silhouetted against the distant sunlit canal. From within the darkness, the form of a metal lantern softly gleams forth, contrasting in its soft reflected light with the bright light-struck leaves falling in the foreground.

The title of this print refers to the fact that this is Whistler's second treatment of this subject. Otto Bacher recorded the short-lived first plate and the genesis of *Traghetto, No. 2*. On his first visit to Whistler's quarters, Bacher saw a particularly beautiful impression of the *Traghetto*, which he praised with vigor and enthusiasm.

fading to nothingness well before its full height and the statue of St. Theodore and his crocodile are reached; and there is no hint of the second ancient Syrian column, that bearing the winged lion of St. Mark.[1] Whistler stands beside Jacopo Sansovino's white marble Libreria, but he draws the building summarily and hastily, with little more purpose than that of channeling the viewer's eye down and toward the center of the Piazzetta, beyond the simply outlined Loggetta and the three enormous flagstaffs. He has formatted his image so that neither the Campanile nor the Doge's Palace are visible. Beneath the cloudy sky, in this one modest print, Whistler has undercut, truncated, obscured, or ignored the central architectural monuments of Venice. In their place, he has focused our interest on the contemporary Venetians as they loiter in the square; the present inhabitants claim precedence, in his eyes, over the remains of a glorious past. Of these, the man in the broad-brimmed, dark hat, a sort of Whistler alter ego who appears in many of these etchings, asserts an empathetic connection with the viewer. Whistler's superb gestural shorthand, with its telling line and characterizing detail, is manifest especially in the figures of the children feeding pigeons in the lower right of the work.

Two formal elements of *The Piazzetta* merit note. Whistler, by means of curving parallel hatchings, clearly intends that the lower section of the column be read, in spite of its broad expanse of plain paper, as rounded. This

105

Whistler offered to show him other impressions of the *Traghetto*, from later states of the plate, and each one seemed to Bacher worse than the preceding:
This last one represented the actual, sad condition of the copper plate as it was then. Horrors! What a shock ran through me! The plate was ruined, irrevocably ruined! I was stunned for a moment, and falteringly questioned him for the reasons that had influenced him to dare to add another line [to the earliest state].
"I changed it because a duffer – a – duffer – a painter – thought it was incomplete." This was all he said, but he seemed very bitter.[1]
Whistler seems not often to have publicly admitted mistakes, and the loss of this plate appears to have weighed upon him. Bacher reports that Whistler mentioned the *Traghetto* several times and, after moving into the Casa Jankowitz, surprised the younger artist one morning by announcing that he was going to do the subject all over again. By means of a counterproof of white ink on black ground, Whistler transferred the old design to a specially made copper plate. From there, he was able to edit the overworked design by constant reference to the original impression, a project that took days, even weeks.[2] Although Bacher reports the procedure a success, it is evident that Whistler was unsatisfied with the result, for he took *Traghetto, No. 2* through more than six states, including major revisions between the second and third one.

    M.M.L.
    M.S.

1. Bacher, pp. 166-169.
2. Bacher, pp. 172, 179.

Exhibition History and Bibliography: Edward G. Kennedy, *The Etched Work of Whistler*, New York: The Grolier Club, 1910, no. 191, iv/vi.

106 The Riva, No. 1, 1880
From the First Venice Set
Etching and drypoint (black ink on oriental paper)
K. 192, iii/iii, sheet 8⅞ × 12½ in. (22.5 × 31.8 cm); plate 8 × 11¾ in. (20.3 × 29.8 cm)
Signed in pencil, in margin lower left: butterfly and *imp*; in plate, upper left: butterfly
The Fine Arts Museums of San Francisco, Achenbach Foundation for Graphic Arts. Gift of Osgood Hooker

The Riva, No. 1 sets forth in lively detail the sweeping curve of the Riva degli Schiavoni (as seen from the Riva San Biagio), ending at the far right with the just-suggested forms of the domes and Campanile of San Marco. Architecture, commerce, and, perhaps above all, the Venetians themselves combine to lend great vitality to the image. This was apt for the scene, as noted by at least one commentator from the 1880s:
Next to the Piazza, the Riva dei Schiaveni is, perhaps, the most attractive place in Venice. It is not only for the sake of the view, although that is magnificent, or for S. Giorgio – best beloved of all lesser Venetian shrines – opposite; but it is because there you see whatever is left of the vivacity and joyousness of Venetian life. . . . On the Riva you have the life of the people.
This is the place for the artist who knows dextrously to combine groups of figures with shipping and buildings. He has but to take his stand on a balcony overlooking the Riva . . . and he will see every type and variety conceivable.[1]
Whistler's working, striding, gossiping Venetians seem the very model for the commentator.
    Scholars have speculated that Whistler compiled this

106

image from at least two different vantage points on the
Riva San Biagio (one on either side of the bridge that
crosses the Rio d'Arsenale) and that the implied elevated
viewpoint is fictive.[2] If, indeed, Whistler's only "balcony" was in his imagination, he has conveyed that
fiction effectively not only by means of the expansive
vista, but also by the empty foreground that, devoid of
activity, raises the viewers' attention to the center of the
sheet as if we were looking out over the scene. But the
elevated prospect we see in this view and such others as
Prendergast's *Rainy Day, Venice* (cat. no. 43) or Sargent's
The Salute, Venice (cat. no. 65) suggests more probably
the use of photographers' tall ladder platforms.

Very close in subject to the later *The Riva, No. 2* (cat.
no. 115), Whistler's images were inspired by the works of
the younger Frank Duveneck, who etched this scene in
the late spring of 1880. Otto Bacher recollected, "It is
only fair to say that Duveneck made the etchings of the
Riva before Whistler made his. Whistler saw them as I
was helping Duveneck bite the plates, and frankly said:
'Whistler must do the Riva also.'"[3] Duveneck's *Riva* was
among the three prints exhibited in 1881 at the Society of
Painter-Etchers in London, sparking the verbal explosion
that occurred when officers from that Society suggested
that the three prints were in fact pseudonymous works
by Whistler.[4]

The Achenbach impression, printed in black, margins
uncut, and signed with a large, shaded butterfly, would
appear to have been pulled in Venice.

M.M.L.
M.S.

1. Julia Cartwright, "The Artist in Venice," *The Portfolio* (1884), p. 20.
2. Getscher, p. 92.
3. Bacher, p. 144.
4. Whistler, pp. 52-65, presents his witty, effective refutation of the
error.

Exhibition History and Bibliography: Edward G. Kennedy, *The Etched
Work of Whistler*, New York: The Grolier Club, 1910, no. 192, iii/iii.

107   **The Two Doorways,** 1880
From the First Venice Set
Etching and drypoint (brown ink on laid paper)
K. 193, iii/vi, trimmed to plate mark, 8 × 11½ in.
(20.3 × 29.2 cm)
Signed on tab: butterfly and *imp*; in plate, upper left:
butterfly
The Cleveland Museum of Art. Gift of Leonard C.
Hanna, Jr.

In *The Two Doorways* Whistler displays his ability to evoke
texture and tone, while simultaneously exploring the ex-

107

tremes of light and dark. The scene shows two doorways
that mark a round-cornered building on a quiet canal.
Although sunlight breaks upon the upper stories of the
distant buildings to the right, the predominant atmosphere of the foreground is dark and dank. To the left,
within the frame of a slightly pointed arched doorway, a
Leonardesque old man stoops to pick something from a
low basket, while two figures stand enshrouded in the
shadows behind him. Lichens and mosses, anchored to
the rough bricks and crumbling masonry, grow upon the
surrounding walls. Further to the right, flanked by two
bricked-in windows, is a closed door, its round arch filled
with a decorative iron screen. The impression of great
age, of glories and vigor long past, finds its root both in
the figures and the buildings.

As in several other plates, Whistler here is giving us an
exercise in positive and negative contrasts: open and
closed apertures, sunlit exterior and unlit interior, a bent
chiaroscuro figure contrasted with a similar silhouetted
figure, and a flat wall parallel to the picture plane juxtaposed with deep spatial recession. This last is perhaps
the most important juxtaposition, for it gives the print
two points of focus, a composition very rare in Whistler's
oeuvre.

The sweeping clusters of parallel lines that Whistler
placed to create the rich shadow in the open doorway
prompted Whistler's biographer, Joseph Pennell, to
write,

*It was in plates like this . . . that Whistler carried his system of
printing further than anyone else. Not only is there in the
dark archway the same elaborate, but much freer work than
Rembrandt put in . . . , but Whistler added richness by cover-
ing the lines, painting on them a tone of ink, and so obtained*
*a quality and depth that no one had achieved before, scarce
attempted.*[1]

These large areas of deep shadow, within which stand
figures darker yet, become all the stronger when juxtaposed to such delicate etching as can be seen forming
the distant sun-washed buildings. One such placement of
dark against light occurs where the edge of the foreground building cuts across the farther buildings, a
particularly vivid gesture that adamantly refuses to resolve into either spatial illusion or flat pattern, but
instead continually teases one's perception.

M.M.L.
M.S.

1. Quoted in "Fifty Etchings by James McNeill Whistler," *The Print
Collectors' Bulletin* (New York: M. Knoedler, 1931), p. 27.

Exhibition History and Bibliography: Edward G. Kennedy, *The Etched
Work of Whistler*, New York: The Grolier Club, 1910, no. 193, iii/vi.

108 The Beggars, 1879/80
From the First Venice Set
Etching and drypoint (warm black ink on modern laid paper)
K. 194, vi/ix, trimmed to plate mark, 12 × 8¼ in.
(30.5 × 21 cm)
Signed on tab: butterfly and *imp*
The Fine Arts Museums of San Francisco, Achenbach Foundation for Graphic Arts. Bequest of Lucie Stern

108

In his Venetian prints, Whistler often utilized figures to animate his scenes, but his population is almost solely composed of types seen from a distance: the gondolier or boatman with his broad-brimmed hat, a playing child, or lithe young women gossiping. In *The Beggars*, on the contrary, he renders a single old woman and barefoot girl in the foreground with all the specificity of two portraits. With her youth made more poignant by juxtaposition to wizened old age, her features softened, and her gaze aimed directly toward the viewer, the figure of the girl borders perilously close to importunate sentimentality and anecdote, qualities rare in Whistler's work. Feeling an unaccustomed and severe poverty while in Venice, Whistler was perhaps susceptible to the plight of the poor. Certainly many commentators on Venice did treat the issue, in tones ranging from a comfortable sanguinity to pettish annoyance. One instructs us that

Il dolce far niente [the sweetness of doing nothing] *is a sensation which can scarcely be realized more completely than in Venice. . . . I never saw poor people who seemed so happy, and who were really so comfortable in their poverty, as the very poorest people here. The softness of the climate, the little on which the comforts of life depend, permit poverty, even beggary, to remain dignified.*[1]

A fellow traveler, however, notes, "The Venetian beggar is the most persistent and annoying of his species . . . and their number is legion."[2] And Whistler, too, seems to have been uneasy about these two figures (and the man walking away from them), for they all three underwent many changes in the nine states (at least) through which Whistler developed this plate.

Balancing the emotional impact of the beggars, the rest of the scene is one of compelling formal and technical beauty. Exploring again the phenomenon of looking from light through a darkened space to a scene of light, the artist delineates the subtle progression of shadows and reflected light that mark the wooden rafters and beams of the *sottoportico*, or covered passageway. The sunlit space beyond, lightly and delicately etched, is filled with architectural elements that echo the larger rectangular shapes of the foreground and in effect aim attention to the center of the composition. There, two elegantly drawn water carriers – faceless, dynamically posed, and vigorous – provide exquisite examples of Whistler's more characteristic figural style.

M.M.L.
M.S.

1. Arthur Symons, *Cities of Italy*, new ed. (New York: Dutton, 1907), p. 109.
2. Elise Lathrop, *Sunny Days in Italy* (New York: James Pott, 1907), p. 303.

Exhibition History and Bibliography: Edward G. Kennedy, *The Etched Work of Whistler*, New York: The Grolier Club, 1910, no. 194, vi/ix.

109 The Mast 1880
From the First Venice Set
Etching and drypoint (brown ink on laid paper)
K. 195, vi/vi, trimmed to plate mark, 13¼ × 6¼ in.
(33.6 × 16 cm)
Signed on tab: butterfly and *imp*
The Cleveland Museum of Art. Gift of Mrs. Malcolm L. McBride

Shaped and proportioned like its dominant element, *The Mast* portrays a *calle* lined with modest buildings and, across the distant low horizon, shimmering trees. In the foreground to the left, a lounging boy mingles with a group of lacemakers, while other groups and pedestrians are visible along the street. Otto Bacher, in speaking of Whistler's etchings, wrote of the additive method Whistler followed in forming his images:

All of Whistler's etchings of Venice were drawn right from the subject, and all the figures in these etchings were drawn from life, although some of them did not pose in the same spot in nature as they are represented as posing in the etchings; these figures were always done from life and out-of-doors, and often near his house. Groups of bead-stringers and lace-makers could be found almost every day in any of the "calles" of Venice. Whistler often worked from these groups of women as they worked daily at their vocation.[1]

As charming as the genre elements of this scene are, more noteworthy is the artist's ability to suggest deep

109

space, convincingly filled with buildings and active figures, on a sheet that is, in many areas, untouched by any line. The second largest of his Venetian plates, the image exemplifies Whistler's preference for the suggestion rather than the depiction of his subject. Land and sky are equally devoid of characteristic markings; it is only the delicate context supplied by the artist that distinguishes the one from the other. An early critic perceived the problem Whistler set for himself precisely:

Having mastered the power of representing form, he set to work to make the objects in his etchings subordinate to the general impression.... Having learned to put in, he became learned in leaving out; and in his later series of Venetian etchings confined himself to a few lines contrasted with large spaces of white paper. But the lines are used with such won-

derful knowledge and skill that they are sufficient to suggest the character of the objects, while the chief meaning is given to the empty spaces. These cease to be mere paper; they convey the impression of water or sky under the effects of atmosphere and light, and, moreover, they stimulate the imagination.[2]

M.M.L.
M.S.

1. Bacher, pp. 97-98.
2. Charles H. Caffin, "How to Study Pictures: Twelfth Paper. Comparing Whistler with Sargent," *St. Nicholas* 32, no. 12 (October 1905), p. 1097.

Exhibition History and Bibliography: Edward G. Kennedy, *The Etched Work of Whistler*, New York: The Grolier Club, 1910, no. 195, vi/vi.

110   **San Biagio,** 1879/80
From the Second Venice Set
Etching and drypoint (warm black ink on laid paper)
K. 197, iv/ix, trimmed to plate mark, 8⅛ × 12 in.
(20.6 × 30.5 cm)
Signed on tab: butterfly and *imp*; in plate, at center left: butterfly
Private collection

Otto Bacher described the San Biagio area, near the Casa Jankowitz, in his account of the months he spent with Whistler in Venice:

This is one of the many calles where lace-makers and bead-stringers could always be found at their work, and where many of us kept our boats moored. Most of the buildings with their beautiful windows and balconies were in a dilapidated condition.[1]

Whistler must have come often into this working-class neighborhood to sketch the bead stringers or needle-workers who would later appear, in different settings, in his prints or in his pastels. Here, however, the workers are dwarfed by the predominant feature of the *calle*, the massive passageway that links the houses beyond to the water in the foreground. This opening, fully two stories high, is where Whistler has concentrated his line work in the print, carefully marking each beam of its ceiling as separate from both its neighbor and its shadow. Viewed from a low vantage point slightly off-center (very likely from a boat), the detailed work on the interior of this arch provides a dark point of focus at the middle of the image. The arch, in fact, finds its eloquent, poeticized counterpart in the reflection at the bottom of the etching, created not through line, but by Whistler's sensitive manipulation of plate tone.

The monolithic character of the darkened archway and its reflection is undercut and lightened by two elements. Hanging from the windows beside the opening are fluttering pieces of laundry, and directly above it are huge tattered sheets, themselves vaguely suggestive of garments on a grand scale. These impromptu festive 'banners' – which also caught Prendergast's attention nearly twenty years later (see cat. no. 42) – reinforce the informal air of the scene. There is, as well, an unsettling shift of scale between the architecture and the inhabitants (the men on the boat at the center of the print are too small to live within those walls or to open those window shutters) that vitalizes the scene and tantalizes the viewer who is unable to make the ostensibly simple image resolve.

M.M.L.
M.S.

110

1. Bacher, pp. 185-186.

Exhibition History and Bibliography: Edward G. Kennedy, *The Etched Work of Whistler*, New York: The Grolier Club, 1910, no. 197, iv/ix.

111 Bead Stringers, 1879/80

From the Second Venice Set
Etching and drypoint (black ink on old laid paper)
K. 198, viii/viii, trimmed to plate mark, 9 × 6 in.
(22.8 × 15.2 cm)
Signed on tab: butterfly and *imp*; in plate, center left: butterfly
The Zelman Collection

Before a modest domestic doorway (the number 37 above the lintel provides a portion of the address) sit three women. Two of them string beads, to judge from their hand gestures and the wooden trays they hold in their laps, while the third holds a round-cheeked baby. Within the confines of this small group, Whistler utilizes a characteristic variety of techniques for drawing figures. At the center, the form of the oldest woman gently emerges from a modulated darkness, bright light touching the foremost portions of her head and hand. To the right, the young mother sits in the daylight, her figure modeled by planes of both light and shadow. The bead stringer to the left, however, the most animated of the group, takes her form not from any internal modeling, but solely from a series of lively, broken contour lines of various weights that exuberantly suggest rather than describe the essential elements of body and dress. Portraying the four ages of life from infancy to old age, Whistler here pictures the range of feminine grace and charm without once succumbing to sentimentality or mere prettiness.

Sunlit figures before a darkened doorway form a motif Whistler often used in his Venetian prints (see cat. nos. 105, 108, 110, 116, 117). Perhaps part of what fascinated him with this pictorial problem is the considerable technical challenge of creating, from nearly overlapping traceries and cross-hatchings, a rich shadow area without blurring the lines or breaking down the surface of the plate. Equally, he must have enjoyed the opportunity to exhibit his virtuosity in modulating from darkness to bright sunlight, describing a number of forms perceived under various conditions of light. In *Bead Stringers*, probably one of his earlier prints in the city, the artist turns this considerable talent to the task of recording a scene of Venetian daily toil – albeit a cottage industry that was somewhat exotic for many visitors.[1] But Whistler's vignette with its dark center, blank edges, and dissolving forms is truly but a glimpse of the activity, the image of a glance or a memory. He captures with his needle the essential gestures of bead stringing and lets the details go unrecorded. These are subsumed within the wonder of seeing vital form built from light and line.

M.M.L.
M.S.

1. Getscher, pp. 47, 282.

Exhibition History and Bibliography: Edward G. Kennedy, *The Etched Work of Whistler*, New York: The Grolier Club, 1910, no. 198, viii/viii.

111

112

112   Turkeys, 1880
From the Second Venice Set
Etching and drypoint (brown ink on laid oriental paper)
K. 199, ii/ii, trimmed to plate mark, 8 × 5⅛ in. (20.3 × 13 cm)
Signed on tab: butterfly and *imp*; in plate, lower left (very faint): butterfly
The Cleveland Museum of Art. Gift of Mr. and Mrs. Ralph King

There is little to identify the scene in *Turkeys* as having an obviously Venetian setting. A slim and winsome young woman stands in a yard near a stone well, feeding the turkeys gathered about her with the grain she holds in a small barrel. Six other figures look on this simple activity from the edges of the courtyard: an old crone, a mother with her babe, a pair of lovers, and a curious young man who turns to observe us as he leans on a window ledge at the extreme right margin of the image. High up to the right, just beneath the vine-trailing trellis, a small cat sits and watches the large birds below. The only specifically maritime element in the scene is at the precise center of the sheet; an enormous anchor, partially hidden by both the girl and the well head, leans against the masonry staircase. With this image, Whistler immortalizes those

Venetians who, away from the canals, away from the monuments, away from the picturesque handcrafts, live and do chores, seemingly untouched by the magic of their city.

The plate, in its first state so scratched and pitted as to suggest a rainstorm, is here largely burnished and wiped clean. The image is summarily drawn, with very few passages of hatching or concentrated reworking. The principal contrast is between the lightly bitten line work of the figures and the buildings and the more deeply bitten work that characterizes the well, the turkeys, and, above, the vine.
   M.M.L.
   M.S.

Exhibition History and Bibliography: Edward G. Kennedy, *The Etched Work of Whistler*, New York: The Grolier Club, 1910, no. 199, ii/ii.

113 Nocturne: Palaces, 1879/80

From the Second Venice Set
Etching and drypoint (brown ink on laid paper)
K. 202, iv/ix, trimmed to plate mark, 11⅝ × 7⅞ in.
(29.6 × 19.9 cm)
Signed on tab: butterfly and *imp*
The Cleveland Museum of Art. Gift of Mr. and Mrs. Ralph
King

113

The site of *Nocturne: Palaces*, while not readily identifiable, contains all the elements that characterize the private sections of Venice: many-storied palazzi with nobly proportioned apertures and balconies, a quiet canal, an arched pedestrian bridge crossing over the still water, a gondola. Only one person is to be seen in the etching, a late-night stroller crossing the bridge just to the left of the glimmering streetlight. He is small and unobtrusive, and does not disturb the quiet that pervades the image.

Whistler has suggested the objects within the print through a web of delicately etched lines, most of them vertical, clustered together in abstract patterns that only imply, never detail, the facts of stone, wood, or metal. Around this linear skeleton the artist-printer has wrapped a shroud of palpable darkness, skillfully manipulating plate tone to create the reflections of masonry on dark water, and to bring the night's darkness down to cover and complete the forms of the palazzi that the etched lines leave unstated.

Throughout his career, Whistler found beauty in the mystery and darkness of the night – the moonlight-evoking title of "Nocturne" appears throughout his oeuvre – but it is pertinent to note that in 1885, long after he last saw Venice, when he wrote of the vespertinal Thames, it was of Venice that he thought:

And when the evening mist clothes the riverside with poetry, as with a veil, and the poor buildings lose themselves in the dim sky, and the tall chimneys become campanili, and the warehouses are palaces in the night, and the whole city hangs in the heavens . . . [then] Nature, who, for once, has sung in tune, sings her exquisite song to the artist alone.[1]

    M.M.L.
    M.S.

1. Whistler, p. 144.

Exhibition History and Bibliography: Edward G. Kennedy, *The Etched Work of Whistler*, New York: The Grolier Club, 1910, no. 202, iv/ix.

114 The Bridge, 1879/80

From the Second Venice Set
Etching and drypoint (brown ink on laid paper)
K. 204, viii/viii, trimmed to plate mark, 11½ × 7⅞ in.
(29.3 × 19.9 cm)
Signed on tab: butterfly and *imp*; in plate, lower right:
butterfly
The Cleveland Museum of Art. Gift of Mr. and Mrs. Ralph
King

Whistler's friend, biographer, and fellow-etcher, Joseph Pennell, saw *The Bridge* as one of the artist's finest prints:
For perfect expression, by the simplest, fewest, yet most expressive lines, this is one of the greatest works of art in the world. . . . And why is The Bridge *a great masterpiece? Because every line in it is exquisitely drawn, exquisitely arranged, exquisitely bitten, exquisitely printed. There is the story in the plate, of the life on the little canals. Those who know them, know that life, that movement, that architecture is perfectly expressed.*[1]
The bridge spans a small canal, perhaps on the Giudecca, that is bordered by relatively modest, vernacular dwellings.[2] Many people, especially children, fill the scene, both on the bridge itself and along the banks of the canal which, in sections of this outlying district, are unlined with stone, the earth of the island here being washed

114

directly by the canal as it meanders to the lagoon. Laundry hangs from the bridge's handrail, lending a festive (if slightly tattered) air to the scene. On the canal, men and boys in their utilitarian sandolos propel themselves into the distance where, far off, a screen of leafless trees closes the vista.

The ease with which this "story . . . of life of the little canals" cloaks Whistler's artifice, hiding his balance and compositional skill beneath a seeming naturalness, has impressed a number of commentators:

Nothing could wear more completely the light and gracious air of a work of art that has 'done itself' than this complicated collection of irregular buildings, river craft and people . . . What does it all seem but the merest accident of a fair day along shore.[3]

Whistler, himself, provides at least a partial explanation of his seeming spontaneity with what he calls "The Secret of Drawing" – a secret with which he shamefully teased poor Otto Bacher while in Venice, but revealed years later to another of his students, who subsequently wrote:

He described how in Venice once he was drawing a bridge, and suddenly, as though in a revelation . . . "I began first of all by seizing upon the chief point of interest – perhaps it might have been the extreme distance – the little palaces and shipping beneath the bridge. If so, I would begin drawing in that distance elaborately, and then would expand from it until I came to the bridge, which I would draw in in one broad sweep. If by

chance I did not see the whole bridge, I would not put it in. In this way the picture must necessarily be a perfect thing from start to finish.[4]

Whistler is not speaking of *The Bridge* here, but the "Secret's" applicability to this and numerous other etchings is readily apparent.[5] *The Bridge* clearly held a special position in Whistler's eyes: originally scheduled to be included in the First Venice Set, he withdrew it at the last moment, to place it instead among the generally more adventurous prints of the Second Venice Set published in 1886.

M.M.L.
M.S.

1. Joseph Pennell, *Etchers and Etching*, 4th ed. (New York: Macmillan, 1926), p. 78. See also the Pennells' biography of Whistler, in which they write, "Probably the finest plate, in its simplicity and directness, is *The Bridge*," p. 281.
2. Maria Naylor, *Selected Etchings of James A. McN. Whistler* (New York: Dover Publications, Inc., 1975), p. xxx, citing Howard Mansfield (*A Descriptive Catalogue of the Etchings and Dry-Points of James Abbot McNeill Whistler* [Chicago: The Caxton Club, 1901], p. 139).
3. Elizabeth Luther Cary, quoted in *The Print Collectors' Bulletin* (New York: M. Knoedler, 1931), p. 38.
4. Bacher, pp. 209-215, the quotation in turn being taken from Mortimer Menpes, *Whistler As I Knew Him* (New York: Macmillan, 1904).
5. Margaret MacDonald, *Whistler: The Graphic Work: Amsterdam, Liverpool, London, Venice* (London: Arts Council of Great Britain, 1976), p. 41.

Exhibition History and Bibliography: Edward G. Kennedy, *The Etched Work of Whistler*, New York: The Grolier Club, 1910, no. 204, viii/viii.

115 The Riva, No. 2, 1880

From the Second Venice Set
Etching and drypoint (brown ink on antique laid paper)
K. 206, i/ii, trimmed to plate mark, 8⅛ × 12 in.
(20.7 × 30.4 cm)
Signed in pencil, on tab: butterfly and *imp*; in plate, upper left: butterfly
The Cleveland Museum of Art. Gift of Leonard C. Hanna, Jr.

In *The Riva, No. 2*, Whistler plays a slight variation upon his *The Riva, No. 1* (cat. no. 106). The season is somewhat hotter (as evidenced by the awning that is now in place to provide shade), the crowd has thinned, there is less shipping along the quay. In addition, the artist's point of view is slightly higher and further back, both from the water and from the bridge in the foreground. Among the consequences of this shift is that, to the far right, the ghostly suggestion of the Campanile of San Marco has been cut from the view, leaving the domes of San Marco (reinforced by the masts and spars of some of the larger ships) to close off that side of the composition. A slightly greater amount of sky above the scene allows the artist to include the top of the campanile of San Giorgio dei Greci in its entirety toward the middle of the plate, rather than to truncate it as in *The Riva, No. 1*. Perhaps the most significant change between the two prints, however, is Whistler's greater concern in *The Riva, No. 2* to create a more coherent, illusionistic space. This is evident in details as diverse as the disposition of the gondolas on the lagoon and the increased order in the arrangement of the people on the Riva (although here again, at least in the first state of the print, Whistler uses a wide arc of blank

115

paper to lift the eye up to the middle distance). The most striking and effective evidence of Whistler's shifted emphasis on the second print is a tightening and strengthening of the imposing building on the left. Because of the inclusion of the roofline of this structure and Whistler's elimination of the second-story molding, its façade here reads far more convincingly as a solid receding in space than it does in *The Riva, No. 1*. Further, he strengthens the wall of the façade that fronts the Rio d'Arsenale by giving it a more regular hatching and a shorter depicted expanse, with the end result that the entire structure reads as a solid block. From this firm anchor we view the sweeping crescent of the Riva, which is not the case in the earlier print where the two walls of this nearest building tend to flatten, drawing attention to the surface of the paper.

    M.M.L.

    M.S.

Exhibition History and Bibliography: Edward G. Kennedy, *The Etched Work of Whistler*, New York: The Grolier Club, 1910, no. 206, i/ii.

116 **The Balcony,** 1880
From the Second Venice Set
Etching and drypoint (sepia ink on laid paper)
K. 207, v/xii, trimmed to plate mark, 11⅝ × 7⅞ in.
(29.5 × 20 cm)
Signed on tab: butterfly and *imp*; in plate, left, on wall by upper windows, and in second window bay from left: butterfly
The Zelman Collection

The Balcony is one of the earliest of Whistler's etchings of the city.[1] He concentrates in this image on making a fairly detailed rendering of a Renaissance Venetian house seen straight on from across the canal. The primary ornament of the building, and the focus of Whistler's attention, is a five-bay balcony that stretches across the *piano nobile*; three figures, a draped swag, and plants of considerable size all share the balcony's space.

    The building is elaborate, albeit narrow, and the passage of time is recorded by Whistler in the brickwork bared of its protective stucco. In the windows are small, ancient glass panes, which clearly delighted Whistler and which were once the pride of Venice, as one Venetian recorded in the mid-sixteenth century:

All the windows are sealed, not with oiled paper or canvas but with the clearest and finest glass enclosed in wooden frames with iron and lead fastenings. They are not only in palazzi and important buildings but in all sorts of places, for ordinary people, much to the amazement of foreigners . . . all this glass comes from the furnaces of Murano.[2]

    On the canal before the house, a large, flat sandolo has just arrived; the boatman appears to greet the woman who stands within the shadows of the doorway. In this area of the print, Whistler distinguishes between the

116

117

bright light of the exterior and the dusky coolness within by filling the space between the woman's figure and the door post with a myriad of small, curving lines, cross-hatched in some portions to create greater darkness, and detailing the out-of-doors with patches of deeply bitten, short, and scratchy lines mimicking the effect of strong sunlight falling across roughened masonry. Whistler leaves a delicately traced plate tone at the bottom of this image to enliven the water.

    M.M.L.
    M.S.

  1. Getscher, p. 95.
  2. Francesco Sansovino, *Venezia: Città Nobilissima et Singolare* (Venice, 1556).

Exhibition History and Bibliography: Edward G. Kennedy, *The Etched Work of Whistler*, New York: The Grolier Club, 1910, no. 207, v/xii.

117 **The Garden,** 1880
From the Second Venice Set
Etching and drypoint (brown ink on antique laid paper)
K. 210, undescribed state between vii and viii/viii, trimmed to plate mark, 12 × 9⅜ in. (30.5 × 23.8 cm)
Signed on tab: butterfly and *imp*; in plate, lower left: butterfly
The Fine Arts Museums of San Francisco, Achenbach Foundation for Graphic Arts purchase

Henry James wrote enthusiastically of Venice in 1883: *When I hear, when I see, the magical name* [of Venice], *it is not of the great Square that I think . . . I simply see a narrow canal in the heart of the city – a patch of green water and surface of pink wall. The gondola moves slowly; it gives a great, smooth swerve, passes under a bridge, and the gondolier's cry, carried over the quiet water, makes a kind of splash in the distance. . . . The pink of the old wall seems to fill the whole place; it sinks even into the opaque water. Behind the wall is a garden, out of which the long arm of a white June rose – the roses of Venice are splendid – has flung itself by way of spontaneous ornament. . . . It is very hot and still, the canal has a queer smell, and the whole place is enchanting.*[1] But for the season, which is autumn rather than spring, Whistler's *The Garden* could easily serve as an illustration, before the fact, to James's lyric reflection. A view into a private courtyard, this etching is among the most poised and, to use Whistler's own word, "lovely" of the artist's prints.[2] From his gondola on an anonymous canal, Whistler depicts an aged and worn gateway, its plank doors widely ajar to reveal within its walls an unexpected vision of rich foliage.[3] A handsome boy sits in the foreground with his foot dangling in the canal. Behind him are five steps that lead up to the garden itself (a cat sits with its back to the artist on the lowest of these). The vines and trees at the rear of the space are almost leafless – Whistler's elaborate clusters of lines denote a profusion of full-grown plants and shrubs.[4] At the back of the garden, in the still-warm sunlight, a woman and three children stand before the open doorway of a large house with impressively arched and overscaled windows. Whistler has carefully detailed the bricks beneath the crumbling stucco of the garden wall, suggested a variety of plants within the overgrown garden, and mottled the walls of the house to record its irregularities revealed by the sunlight.

He hangs this narrative upon a framework of considerable formal strength. The series of comparably proportioned rectangles (of sheet, gate, doorway, and window) clearly defines the illusion of space and recession, which the tonal shift from near dark edge to lightened, distant center reinforces. Whistler artfully compromises this perception, however, by stretching a linear web of tree branches across the house's façade. This tracery not only imposes a flat pattern across the back but, finding echoing forms on the outside of the garden wall, pulls the scene within forward to the surface. This formal play invigorates the image without negating its illusionistic core.

Whistler's attention to the material facts of age and benign neglect throughout the image establishes a pervasive mood of nostalgia. He reinforces this effect by the muted, atmospheric depiction of the scene in the background which is almost dream-like when juxtaposed to the foreground garden wall with its strong, deeply etched lines (the plate tone across the bottom of the image, by heightening the illusion of the water, again strengthens the reality of the foreground). By viewing the garden through a gateway, Whistler further enhances the sense of the transitory, for the doors must soon close, the gondola float on, the private garden again be concealed by the impersonal wall. Like James's visionary site, *The Garden* wears already the air of a memory.

M.M.L.
M.S.

1. James, *Portraits of Places*, pp. 16-17.
2. Whistler wrote to Walter Dowdeswell in September of 1886, asking, ''How do you like the proof? Isn't 'The Garden' lovely?'' (quoted in Fine, p. 109).
3. Bacher records, ''The Garden as seen through the open door of the water entrance was etched from Whistler's gondola. The figures were drawn from life as they were found in the subject,'' p. 112.
4. Getscher, pp. 52, 53, and MacDonald, p. 44, state that the plate is one of the later ones from Whistler's trip.

Exhibition History and Bibliography: Edward G. Kennedy, *The Etched Work of Whistler*, New York: The Grolier Club, 1910, no. 210, undescribed state between vii and viii/viii.

118   Nocturne: Furnace, 1880

From the Second Venice Set
Etching and drypoint (brown ink on modern laid paper)
K. 213, vii/vii, trimmed to plate mark, $6^5/8 \times 9$ in.
$(16.8 \times 22.8$ cm)
Signed on tab: butterfly and *imp*; in plate, center left: butterfly
The Fine Arts Museums of San Francisco, Achenbach Foundation for Graphic Arts. Gift of Osgood Hooker

But for the omnipresent gondolier, Whistler seldom showed Venetian men at work. A singularly beautiful exception to the rule is in *Nocturne: Furnace*. From across the still water of a narrow canal, the artist looks through a great square doorway into a massively beamed room aglow with heat and light. The man's figure before the furnace, reduced to a few contour lines by the glaring light, appears poised to act, tools in hand. He is a glassworker, manipulating a molten gather of glass in front of a heavy protective leather apron. To the left of the door, above a suggested stern and oarlock of a gondola, a figure with a lamp stares out of a window into the dark night, the scene at the window providing a gentle echo of that within the doorway. These three elements, nightwatcher, gondola fragment, and glassworker, are unconscious of each other and constitute an abrupt series of visual non sequiturs which, nevertheless, are yoked and compose themselves into an aesthetic unity in the artist's organizing imagination.

In *Nocturne: Furnace*, Whistler has concentrated considerable energy in depicting the humble architecture with etching and drypoint lines. Long clusters of vertical lines suggest the modulation of the masonry, while diagonal lines falling from doorway and window not only indicate areas of rougher texture, but also seem to materialize the light emitted from within. Dark night air finds its form in the plate tone that lies everywhere across the image, save in the bright interior before the open furnace.

M.M.L.
M.S.

Exhibition History and Bibliography: Edward G. Kennedy, *The Etched Work of Whistler*, New York: The Grolier Club, 1910, no. 213, vii/vii.

118

119 **Little Salute,** 1880
Drypoint (dark brown ink on antique laid paper)
K. 220, ii/ii, trimmed to plate mark, 3¼ × 8⅜ in.
(8.2 × 21.1 cm)
Signed on tab: butterfly and *imp;* in plate, lower right:
butterfly; on reverse: *Little Salute Drypoint* and butterfly,
in artist's hand
The Zelman Collection

Near the center of the *Little Salute,* short strokes of soft,
velvety drypoint combine to show the main bulk of
Longhena's Santa Maria della Salute surrounded by
boats. To the left we see into the long vista of the Grand
Canal, while to the far right the wide Giudecca Canal,
punctuated by small craft, extends generously to the
dome and portico of Palladio's Redentore rising above
the structures on the Giudecca island and closing off the
scene. Whistler, perhaps viewing the scene from his room
at the Casa Jankowitz, has used an eccentrically wide
plate format to encompass a larger vista than he normally
allowed himself, invoking memories of topographical
views from earlier centuries.[1] Perched upon the high
horizon, however, the buildings and other forms are
summarily treated, suggesting in their lack of detail that
accurate and minute recording were immaterial to Whistler. His goal seems instead to have been centered on
capturing a particular condition of light and weather, an
impression of a specific glance across the water. In this
instance, by utilizing the shape of the plate, the ink-re-
taining ability of drypoint's burr, and the wide, lightly
inked marks to either side of the plate left by a scraper,
the artist has suggested a blustery, overcast day. The wa-

ters of the lagoon are choppy beneath the strong wind
coming from the south – Whistler has even wiped the
plate to suggest that the very ink is being blown out from
the incised lines from right to left, while his butterfly
signature at the bottom right seems a gauge to test the
strength of a wind that transcends two levels of illusion.
M.M.L.
M.S.

1. Bacher, p. 184, ill. 254, writing of *Upright Venice,* K. 205 (although
confusingly calling it *Little Salute*), says that the view was done from the
Casa Jankowitz. The distant view in *Upright Venice* is, in fact, comparable to the left two thirds of *Little Salute.* See Paul J. Karlstrom, *Venetie:
Venice Panorama* (Los Angeles: Grunwald Graphic Arts Foundation, University of California, 1969) for early views of the city.

Exhibition History and Bibliography: Edward G. Kennedy, *The Etched
Work of Whistler,* New York: The Grolier Club, 1910, no. 220, ii/ii.

119

120 Nocturne: Salute, 1879/80
Etching (dark brown ink on wove paper)
K. 226, v/v, trimmed to plate mark 6 × 9 in.
(15.2 × 22.9 cm)
Signed in plate, lower left: butterfly; tab unsigned
Private collection

For *Nocturne: Salute*, Whistler stood on the Molo or quay in front of the Piazzetta and looked toward the mouth of the Grand Canal. There in the distance, formed from simple masses of cross-hatched lines, Santa Maria della Salute and its reflection hang upon the horizon. To the right, the Dogana is clearly suggested; its large gilt orb reads as a complementary sphere against the night sky, while masts of moored ships and a ghostly gondola hover on the broad Bacino. But these monuments and objects are not Whistler's primary concern in this, one of the first prints that he did in Venice.[1] Instead, light – both natural light, glowing from the horizon, and artificial light, such as that cast from the lamps in front of the Salute – forms the subject of this delicate, ephemeral image. Otto Bacher, when writing of *Nocturne: Salute*, spoke of "that tentativeness of feeling waiting on perfection" and continued by saying that the first impression of this image was "like a breath in its delicate elusiveness."[2] In the combination of the suggestiveness of the linework and the delicacy of the plate tone, *Nocturne: Salute*, comparable to the First Set's more monumental *Nocturne* (cat. no. 99), justifies Bacher's emphasis on the transitory in his criticism.

One need only briefly compare Whistler's *Salute* to the chromatic enthusiasms of Haseltine (cat. no. 18) and Moran (cat. no. 27) to see how radically this nocturne differs in scale, definition, and tone from the better-known views of the church. But like them, Whistler's image depends on our preknowledge and recognition of the domed monument, and on our visual pleasure at catching his subtle mnemonic clues.

More evocatively than in any other image, Whistler captures here the seeming insubstantiality of Venice, a characteristic often noted by others including such contemporaries as Henry Wadsworth Longfellow who, in his "Venice," invokes the "White phantom city, whose untrodden streets/Are rivers and whose pavements are the shifting/Shadows of palaces and strips of sky."[3]
M.M.L.
M.S.

1. Betsy Fryberger, *Whistler: Themes and Variations*, exh. cat. (Stanford, Ca.: Stanford University Museum of Art, 1978), p. 47.
2. Bacher, pp. 199-200.
3. Henry Wadsworth Longfellow, *The Complete Poetical Works of Henry Wadsworth Longfellow* (Boston: Houghton Mifflin, 1893), p. 319.

Exhibition History and Bibliography: Edward G. Kennedy, *The Etched Work of Whistler*, New York: The Grolier Club, 1910, no. 226, v/v.

120

Whistler 169

Production notes:

Venice: The American View, 1860-1920 was designed by Jack Werner Stauffacher of The Greenwood Press, San Francisco, California. Editing and production management by Ann Heath Karlstrom, The Fine Arts Museums of San Francisco. Type is Méridien, designed by Adrian Frutiger, display type handset at The Greenwood Press, text photocomposed by Mackenzie-Harris Corporation, San Francisco, California. Printed on Quintessence Dull 80 by Gardner/Fulmer Lithograph, Buena Park, California.